# Unfinished People

# Unfinished People

*Eastern European Jews Encounter America*

Ruth Gay

W. W. Norton & Company
New York • London

Lines from the Passover Haggadah with English translation, edited by
Nahum N. Glatzer, translated by Jacob Sloan. Copyright 1953 by Shocken
Books, Inc. Reprinted with the permission of Shocken Books, a division of
Random House.
For information about permission to reproduce selections from this book,
write to Permissions, W. W. Norton & Company, Inc., 500 Fifth Avenue,
New York, NY 10110.
The text of this book is composed in Fournier
with the display set in Koch Antigua
Composition and manufacturing by The Haddon Craftsmen, Inc.
Book design by Chris Welch

Library of Congress Cataloging-in-Publication Data
Gay, Ruth.
Unfinished people : Eastern European Jews encounter America /
by Ruth Gay.
p.   cm.
Includes bibliographical references and index.
ISBN 0-393-03991-9
1. Jews, East European—New York (State)—New York—Social life and
customs.   2. Jews—New York (State)—New York—Social life and
customs.   3. Immigrants—New York (State)—New York—Social life
and customs.   4. Bronx (New York, N.Y.)—Social life and customs.
5. New York (N.Y.)—Social life and customs.   I. Title.
F128.9.J5G39   1996
305.892´407471´09041—dc20
96-13924
CIP
ISBN 0-393-32240-8 pbk.

W. W. Norton & Company, Inc., 500 Fifth Avenue, New York, N.Y. 10110
http://web.wwnorton.com

W. W. Norton & Company Ltd., Castle House, 75/76 Wells Street,
London W1T 3QT

1 2 3 4 5 6 7 8 9 0

*To Peter*

# Contents

# Part I

# Introduction

At the height of the immigrant flood from Europe (1880–1920), when New York was the great mother port for immigrant ships, 17 million immigrants, three quarters of all those who came to the United States, were sluiced through the narrow gates of Ellis Island and Castle Garden, the two receiving stations in New York. In the same period, when nearly 2.5 million Jews left Eastern Europe, nine out of ten chose the United States as their destination, and they also saw New York as the inevitable way into the new Promised Land. Most went no further. In the thirty peak years of Jewish immigration (1881–1911), nearly three quarters of the 1 million Jews who entered the harbor remained in the city.

They were for the most part young, single, unskilled, uneducated, and boundlessly optimistic. Many of them were no more than children—twelve or thirteen years old—who came without their families to stay with older sisters or brothers, or with *landslayt*—countrymen—who were as good as relatives. But those to whom these children came were themselves poor immigrants, just able to find a place for the newcomer to sleep. Within a few days, with or without any English, they went to work, literally to earn their daily bread. These children, with the thoughts and cares of adults, left their childhood behind in the Old Country and came to find a place in the New World.

They did not feel sorry for themselves. They did not think that they deserved to be coddled and cared for. Some who wanted more schooling managed to find their way to the night schools run by the public school system in New York where they could learn English more systematically than on the streets. The Educational Alliance on the Lower East Side offered an even wider range of courses in a homier atmosphere. In their eagerness, they formed a remarkable generation of autodidacts, who found expression and companions in the myriad of political and cultural organizations and in the burgeoning trade unions. But there were others who would never again open a book—whose literacy in Yiddish did them no good in America, where even the alphabet was different and in this as in other enterprises remained between two worlds, not competent enough to enjoy reading Yiddish, and barely making their way with minimal English.

Literacy, or the lack of it, was only the most obvious of their gaps in knowledge. When we think of twelve or thirteen-year-olds even a century ago, when children, especially poor children, early took on adult responsibilities, they were nonetheless far from expert in the nuances and mores of their culture. The static, traditional world out of which they came was far more stylized, far more formal than the world to which they were going. And here is where their lives came apart. They had not yet really learned how to be adult in their own culture. They were lacking in manners; they did not know the ceremonies; they often did not know the most obvious customs because they had simply left their homeland too young. Yet with only this partial apprehension of the world out of which they came, they expected to go on and build their adult lives, raise and teach their children, and grow into respected elders. How superficially they were rooted in that old culture would sometimes catch them up in surprising ways.

Several years after I married, my father-in-law called me aside for a confidential talk. He and his wife were of an older generation than my parents. They had come to America in their early thirties with two children and had already seen something of the world. My father-in-law had, in fact, served in the Russian Army during the Russo-Japanese War of 1904–05. Now he was disturbed over a matter of some delicacy. It turned out that my parents had failed to present their new son-in-law with a *tallis* (prayer shawl) on our marriage. This was a source of steady personal embarrassment to my father-in-law since his son came frequently to his little *shul* to join him in the services, and was still wearing his little boy's *tallis* given to him when he was thirteen. Upon his marriage he should have put on an adult *tallis*, made of wool and that hung to the knees.

The cause of the problem soon became clear. There was no ill-will on the part of my parents; this was not a subtle display of displeasure with their son-in-law. Their omission of this traditional gift was due to sheer ignorance. When they had left the Old Country, and its intricate social web, my parents had each been too young to have noticed this custom. For them—as for their children—it was lost, like so much else. What they had not learned, what they did not know, they could not transmit.

Culturally, then, these children as adults skated on very thin ice—wedded to the culture they had brought with them and its language, yet not really adept in it. And once in America, it was too late to learn any more. But how American were they? Once again, there is a whole spectrum of examples: there were those who persevered in making themselves American, went on to high school, even to college, and entered professional careers. Others lived their whole lives in a strange never-never-land, speaking a very shallow version of the language they had brought with them, and later learning an equally shallow version of the language of their new country. For all of them, it took heroic efforts just to stay afloat, to keep their jobs, and it took a very adventurous temperament to move ahead.

Sometimes, when he reflected on compatriots who had grown

rich in this country, my old father-in-law used to say, with a satisfied twinkle in his eye, *"I'm* a rich man because I have no debts."* It was a cautious frame of mind, and for those whom it suited, it was a moral refuge. He did not have to measure his success against the rich and powerful. By the standards of the Old World, of the shtetl, he *was* a success—he had employment, he had a home, he and his family did not live in want.

There was another kind of refuge. In the many densely populated Yiddish-speaking neighborhoods of New York City, it was often unnecessary to worry too much about the American world. From the perspective of Brownsville or the Bronx, in fact, that world seemed very far away and often quite unintelligible. In these neighborhoods one could spend a lifetime and never have to speak a word of English—at the stores, at work, even the doctors at the Board of Health clinics if you picked the right one—everyone spoke Yiddish. Living in this dense Yiddish-speaking world, my mother was convinced that young doctors were taught Yiddish in medical school as one of the indispensable tools of their trade.

In 1870, a decade before the great influx from Eastern Europe began, the 80,000 Jews in New York City were largely of German origin. They were joined after 1830 by some 200,000 German Jews who abandoned their homeland, and of whom more than a third had landed in New York. The landscape of Jewish life in America, however, was permanently changed by the sheer number of the new arrivals from the East.

By 1915, there were 1,400,000 Jews in New York City, half of the Jews in the United States, publishing four Yiddish-language newspapers daily, as well as countless additional journals and magazines representing a broad array of social, cultural, and political convictions. There were cafés, restaurants, and cabarets geared to the Old Country taste; there was a thriving Yiddish theater. There seemed to be a landsmanshaft organization for every town in Eastern Europe, and a very large number of vehement political groups—

Socialists, Zionists, anti-Zionists, and many shades in between. For many immigrants, the landsmanschaft organizations were a kind of substitute family, where they heard again the accent of their home and felt the warmth of shared memories with their fellow members. More practically, these self-help groups also looked out for the newcomers, paid sick and unemployment benefits, and bought group plots in cemeteries in the outer boroughs where their members could remain together through eternity.

The uncertainty of these child immigrants colored and shaped their adult lives. Much of the intensity and hysteria that became the hallmark of Jewish family life was less extravagant warmth and love, as it has often been seen, than a true representation of the fear and double incompetence of these children: double because they had not been able to master either of the cultures in which they lived. *Their* children early came to recognize this incapacity as, at an early age, they were required to read and interpret notices from the gas company, from school, as well as other official communications that came in the mail. The very appearance of these letters would throw the parents into a panic, only allayed with difficulty when it turned out that the gas company was notifying its subscribers that there would be a temporary suspension of service on the next Tuesday between 9:00 and 11:00 A.M.

Very, very early, very quietly, the children of this generation developed an area of reserve that widened with time as their own world grew more complex. Then they turned to teachers, to their peers, to the leaders of clubs that they had joined—to almost anyone else—for advice.

But not to their parents. They learned to bring home only the good news, to suppress anything that had any ambivalence, that would arouse an outburst of anxiety, an emotion that went nowhere and solved no problems. Their parents could offer passionate feelings and unlimited devotion, they learned, but what they needed was a cool consideration of the facts against a background of worldly experience. By and large, these children of children had to learn to negotiate their own way in the new world to which they had been born. They sought advice at home at their own peril.

Studying that other world became a lifelong occupation, and one never knew when something seemingly trivial, but totally new, would illuminate an entire area of experience. I report all this at first hand. My own parents were just such immigrant children when they came to this country. My mother, from a tiny town in Galicia, arrived with her sister, Chana, when she was thirteen and Chana fourteen. Taking advantage of the opportunity to travel across the ocean with a woman who was their neighbor, they were the last of the five children in their family to leave for the New World. Their pious old father, a follower of the Chortkover rebbe, remained behind rather than live in what he called *"a treyfe medina*—an unholy land."* Later, when his children sent him money from their earnings, he implored them to desist, sure that it came from tainted labor, that is, money earned on the Sabbath.

My father arrived at Ellis Island as a boy of sixteen or seventeen—he was never certain of his age—and came from a small town near Bialystok. It was so small that he was ashamed to tell us and at first would always say that he came from Bialystok itself. In time he spoke of Tiktin (Tykocin), still a town of some size. And finally, when he was in his nineties, he admitted that he had been born in Rutki, a village a few miles west of Bialystok. It took a long time before we realized that these evasions were about something that was invisible to us. For him it was somehow shameful that he came from a village, a shtetl, and like much else he suppressed what he considered unsuitable in America. Discovering the world—our world—under these circumstances also took a long time. Without a map in hand, we were constantly plotting new points and trying to discover what kind of terrain we were standing on.

One weekend when I was in my twenties, I was invited to visit some friends in their summer house in New England. They had three children and lived very comfortably in an old farmhouse that they had made delightfully livable. It had, unobtrusively, all the mechanical conveniences of modern life but all the charm of the nineteenth century. Here and there they had found furniture appropriate to the size and style of the house, some of it family pieces and some bought at country auctions—a horsehair sofa, a square rosewood piano, some straight chairs and some comfortable ones disposed informally and invitingly around the living–music room.

I was a little nervous about this weekend because this was the first non-Jewish family that I had ever visited as a house guest, and I was sure that there were differences between their life and mine of an order that I could not even fathom. In the highly stratified America of the thirties and forties it was possible to live a tightly segregated life in a place as big as New York. And although I went to such worldly institutions as Hunter High School and then Queens College, all my friends came from identical immigrant families. Our experience of the outside world, of the other world, was very narrow, and we knew it. But we also did not know the others and were too shy to break out of the comfortable circle of people like us. I was prepared, therefore, for all kinds of revelations during my country weekend, and I was right, but they came on far more mundane levels than I would have thought.

The first surprise that awaited me was how the parents treated their children. Their style was something that I did not know— good-tempered, considerate, gentle. One day the mother observed that one of the little girls was not looking well. She had no fever, but did not seem to be her usual self—somewhat subdued and limp. Her mother suggested that she would make up a bed on the sofa where her daughter could lie and read and be comfortable. The little girl agreed, and snuggled down on the sofa under a paisley shawl with a sigh of relief and contentment. I watched all this closely and, I must confess, with a pang of longing for the quiet attentiveness I had never experienced.

Here, the child was regarded as someone who had wishes and

thoughts and desires—all of which were legitimate and to be considered in any dispositions made concerning that child. As to the child's sickness, the mother was responding by taking a simple first precautionary step. But what impressed me was that she was thinking about the *child*. When I considered the world in which I had grown up, I saw a remarkable contrast.

When I was sick, my parents responded first to the *sickness*—and always with alarm. They then took measures to allay their fears, but they were too frightened, paradoxically enough, to think about me. They watched the thermometer to see whether the fever was going down or up. But they did not ask me how I felt. My mother would wander white-lipped through the house, wringing her hands and murmuring in alliterative Yiddish, "Dear God frighten me, but do not punish me." On such occasions, my parents did not trouble to make fine distinctions between a fever brought on by a chest cold or by diptheria; the response to illness was always to declare a state of emergency. Even as children, my friends and I perceived this disproportion between our common ailments and the storm of concern that they aroused. We mistook this intensity for love.

With any illness, our parents' underlying panic came out of hiding and expanded to visible proportions, although in actuality it was always there, woven into the fundamental texture of daily life. Who among the children of that generation does not remember the phrase: "Don't run, you'll fall"? And since children do not on the whole make their way gravely with their hands clasped behind their backs, this sentence was repeated a thousand times, losing force with every utterance. Whoever has watched a toddler get up on its feet and begin to move, suddenly rediscovers the history of the human race, the difficulty and the intricate balancing that is required to walk in an upright position. Since toddlers are also uniquely designed to absorb all the shocks of their sudden collapses, calmer parents can enjoy this unique moment of learning. But the warnings of these immigrant children—now parents—had little to do with the reality of childish locomotion, and everything to do with their fears and their sense of inadequacy: their fear that the child might hurt itself, and their helplessness in the face of harm.

This mood of watchful waiting did not make for an easy atmosphere, and as the children of the immigrants sought to escape to the wide world opening to them, their parents felt or knew that something was slipping away. It only increased their anxiety. Alfred Kazin once described this atmosphere very vividly when he said about Yiddish that it was the sort of language where one smashed a chair through a window to let in a little air. By contrast, life in the world of the "others" was so much calmer—where one had only to lift the sash. It was less colorful, perhaps; it was less intimate; but it was so much more restful.

Unfortunately, those immigrants who came as adults, firmer in their convictions, more certain about how to organize their lives than their younger friends and relatives, and calmer in their certainty, did not fare much better with their children. What was unavoidable for both groups was the alienation that came between people who lived in different cultures. Love and respect were inevitably tempered by difference.

This has been a well-documented immigration. The arrivals have been counted in government statistics. The newcomers have been analyzed in learned journals and works of sociology. They have written their own memoirs, and their newspapers and journals provide a lavish record of their thoughts and feelings during their first turbulent decades in this country. Their songs, plays, poetry, novels, all help to round out the picture. But oddly enough, unless we take the trouble to look for it, we are left not with the nuanced portrait that such riches of material should have produced. Instead, on a popular level, we have before us a meager caricature—as presented to us by comedian after comedian who seem to have listened only to one another, until we are finally left with the latest exponent:

Jackie Mason. Speaking in a way that is supposed to evoke the accented English of the immigrant generation, he wraps himself in the recognizable mantle of their artless innocence while expressing the harsh and oversimplified prejudices of his own time. In another distortion, the immigrants have been sentimentalized as the saintly and characterless grandparents, the *bobe* and *zayde* (grandma and grandpa) who smile indulgently and uncomprehendingly at the antics of their descendants. But they have also been vilified, notably in the images of the ugly, narrow-minded Jewish families flashed around the world in many sequences of Woody Allen's movies.

Three generations away, their grandchildren and great-grandchildren have begun to rediscover and recreate the "klezmer" music that their ancestors themselves quickly abandoned in their yearning to be "up to date." Just as earnestly, they attempt to recapture the language that was annihilated not only by Hitler but also by modernity. On the Lower East Side, now itself in a state of decay and disarray, New York City has established a Tenement Museum; Aaron Lansky has collected over a million old Yiddish books for the National Yiddish Book Center; the Yiddish movies of the twenties and thirties are all being repackaged for video—with English subtitles; and the old *Forward* has begun publishing a successful English-language weekly to pick up the audience that yearns for the atmosphere of its Yiddish prototype. Courses in Yiddish are springing up in universities everywhere, from California in the United States to McGill in Canada to Oxford in England and even in Germany. It is all something that would have been incomprehensible to their forebears. The last of that immigrant generation have all but slipped away, but the effect of the broad strokes of the comedians and caricaturists has been to tamper with memory. Unthinkingly the descendants accept the stereotypes, and squeeze their ancestors into the narrow and rather condescending mold that others have created for them.

In the chapters that follow, we will explore the daily lives of these immigrants again—particularly those "unfinished people" who were easily overwhelmed and intimidated in a world that they never quite grasped. In order to capture and recreate the years of the twenties and thirties when they were establishing themselves in New York, I will draw upon my own memories of life in the Bronx. The anecdotal method is not in the best repute, but perhaps we can make it more respectable by calling it "testimony." I must confess that having passed the age of seventy, I sometimes feel like one of the last who actually heard and spoke Yiddish, who participated in this life and did not just hear about it in Borsht Belt jokes. But I do not want to offer only impressions or reminiscences, and will therefore augment my own observations with two framing essays on the life and times of the East European Jewish immigrants in their homelands and then in New York. My own angle of vision was, after all, very narrow, and I would like to set what I saw against the larger background. The place to begin is in the Old Country, in the much misunderstood shtetl from which so many of the immigrants came; then in succeeding chapters I want to sketch in a portrait of that striving, struggling immigrant life that marked New York in the early decades of this century. I hope that this book will present these immigrants afresh, without either the sentimentality or the hostility that has diminished them in the past.

In homage to the musical culture of the immigrant era, a companion CD and cassette have been made expressly for this book. Produced and performed by the Grammy-nominated dean of Yiddish musicians, Henry Sapoznik, the recording features some of the most gifted players in the contemporary klezmer music scene. In turn sentimental, satirical, or wildly exuberant, the songs and dance tunes re-create the immigrant favorites mentioned in the book. *Unfinished People: The Music* is available directly from Living Traditions, 430 West 14 Street, #514, New York, NY 10014.

# Part II

# There

A simple logic was behind the move of most European immigrants to the United States at the end of the nineteenth century: economic hardship at home and unlimited opportunity in America led irresistibly from the one place to the other. For Jews, the forces were more complex. Living as unwanted or barely tolerated strangers in the lands of their birth, they had long been subject to legislation that thwarted every impulse toward a useful and self-sustaining life. The details of these restrictions differed from country to country, but the net result was to place barriers everywhere: from ways of earning a living, to where they might live, to access to education—all were circumscribed so closely that ordinary Jews felt driven back from the world around them at every point. As a consequence, Jews in Eastern Europe lived in a tightly enclosed society that had changed little since the Middle Ages. Dominated by Jewish law and custom, it was governed from within by an oligarchy of the rich and learned. Poor Jews had very little to say about the course of their lives, ruled as they were by two masters: the state, which determined their very right to existence; and the Jewish community council, which determined their place in their own society.

Jews had two ways of thinking about their fate: to be born a Jew was to be counted among God's Chosen People, a privilege that placed them at the pinnacle of Being. Or, and simultaneously, it was a passport to Hell, since they were condemned for life by the accident of birth to hardship, scorn, and not infrequently physical harm. *Kiddush ha Shem* is a ready phrase in Yiddish—the holy death of martyrs for the sake of the Holy Name—and the prayerbook is filled with poems memorializing the horrid events that periodically took Jewish lives in the past. This martyrdom or persecution was something that Jews learned from an early age was part of the meaning of being Jewish. *"Me shlogn yidn*—They are beating Jews" was the frightening alarm that was raised as marauders began their work, a sentence that conveyed fear, helplessness, and the utmost fury. There would come a time when it could no longer be borne.

By the end of the nineteenth century, two internal forces had been disturbing the peace of the Jewish communities in Eastern Europe for a century. A new ecstatic Judaism, Hasidism, that had emerged in the early eighteenth century, was winning followers away from the conventional synagogues. And at the other end of the spectrum, the followers of the Enlightenment, an insidious and seductive way of thinking about the world, had been troubling the Jewish communities of Eastern Europe since the days of Moses Mendelssohn. This eighteenth-century philosopher who settled in Berlin had become a model to all those who wished to master both the Western and the traditional Jewish worlds of learning. In Eastern Europe, the movement, which had taken fire from the modernists in Germany, was known by its Hebrew name, the *Haskala*—the Enlightenment. As in the West, earnest young scholars worked in a new secular Hebrew, creating a literature built on passionate national feeling. They published books and periodicals, used modern forms in poetry and novels, and ransacked the learning of the Western world. But in Eastern Europe, as in Germany, it remained a movement confined to a small, educated elite. Not only did the participants have to command Hebrew fluently, they also had to share what seemed a daring idea—to use the Holy Tongue for profane purposes.

By the nineteenth century, when the Jews in Eastern Europe could trace their history in the region for a thousand years, they had reached their height in numbers—some 7 million—and their nadir in the conditions of their lives. In the 1880s, when the great exodus to America began, there were 5 million Jews in Russia—which included Poland, Lithuania, Latvia, and Estonia—more than 1,500,000 in the Austro-Hungarian Empire, and another 280,000 in Romania. Under each of these governments, the Jews together with the gypsies were perhaps the least favored inhabitants, and while details differed from country to country, the outcome in each was a poor, socially isolated population.

Romania, the smallest of the three countries, with the smallest number of Jews, nonetheless took the severest legal position toward its Jewish inhabitants. Established as an independent kingdom in 1878 by the Treaty of Berlin, which marked the end of the Russo-Turkish War, the Romanian regime adamantly refused to grant its Jewish inhabitants the right of citizenship, even though this had been one of the conditions of the treaty. Taking the strict position of a nation-state, the government declared that it was impossible for Jews to be Romanian subjects because they were neither Christians nor descended from Romanians. Some eight hundred men who had fought in the war for liberation from Turkey were grudgingly granted citizenship, and ever after, every application was scrutinized on a case-by-case basis. When at the end of the nineteenth century all of Europe seemed to be pouring into the United States, 90 percent of the immigrants from Romania were Jews.

By 1902, the United States was alarmed enough at such an influx for the Secretary of State, John Hays, to write in protest to the Romanian government. After reminding the government that under the Treaty of Berlin it was obligated not to discriminate because of differences in "religious creeds or confessions," the note pointed out that "by the cumulative effect of successive restrictions, the Jews of Roumania have become reduced to a state of wretchedness. . . . Human beings so circumstanced have virtually no alternatives but submissive suffering or flight to some land less unfavorable to them." And here, of course, was the nub of Secretary Hays's concern: the consequence of Romania's maltreatment of its Jews brought to the United States what seemed to him thousands of undesirable immigrants, or, as he put it, it brought about the "transplantation of an artificially produced diseased growth to a new place." While the note was eloquent in its protest against the persecution of Jews in Romania, it altered neither the government's policies nor the Jewish yearning to leave. In 1905, the *Jewish Encyclopedia* reported that "at least 70 per cent [of the Jews] would leave the country at any time, if the necessary travelling expenses were furnished." As late as 1916 in the midst of World War I, and still unenfranchised, the Congress of Romanian Jews doggedly drafted yet another petition to the government for equal rights.

Yet in New York in the 1920s, when the entertainer Aaron Lebedeff sang about his home, the inevitable nostalgia of the emigrant prevailed as he mourned Bessarabia, the place where he was "at home" and "at ease." ("Bessarabia iz mayn haym. Dort fil ikh sikh bakveym.") Odessa was characterized as a veritable "Garden of Eden," while his ultimate apostrophe was to *"Romania, Romania, a land a ƶise, a shayne* . . . a sweet and lovely country." Endlessly heard on records and in the Romanian cabarets of New York's Lower East Side, the song praised the special dishes, the delectable wine, and the carefree life of that very Romania from which its listeners had fled. Whether it was the song itself or Lebedeff's exuberant style, it certainly helped to fix the reputation of Romanian Jews as people who knew how to enjoy life. It was not for nothing that the most raffish of the restaurants on the Lower East Side were in Romanian hands, just as Romanian women were regarded as the most voluptuous. That myth may have been helped by the fact that the last king of Romania had a red-headed Jewish mistress—Magda Lupescu—whose name was a household word, pronounced by Jews in America with a mixture of shame and pride. All of this—the sentiment, the vision of the good life, the scandal, the nostalgia—came later, of course, after the high tide of immigration between 1881 and 1910. In those soberer years, Romanian wine notwithstanding, one in four Romanian Jews left their land, "a zise, a shayne"; in all, 67,000, to come to America.

Austro-Hungary, that great creaking agglomeration of peoples united under Franz Joseph, its emperor from 1848 to 1916, emancipated its Jews in 1867, the only country in Eastern Europe to take this step. While Franz Joseph's Jewish subjects may have been appropriately grateful, those in Austria, at least, were not less poor or wretched than their brethren in Russia and Romania. As in the other countries, the restrictions on Jewish occupations, on their admission to universities or guilds, on their right to own land continued to thwart any free development. The result was that these exclusions kept all but a small minority in a state of destitution. The largest concentration of Jews in the sprawling empire were the 800,000 in Galicia; another 600,000 lived in Hungary; while smaller numbers were scattered from the western border in Silesia, across Bohemia, Moravia, down the Adriatic Coast to Croatia, to an outpost of some 7,000 in Trieste.

Galicia, the major center from which the emigrants left, was home to the poorest and most Orthodox Jewish population in Eastern Europe. This region was also the stronghold of the relatively new Hasidism. Originating in the 1730s in Podolia under the inspiration of Israel ben Eliezer, better known as the Ba'al Shem Tov, the Master of the Good Name, Hasidism quickly attracted followers in the neighboring regions of the Ukraine and Bessarabia. Resisted at first by the traditional rabbis, who condemned its practices as outlandish if not scandalous—the dancing, the ecstatic transports, the "wonders" performed by the leaders of the movement, the inattention to the niceties of rabbinic law—it nonetheless developed an overwhelming following as the dynasties of the wonder-working rabbis flourished. Scorned and mocked by their "rational" Opponents—the Mitnagdim of the north, especially in Lithuania—by the mid-nineteenth century the movement was firmly established, and its earlier laxness on matters of ritual had given way to a punctiliousness with which even the traditional rabbinate could no longer find fault.

While the Hasidim rose to ecstasy in the throes of wordless song, their Opponents did not hesitate to ridicule them in sardonic verse. In a song now frequently misunderstood and sentimentalized, they derided the exaggerated devotion of the Hasidim who, in their zeal, outdo every movement, every act of their leader. "When the rebbe dances," runs the song, "the Hasidim jump; when the rebbe eats, the Hasidim gobble . . . " and on in this vein.

In otherwise undistinguished small towns, the leaders of the various branches of Hasidism created major centers of pilgrimage as their followers came to ask advice, to celebrate the holidays, or simply to rejoice by being in the presence of *their* rebbe. Arthur Ruppin, a German-born sociologist, visited several of these famous centers in 1903 to gather material for his projected *Sociology of the Jews*. Traveling from Vienna to Cracow, he sees, as he reports in his memoirs, "for the first time *real* Jews with earlocks and caftan." Further east in Tarnapol, he meets the head of a secular Jewish school who is "delighted to see a doctor from the West. The conditions in Galicia," he tells Ruppin, "must be made known to the world. They call out to heaven for a change." On his way to the synagogue with his host, Ruppin experiences the famous *blote*—the mud of the unpaved streets in the Jewish towns, which is so deep that he loses his footing and falls into it.

He travels on to visit the head of the Hasidic dynasty at Chortkov. Although he is impressed by the rabbi's palace and his sumptuous private room for prayer, he remains the detached observer. The visit goes badly since Ruppin's German and the rabbi's Yiddish are too far apart for communication. Then, because the rabbi has been misinformed about the purpose of his arrival, Ruppin finds himself being blessed for a nonexistent forthcoming examination.

His next stop is Belz, which he reaches just as thousands of Jews have come on pilgrimage to see the rabbi. With a normal population of 6,000, of whom half were Jews, the town could hardly provide accommodations for the visitors. But the Hasidim were uncomplaining, and lay down to sleep wherever they could find space, wrapping themselves in blankets, and covering the floor of the inn, which is where Ruppin finds some of them when he returns to his room late one night. In the synagogue itself, where he attends evening services, he observes that there are no benches. "Several thousand Jews stand pressed together," he reports, "in a frightful crush, and bend during prayers like stalks of wheat in a field. The service begins with the appearance of the rabbi and everyone tries to get as close as possible to him. His prayers," Ruppin observes, "seem to call forth a kind of ecstasy. They close their eyes and sway violently back and forth. . . . Whoever sees the Jews here at their prayers, must say that they are still the most religious people in the world."

But apart from this tribute, Ruppin does not take fire from what he sees. Indeed, when he interviews some of the visitors, he characterizes their attitude toward the rabbi as one of "unbelievable superstition." One man has come from Russia to discuss his business affairs with the rabbi, while another, a Galician Jew now living in London, comes twice a year for advice, each trip costing him 800 gulden. Ruppin, ever the scientist, discovers that 600 gulden is the annual income of the "richest" Jews in Belz—some 10 percent of the population. This wealth, he explains, suffices to rent one room with a kitchen and provide just about enough food for a family's survival. The remaining 90 percent of the Jews manage on 3 to 6 gulden a week. His final sentence on Belz, seemingly objective, contains the barely suppressed indignation of the nineteenth-century European confronting the primitive. "There is a great deal of typhus," he concludes, "because of the lack of a sewer system."

Decades later, in America, with pilgrimage a thing of the past, Belz was remembered differently in the most sentimental of all the Yiddish songs about home: *"Belz, mayn shtetele Belz* . . . Belz, my little town Belz, where I spent my childhood years . . . " Even for those who had lived nowhere near Belz, once in America, the song was able to arouse the longing and sadness—less for the town than for those few childhood years that the immigrants retained in their hearts.

Three years after Ruppin's visit, the philosopher Martin Buber, who had studied with the sage of Chortkov, was the first to make a bridge to the West by publishing the *Tales of the Hasidim* in German translation. And in Warsaw, at about the same time, one of the luminaries of Yiddish letters, I. L. Peretz, tried for yet another kind of reconciliation, portraying the Hasidim in his stories with something of the affection of the folklorist. In his "If Not Higher," a *Litvak,* a Lithuanian Jew who is, of course, a skeptic, seeks to discover where the Nemirov rebbe goes at night during the penitential period before the Day of Atonement. His followers are convinced that during his mysterious absences he is visiting the heavenly realm. The *Litvak* secretly follows him and discovers that in the early hours of the morning the rabbi is actually cutting wood for a poor bedridden widow and delivering it disguised as a peasant. The *Litvak,* with his rational system intact, thereupon becomes a follower of the Nemirover. As in the case of traditional Orthodoxy, Hasidism created both a world and a world view, and its adherents lived totally within its confines. While the older generation might have been persuaded to stay close to the rebbe, to avoid the contamination of the New World, the younger generation could not be held back. In all some 340,000 Jews emigrated from the Austro-Hungarian Empire between 1881 and 1914.

What made all these communities resemble one another, whether Hasidic or Mitnagged, was the prevailing poverty. But in Russia the hardships of the poor were compounded by a particularly punitive system of conscription, specifically devised to wean Jewish children from their religion. Although it was the home of three quarters of the Jews in Eastern Europe, never was there a worse match than Russia and the Jews.

As early as the sixteenth century, Ivan the Terrible had set the tone for what was to come. When, in 1563, his troops had conquered Polotsk, a city on the Polish border, he ordered the Jews to be baptized into the Greek Orthodox faith. Those who refused were to be drowned in the Dvina River and three hundred met their death in this way. The Tsars could never understand Jewish stubbornness in refusing Christianity, while the Jews wanted no more than to observe their religion in peace.

Russia acquired the major part of its Jewish population inadvertently, as it were, along with the territory carved from Poland by Russia, Prussia, and Austria between 1772 and 1793. With Catherine the Great's portion of land came its 400,000 Jewish inhabitants, but Catherine had no wish to add more Jews to the population of Holy Russia and determined on a policy of containment. Certain territories along the western border of Russia where the newly acquired Jews lived were designated as the Pale of Settlement—and there the Jews were to be confined.

This began a vicious mixture of limited space and infinitely expanding restrictions on how Jews could live that characterized Tsarist policy for the next century and one-quarter. The success of Catherine's policy can be measured by the fact that the census of 1897 found that 3,558,000 of Russia's 5,000,000 Jews lived in the Pale, while only 300,000 lived in Russia proper, where they accounted for less that one-half of 1 percent of the population. The remaining million were in Poland and the Baltic states, also under Russian rule. One of Catherine's first actions after her acquisition was to impose a double tax on the Jews, a law that was never officially abrogated and put Jewish communities in a position of eternal arrears to the government, borrowing money to pay what they owed and eventually paying interest on interest. This had fateful consequences, as we shall see, for Jewish conscripts. It was under her rule, also, that the principle that everything that was not explicitly permitted the Jews by law was denied them.

Catherine's grandson, Nicholas I, is best remembered in Jewish history for his ukase of 1827 that conscripted Jews into the army under the so-called cantonist system, named for the cantonments or barracks in which the recruits lived. The system encouraged the recruitment of Jewish children as early as the age of twelve, but their required twenty-five years of military service was only reckoned from the age of eighteen. Its actual purpose, of course, had nothing to do with the military, and everything to do with religion and the desire of Nicholas I to convert the Jews. Where better to begin than with children?

The Russian writer and political activist Alexander Herzen, in a famous description of a group of newly inducted cantonists whom he meets on the road in 1835, questions their guards, who tell him that a third of the original group has already died. "They've collected a crowd of cursed little Jew boys of eight or nine years old," reports one of the guards. "Whether they are taking them for the navy or what, I can't say. . . . Not half of them will reach their destination . . . they just die off like flies. A Jew boy, you know is such a frail and weakly creature, like a skinned cat; he is not used to tramping in the mud for ten hours a day and eating biscuit, and then again, being among strangers, no father nor mother nor petting; well, they cough and cough, until they cough themselves into a grave." This law remained in force until the death of Nicholas in 1855.

In all, about 70,000 Jews passed through the cantonist system during its thirty years of existence. Some 25,000, perhaps half of those who were still children when they were recruited, converted; others married Russian women and left Jewish life; still others returned to their villages. Sholem Aleichem describes such an old cantonist, Jonah, who becomes a bathhouse attendant in his old village, in the end neither Jew nor Russian, speaking a strange mixture of both languages and finding himself at one with the community only on Purim. On that holiday, a day of masks and make-believe, he, too, has his place among the revelers.

The terror inspired by those thirty years under Nicholas I was heightened by the random and ferocious way the recruiters went about filling their quota. They were called, with reason, *khappers*, or kidnappers, since they had the power to invade a house to carry off a child, or simply capture a young man on the street. Although after 1857 the term of service was only four years, in folk memory the horror associated with military service persisted. Yet there was reason enough to avoid even four years as a soldier of the Tsar where Jews not infrequently found themselves the target of anti-Semitic officers and fellow soldiers. The ballad of "Yoshke's Departure" sung by his betrothed poignantly conveys her fears as she bids him goodbye at the railroad station.

> *Don't buy me any trinkets*
> *Or tell me that I'm pretty.*
> *Buy yourself a good pair of boots.*
> *You've got to join up . . .*
> *Oy vey, oy vey*
> *Yoshke is going away.*
> *One more kiss, one more touch.*
> *The train is about to leave.*

The periods of recruitment were dreaded in the Jewish villages like the coming of the Angel of Death because the power and favoritism of the ruling oligarchy showed itself then, finding ways to exempt the rich and enlist the sons of the poor. The first part of the quota, based on population and subject to change from year to year, demanded four to eight recruits for every 1,000 taxpayers in the community. In addition, an extra recruit was required for every 2,000 rubles of tax arrears owed by the community. These had swollen tremendously in the century since the double tax of Catherine the Great, so that by 1860 Jewish community arrears were estimated at 1,300,000 rubles—a serious sum when measured in lives. And then there was the penalty exacted for every recruit on the list who did not appear. For each such failure, his fellow Jews were required to supply three men in his place.

The system of exemptions for the educated, for the sons of rich merchants, for only sons, for rabbinical students and rabbis, as well as the arbitrary favoritism of the community leaders, put poor Jewish families with many sons at a disadvantage. In addition, the rich had the option of buying a substitute. Some of those who expected to be called up maimed themselves; others starved so as to fail the physical examination; and many fled abroad.

There was another kind of violence that also darkened the lives of the Jews in Russia, the ever-recurring pogroms—significantly enough, a word of Russian origin. Sometimes officially inspired by the state, or encouraged—especially at Easter—by the Church, sometimes a spontaneous outbreak following a quarrel, these hung in the air and Jews never felt secure in a world where neighbors could turn into enemies.

By 1881, the Jews in Russia had begun to see emigration as a solution to their problems. In April of that year—a month after the assassination of Alexander II—a series of pogroms broke out, beginning at Elisavetgrad in the south and gradually spreading to every part of Russia and Poland, including Warsaw. In all, 265 Jewish communities were attacked, one by one, as the violence moved from village to village, month after month, until the last one of the year in Warsaw broke out on December 25, 1881. When, in January 1882, the Minister of the Interior Count Nicholas P. Ignatiev was questioned on the future of the Jews in Russia, his reply was an invitation to leave. "The Western frontier," he said, "is open for the Jews." In that year 10,489 Jews took the hint, tripling the number who had left the year before.

A few months later, in May 1882, a year after the onset of the pogroms, the government responded to the disorders by blaming the victims. It issued the "Temporary Laws" which required Jews to move out of their villages to the cities, a move that increased the instability of Jewish life since new residence permits were issued for only a limited term. Further, the percentage of Jewish students allowed to enter the high schools and universities was drastically reduced. Then, in 1894, a new law put the liquor trade under government monopoly. Since the Jews had for generations leased the right to make liquor and run the inns in the villages, they became the true target of the law. As its consequence, 200,000 families lost simultaneously their means of livelihood and their right of residence.

The result of this total dislocation was that by 1897, more than 50 percent of the Jews living in cities were without any occupation. Although the pogroms gradually died out, they continued to reappear sporadically over the next decade in various parts of Russia. In 1903 the Kishinev Massacre, which claimed forty-five Jewish lives, some six hundred wounded, and one thousand five hundred houses and businesses destroyed, again aroused worldwide indignation. In Russia, this latest pogrom was less surprising to the Jews than to the rest of the world.

Since the pogroms of 1881 there had been a new resoluteness in the Jewish appraisal of their situation. Some among the students and intellectuals had turned to the underground revolutionary movements. Others simply left. After centuries, the Jews had begun to throw off their long acceptance of suffering, their view of death at

the hands of hooligans as a holy Sanctification of the Name—
*Kiddush ha Shem.* The prevailing mood was expressed by the young
poet Chaim Bialik, writing in Hebrew:

> *Your dead have died in vain, and neither you nor I*
> *Can say for what they gave their lives, and why . . .*
> *No tears shall flow for you!—the Lord swears by His Name—*
> *For though the pain be great, great also is the shame.*

But the Jews no longer needed the reminder of Kishinev or Bialik. By 1903, more than 1 million had already left, and in the year
of the massacre another 125,000 gave up on Russia and sought their
fortunes elsewhere. They did not wait to hear Nicholas II say, in
1906, using the perjorative for Jews, "So long as I am Tsar, the
Zhyds of Russia shall not have equal rights."

External forces were not the only ones propelling Jews out of
their villages. Inside Russia, the government decrees affecting Jews
filled a book of nearly 1,000 pages, providing an airtight administrative and legal basis for the restrictions on life and liberty. As we
have seen, life within the Jewish villages and the Jewish enclaves in
the larger cities was often squalid and brutal, in addition to being
desperately poor. Surprisingly, in the last few decades, long after
the fact, as the voices of the immigrants themselves have weakened,
popular writers in the United States have invented a romanticized
image of these villages that satisfies the contemporary American
wish for a picturesque past.

In these rosy accounts, arranged marriages produce perfectly
matched pairs; children are tenderly educated in their schools;
women are happy to stand at their market stalls all day so that their
husbands can study. It is the best of all possible worlds. But it was
the reality in these villages, unaccounted for in the fairy-tale
retellings, that our young emigrants were escaping as much as the
hostile forces outside. Jewish life, this seemingly secret life, conducted in two strange languages that aroused so much suspicion and

enmity among their neighbors, was for centuries the source of Jewish cohesion and strength. But by the nineteenth century the protective fence was becoming a prison wall.

In part by choice, in part by the pressure of external forces, Jews lived separately from their neighbors in Eastern Europe. It was a life self-absorbed, self-contained, and governed by laws made by God and interpreted ever more closely by man. At the center of this system was education, not the education offered by the state, if and when it existed, but the education in the *heder*—the schoolroom where the schoolboy was inducted into the Hebrew alphabet—and the sacred texts, the Bible and the commentaries. Many spent their lives in the study and elucidation of these fundamental texts, ordinary men whose families or wives found it right to support them to this end. Girls seldom received any formal education, but were taught at home by their parents or by tutors to read Yiddish, also written in Hebrew script. They were taught, too, the fundamental blessings and prayers, which they recited year after year, often never understanding a syllable of what they were saying.

In time it became increasingly clear that this learning was totally remote from the outside world. In this scheme, there was no room for secular education, for mathematics, history, science, nor even for the language and literature of the country in which the students had been born. These *hedarim*, the prison houses of so many children for years on end, through long days of winter and summer, suffered from other deficiencies, as their former pupils attested. They were often in the hands of incompetent, poorly paid teachers whose schoolrooms were generally no more than a corner of their own wretched living quarters. There the children spent the day, crowded together on benches chanting their lessons aloud, in a pedagogical system that depended on blows to command discipline or to respond to error. Then again a pupil might be put to work tending a baby, or fetching water, or fulfilling some other domestic function for his teacher's wife.

Mendele Mokher Seforim (Shalom Jacob Abromowitsch), the

founder of modern Yiddish literature, was himself an exceptional student who enjoyed the attention of gifted teachers. But he had seen what ordinary students suffered. "Everyone knows, what a Talmud Toyre (a beginners' school) is," he wrote in his bitter satire *The Little Man*. " . . . It is a grave in which poor Jewish children are buried, where their minds are mutilated and where they are removed from all contact with the world in which they live. It is a factory that manufactures good-for-nothings, ne'er-do-wells, and spineless unfortunate creatures. It is a vast pit, an abyss, an unclean hovel standing on wobbly supports . . . a shame and a disgrace for other people to see."

No wonder that many Jews came out of these schools not able to do more than read their prayers and follow the services in the synagogue by rote. Nonetheless, it was a society in which learning occupied enormous prestige, where a truly able student could advance to the renowned yeshivas, and even a poor boy could hope for recognition on the basis of his talents. A rich family might well seek out a talented student as a son-in-law, and then keep him and their daughter and subsequent children for years while he continued his studies, feeling repaid for their efforts in the renown his learning brought to their family.

Even more than the way this system rewarded the gifted, it was the basis of continuity in Jewish life. It gave Jews their sense of history; it was the source of Jewish law and ethics, the fount of Jewish custom. It was the guide to manners and morals. But above all, learning was so central that it became the measure by which rank and honor were determined. In an impoverished and underemployed population, the study of the Bible and its commentaries provided an unending occupation. Even a poor workman at the end of his working day would turn in at his little synagogue, which was as much his club as a place of worship, to study *"a blat gemore*—a page of commentary"* for an hour before the beginning of the evening service. It refreshed his spirit, but more than that it restored to him his sense of dignity in a hard world. When Tevyea, Sholem Aleichem's imperishable dairyman, daydreams about his future life should his daughter marry a wealthy suitor, his fantasy places him at the head of a table with fellow Jews who are studying *"a blat gemore."* As he relishes the scene, they ask his opinion, and defer to his interpretation of a knotty passage. What is significant in this fantasy is not the deference that he assumes is paid to wealth, but that the most luxurious recreation he can imagine is the study of a sacred text.

Yet this reverence for study, which for so long had been the binding force in Jewish life, was predicated on a self-contained society. The nineteenth century brought changes to Europe unimaginable in the epochs that had preceded it. Monarchy was no longer sacred; revolutionary movements were springing up in dark places; the increasingly popular creed of national self-determination was awakening novel thoughts among Jewish intellectuals. Moses Hess broached the idea of Jewish nationality as early as 1862, and later Theodor Herzl galvanized the forces that sought a return to Zion by postulating a Jewish state. But most important was the spread of the doctrine of the natural rights of man. Slowly, slowly, the echoes of these theories percolated into the yeshivas. In response, as the lure of other cultures grew more dangerous, the rabbis sought to close the intellectual gates to new ideas. They could not imagine a way in which Jewish life and learning, as they knew it, could accommodate to the surrounding world. This rigidity, however, this incapacity to change, contributed to driving millions of young Jews from their homes.

Over and over again we learn in the memoirs of the period how yeshiva students had to read secular works by stealth, often having laboriously taught themselves the forbidden profane languages. To the guardians of the faith, however, even to read Latin or Cyrillic script was the beginning of heresy. Pauline Wengeroff, who came from a well-to-do family in Bobruisk, near Minsk, wrote her memoirs at the end of the nineteenth century describing the gradual decay of the strict traditional society in which she had grown up. She lived in a large and wealthy household that included her two married sisters. Their husbands, in accordance with good old custom, spent their days immersed in the study of the Talmud, which was customarily chanted aloud. These young men, who knew German, one day hit on the device of placing Schiller's *Don Carlos* inside their Talmud folios, which they then read with the Talmudic chant. Although they were caught and reprimanded, they were not to be stopped and continued their secret intellectual forays, studying Russian grammar, natural history, and even collecting and cataloguing insects. Later in the century, Shmarya Levin, a Zionist who was a passionate Hebraist, and who became a representative in the Russian Parliament, wrote in his memoirs that if a student in his yeshiva were caught reading even a modern Hebrew newspaper, "his dismissal took place on the spot." As early as the eighteenth century, Salomon Maimon, who fled to Berlin to study philosophy, used the words "barbaric" and "superstitious" to characterize his world, words that recur again and again among later emigrants.

In the West, a century ahead of the Jews in the Tsarist lands, German Jews had begun to wrestle with ways to bring their two cultures together in their lives. By the end of the eighteenth century, they began to establish secular schools that taught German language and literature, history, mathematics, science, and the traditional subjects of Jewish learning. New prayerbooks were written; rabbis began to preach their sermons in German. In the mid-nineteenth century Samson Raphael Hirsch, the founder of Neo-Orthodoxy in Germany, introduced the idea of "*Torah im Derech Eretz*—the Bible in the way of the world." This was an approach that kept both worlds in balance, excluding neither.

In Eastern Europe, where there was no comparable movement toward change, and faced by a choice between absolutes, many of the young responded by rejecting traditional Jewish life entirely. During the nineteenth century they had many alternatives. A group of enthusiasts in St. Petersburg who called themselves the "Lovers of Zion" adopted in 1882 a program of national revival, with its corollary, settlement in Palestine, as the way into the future. Despite their inexperience in farming, they managed to send a trickle of pioneers who established colonies under the most arduous of circumstances. There were Russian revolutionary movements that attracted Jews; there was a Jewish Socialist movement—the Bund—and in 1897 the founding of the Zionist movement drew thousands to its banner.

While in the cities such as Odessa and Vilna the ideas of these movements, and their newspapers, were common currency, in the remote villages where more than half the Jews lived all this echoed only faintly. The well-to-do or well-educated might subscribe to a newspaper, but it was hardly as if this was part of the regular reading matter of the ordinary Jew. Sholem Aleichem describes how the Dreyfus Case is followed in his mythical village of Kasrilevke. "Zeidel, Reb Shaye's son," Sholem Aleichem tells us,

> was the only person in town who subscribed to a newspaper, and all the news of the world they learned from him, or rather through him. He read and they interpreted. . . . As the case went on, they got tired of waiting for Zeidel to appear in the synagogue with the news. They began to go to his house. Then they could not wait that long and began to go along with him to the post office for his paper. There they read the news, discussed, shouted, gesticulated, all together and in their loudest voices. More than once the postmaster had to let them know in gentle terms that the post office was not the synagogue.

In these Jewish villages in the Pale, in the Ukraine, in the countryside in Galicia, the process of acculturation which so gradually but ineluctably overtook the Jews in Western Europe, as it did also in Vienna and Budapest, was neither a temptation nor a possibility.

What could be more remote for the Jews in the countryside than the peasant life around them? Tightly bound to the rhythms of the Russian Orthodox Church, imbued with an endemic anti-Semitism, and, as it seemed to the Jews, without culture, peasant life could not invite emulation. The weak links in Jewish society, of course, were the intellectuals who discovered and deciphered other languages, whose heads were turned by new literature and new ideas. They soon had ambitions that transcended their village—the shtetl.

And yet the boundaries of these Jewish villages in the peasant countryside were more porous on the level of daily life than either side knew. In their diets, the staples of the Jewish cuisine mirrored those in the peasant household, without the pork, of course, and with the addition of the Sabbath challah. But at both ends of the village, Jews and peasants ate borsht in Poland, kasha (buckwheat groats) in Russia, marmaliga (corn meal) in Romania. Folk medicine easily crossed religious boundaries when doctors were few and unreliable. And superstitions were also not stopped by the guardian amulet—the mezuzah on the doorpost. Fears of the evil eye, of the well-aimed curse, of malign spirits, of the portents in dreams were all part of the universal beliefs, shared by Jew and peasant alike.

In Jewish life it was sometimes hard to know where law and custom left off and superstition began—and it was just this unthinking enslavement to ritual that exasperated the younger and more adventurous members of the community. But far more serious was their desperate and chronic economic situation. With the exception of a thin layer of well-to-do families—merchants, manufacturers, professionals, along with a few millionaires and ennobled families—few young Jews could see a future for themselves. In the spring of 1882, one young yeshiva student, Isidore Kopeloff, and his friend Israel Mendel in Bobruisk knew that they had to leave.

We had no definite plans [he wrote] as to where to go or what to do. We did not even know what we might be suited for. We left because we were driven by necessity. In Bobruisk we did not see any possibility of employment, unless we sat and waited for a match with a dowry, and then after the wedding became a broker, or a small shopkeeper, or just hung about the streets all day long—something that for us as modern, worldly, enlightened, and socialist-thinking fellows was simply out of the question. We wanted to accomplish something, to work, to create, and above all to become useful both to ourselves and to others. At the least, we wanted to earn our bread honestly. It was a pain and shameful to us to exist as a burden to others—I on my poor mother, and Israel Mendel on his father.

Jakob Fromer, who escaped to Berlin from Poland about the same time, also wrote about how debasing the lack of real work was for the young men, and how purposeful and desirable the West seemed to them. There, he wrote admiringly, "everyone has his own recognized profession and does not need, as in the ghetto, to puzzle out every morning when he wakes up, how he will make his living that day."

In Russia, where more than 95 percent of the population made its living in agriculture, the Jews, who were not allowed to own land, occupied a strange middle position in the countryside as the stewards of estates and sometimes as lessees of orchards or forests. These were the lucky ones. Others had literally no occupation, living from hand to mouth by casual employment as porters, wagon drivers, and occasionally earning a commission for acting as a broker in whatever transaction came to hand. Mendele Mokher Seforim, in one of his mordant vignettes about Jewish village life, describes just such a desperate figure who comes to a weekly fair and tries to earn some money making a match between the children of two rich merchants. All day long, as he tells it, he runs between the two, praising the merits of each party until they finally sit down to write an agreement. "Just as we were ready to break a bit of crockery in the customary gesture of celebration," he recalls ruefully, "we happened to remember the bride and groom, and what do you think? Believe me, it hurts even to talk about it. The whole thing was a disaster! No, it was ten times worse than a disaster! It just blew up in my face! Listen to my misfortune and how the wrath of God descended on me: the two merchants each had—what do you think they had? They each had a son!"

The misery of these little villages was corroborated both by travelers from abroad and by Jewish writers who with more passion and engagement than the occasional visitor were able to describe the fine details of Jewish poverty. In the summer of 1905, just a few months before the Revolution, a British diplomat, Henry Hammond Dawson Beaumont, traveled through the Pale of Settlement and Poland to inspect the situation of the Jews. He wrote a diligent report filled with statistics and acute observations of how they lived. Typically, in Vilna, called by the Jews "the Jerusalem of the North," he was struck only by "its narrow streets, its overcrowded houses, its dirt and unsavoury smells." Karl Emil Franzos, a Jew from a Westernized German-speaking family who grew up in Chortkov, wrote obsessively about the misery of his Yiddish-speaking compatriots. Disguising the town under the name of Barnow, his stories pointed out not only the physical wretchedness in which the Jews lived but also the price that many paid for the rigid rules of Judaism, whose infringement could bring ostracism or even, as in one of his stories, death.

Life in Eastern Europe was chronicled by scholars and literary figures, but also by ordinary members of the community, who were sometimes inspired by the distance of emigration. Women were far fewer among the memoir writers, but far more impassioned. To read them is to experience an explosion in words, celebrating above all their liberation in America. All of them were child workers who, with a sharp eye for social injustice, recorded the dual helplessness of being working female children.

In the early years of this century, childhood seemed to end at the age of fourteen. At least the keepers of immigration statistics in the United States so classified the world. And here, as in much else, Jewish immigrants differed from the others. Whereas only 8 or 9 percent of other nationalities were listed in this category, nearly 30 percent of the Jewish immigrants were under fourteen. There are several explanations for this striking difference. The most common is that Jews came to America with their families, which included large numbers of young children, with the intention of settling in this country. Among other nationalities, the more common pattern was for the young men to come and stay only long enough to earn the money that would permit them to return home as "rich men." For the Jews caught up in the large and growing flight that began in 1881, however, it was permanent. In the pattern of emigration that quickly developed, the young and strong went ahead—single young men, young married couples—and then gradually brought the rest of the family over.

Less often noticed, except by the statistics keepers at the Immigration Bureau, are the large number of children thirteen or fourteen years old who traveled alone to America. As we have seen, the arriving thirteen-year-olds did not think of themselves as children. Many had already spent several years as apprentices in the Old Country, providing themselves with a basis for a life that they could not even imagine. But in their dreams it was the opposite of everything they were leaving behind. Except for the work. They knew that they would labor for their livelihood from their first day in the new country.

In the factories where they found jobs, they also found one another, talked and laughed, and formed friendships. One girl who worked in a shop that prepared ornamental feathers for the millinery trade remembered how the girls were fined by the foreman for laughing. But sometimes, she said, in spite of the prohibition or perhaps because of it, the tables lined with girls would be swept with paroxyms of laughter over some trifle, and the more the foreman threatened, the harder it was for them to stop.

They looked after one another, as another woman who worked

most of her life in a clothing factory remembered. "We were very young," she said.

> I was only thirteen when I went [to live in a union-sponsored settlement house]. Most of us didn't have families. We were each other's family. One little girl was only twelve. That was Rivke, a quiet shy little thing. She was working in an electric factory. She was in there sixteen, eighteen hours a day. She never complained but at night she would sit and cry. Her fingers were tied up in rags full with blood. We made her quit that job and she learned sewing from one of the other girls. That same little girl, we didn't save her nothing. Later on she got killed in the Triangle Fire.

In this fire in 1910 at the Triangle Shirtwaist Company in New York City, 146 young workers, mostly Italians and Jews, were burned or fell to their deaths.

Young as they were, these children had seen and endured a great deal in the Old Country. But in their villages there was no remedy for their afflictions. It was only much later, in the New World, that long-buried secrets came out of hiding, often in the anonymity of the letter columns of the *Forward*, in Yiddish the *Forverts*, one of the daily newspapers in New York. One young woman who had been raped in a pogrom and had lived for years with a sense of shame wrote to say that she was now engaged to a young man, but tormented by this terrible event in her past. Should she tell him? Would he reject her? What should she do? These children had come to America to start anew. But sometimes the past would not let them go.

# Part III

# The Bronx

# 1

# Floors

In the Old Country, my mother lived in a house with a beaten earth floor. She never told me this. I only learned it by chance when my father taunted her with it in response to her fine airs and manners. My mother-in-law, on the other hand, came from Warsaw, where she had lived in an apartment building made of stone. The stories of these floors became a talisman of sorts, for one the source of shame, for the other of amusement. My mother-in-law loved to tell the story of how she prepared for her first Sabbath in the new country. Wanting to wash the kitchen floor, she filled a bucket with water, and preparatory to wielding the mop, flung the contents on the floor. Shrieks from her downstairs neighbors, pounding on the door, protests about the *grine*—the greenhorn. In Warsaw, she had lived with stone floors; how was she to know that in the New World they were made of lesser stuff.

Even in the New World, floors—the linoleum-covered kitchen floors especially—were sure barometers of a housewife's standards and ability. When I came home from school on Friday afternoons, it was at the culmination of the day's and the week's race with the clock to bring the apartment to a state of perfect cleanliness before Sabbath rest overtook us. I would arrive to find the kitchen chairs stacked in the living room while the freshly washed linoleum was drying. It would then be covered with pathways of newspapers, to prevent marring the perfect surface, until finally at some point when the papers themselves created a mass of crumpled debris underfoot, they would be lifted up to expose the pristine floor. Cleanliness was more than a good in itself. It was a test of character, a measure of worth, a yardstick of competence. One of the most devastating judgments of that time was the whisper that a certain neighbor was "dirty." Now, cleanliness did not have anything to do with orderliness or repose; in fact, I mostly remember it being achieved at the cost of immense upheaval, bad temper, and tension about time, since Orthodox housewives set themselves rigorous standards of work to be accomplished by the end of every Friday, the "end" being measured inexorably by the time that the sun set. And a winter Friday was heartbreakingly short for the amount of work that had to be compressed into it.

I would awaken early in the morning to the sound of my mother wielding the *hakmeser*—the round-edged chopping knife—as she pounded the gefilte fish mixture. Although the fish had already been ground, the last stages of preparation called for a final maceration by hand in the wooden chopping bowl reserved for this purpose. As I left for school, I would see the parts of the stove dismantled in the sink in some terrible lye solution that required my mother to use heavy rubber gloves. Then the beds were treated to their weekly spraying of kerosene against bed bugs. Only much later did I realize what a terrible fire hazard was being prepared here in the name of cleanliness. The fear of bed bugs—*vantsen*—organized the housewife's working day. Beds were not made in the morning. It would only encourage the spontaneous generation of these vermin, it was believed, to enclose the warm, breathing air in which we had slept inside tight covers. Instead, the windows were flung open— even on the coldest winter days—the mattresses folded in half (this was before the days of innersprings, of course), and the pillows and featherbeds put out on the window sill to air. Air and sun were the great panaceas and healers of New York tenement life. They prevented bed bugs; they forestalled tuberculosis; they brought good health. They were the hallmark of respectability. It was the search for air and sun that led to the migration from the Lower East Side, and even from Harlem, to the quiet streets of Brooklyn and the heights of the Bronx.

Only in late afternoon was the bedding taken in, the windows closed, and the beds restored to some semblance of normality. Bed bugs were in themselves a troublesome and unhealthy plague. More than that, they were a source of shame—and it was shame rather than hygiene, I think, that drove the housewives to scour their apartments and vie with one another in setting absolute standards for their cleanliness. This was not the only area in which shame played its part in modulating the behavior of the immigrants. It was shame about their poor, primitive origins that affected the way the newcomers accepted America, just as it prevented them from telling their children very much about their own lives in the Old Country. The anecdotes that survived filled in very little of the background, but took the form of an adventure tale that ended fortunately (or badly), a clever exchange of words, a family narrative. But what people wore or ate, what kind of beds they slept in, what sort of furniture was in the rooms they talked about was all left in the shadows.

My mother was actually a poor housekeeper—no housekeeper at all by American standards—but she too was drawn into its simulacrum by her need to assert her standing as a housewife. In that community, to be a *berye*, the Yiddish superlative for housewife, was the highest compliment for a woman. It conveyed skill, shrewdness, accomplishment, a capacity for getting things done. To tell the truth, my mother's gefilte fish was terrible, and we lived all week long in a welter of disorder and makeshift arrangements. But Friday, the climax of the week, the day of preparation for the Sabbath, exerted its power even over her. However inept she was in her household management, old memories stirred; the atmosphere of our neighborhood, which took on an extraordinary bustle on Friday mornings, also motivated her to take what was largely symbolic, if drastic, action.

She had come to this country as little more than a child and arrived to be taken in by her oldest brother, Asher, now Harry, and his wife, Feigele, now Fanny. My mother was prepared for marvels in the Golden Land. But her first great puzzle came as they were driving from the ship in her brother's buggy through the Lower East Side and she saw the high, closely packed tenements. These were understandable. She had heard of the tall buildings in New York. What she couldn't understand were the lines of washing hung out to dry, four and five stories above the ground. How did anyone reach them?

Her bewilderment about the laundry and embarrassment about asking, like my mother-in-law's miscalculation about the floors, marked the beginning of a pattern of confusion and disorientation. What it elicited was a style of caution and withdrawal to safer ground, where the hazard of making mistakes or of being mocked as a *grine* was reduced. But it left a residue of uncertainty, a loss of confidence that stamped their experience with "America." My mother-in-law, after all, arrived as a married woman with two children. She, unlike my mother, could and did remain safely embedded in her family, never learning much English and never needing to, living as she did in an entirely Yiddish-speaking world. There she could be expansive, authoritative, dramatic.

For my mother, however, who arrived in the country having just entered her teens, and immediately went to work in a shirt factory, wariness became a way of life. In her shop the other operators at the sewing machines were young Jewish girls like herself, and some, like her, went to school at night to learn English. For a long time, however, it remained the language of strangers. In her family, as in the shop, she lived in the self-enclosed world of the immigrant. From moment to moment, her life went on in Yiddish, and not only in conversation. New York at that time was rich in its offering of

Yiddish newspapers, magazines, cabarets, and theaters. The theaters especially were the magnet of the working girl, with their stars and matinée idols such as Boris Thomashevsky, my mother's favorite.

In the years just before World War I, the Yiddish theater in New York was at its height, and its eager patrons were none other than the shop workers like my mother, storekeepers, artisans, laborers, peddlers—in a word the whole immigrant generation, newly arrived and passionate about the theater, which gave them back their lives, heightened, beautified, in elevated language, dramatized. Of course my mother had never experienced the theater in her tiny shtetl in Galicia. And certainly her father would never have approved of the happenings on stage. Women singing in revealing gowns, couples kissing on the stage, children speaking disrespectfully to their parents—all this would only have confirmed his view of America as an unholy land whose embrace corrupted life itself. His was not the only family that lost its children to the New World, yet he seems never to have repented.

This was a sorrow to my mother, who adored her learned and saintly father. But it did not interfere with her newfound pleasures. In her late teens, as an experienced "operator" she began to specialize in the shop, and at piecework rates set collars on the body of shirts from morning to night. This meant high earnings, and living under her brother's roof she had money left over for finery on a grand scale. She patronized a dressmaker and ordered elegant evening wear for the theater, for *simkhes*—celebrations—and for weddings. I saw two of these fantasies that survived into my own childhood—one a heavily beaded, sleeveless pink satin dance dress; the other an elaborate, full-skirted, full-sleeved confection in black velvet dévoré, a fabric whose like I have seen only rarely since.

It was a hybrid world, of course, where old customs and new opportunities were blended, and in the rich Jewish culture of New York City during the first decades of this century, new rules began to govern the habits of Jewish life. It was understood that the Yiddish theater would not give performances on Friday night or Saturday. But Saturday at sundown and Sundays, the box offices opened to great crowds. As my mother told me, people didn't buy tickets in advance—a remnant of Old World fearfulness, where one didn't tempt fate by making advance preparations. So the hubbub and excitement in the lobbies of these theaters before performances were heightened by the anxiety over whether one would reach the head of the line before all the tickets were sold.

What the public loved above all were the melodramas that reflected the all-too-vivid moments in their own lives: stories of abandoned wives, estranged American children, neglected parents, interspersed with heady musicals and tales from the Old Country—a mixture that reflected the homesickness already being translated into nostalgia. Is it any wonder that Shakespeare's *Lear* was a tremendous hit on Second Avenue? Shakespeare was, in fact, a familiar playwright to Jewish audiences, so familiar that translators took liberties. One announcement for *Hamlet* advertised that the play had not only been translated but also improved for its presentation in Yiddish— *"iberge*z*etst un farbesert."*

The immigrant audiences of the 1920s were easily reduced to tears either by happy endings or by tragic ones. This was a young audience, uprooted from "home," anxious about their livelihood, about making their way in the New World, struggling to reconcile what they had been taught in the Old Country with the unexpected freedoms and possibilities of America. For many who came as young teenagers, "home" as a place, as a way of life, faded. What remained were the memories of parents left behind, memories of themselves as children. But these were rapidly overlaid by the configuration of a totally different society, and the wish to enter somehow into that new world.

When they had grown up enough to marry, few of these children had family mementoes with which to start a household. At best, like my mother, they had brought a down quilt—a *perene*, covered in a sturdy red chambray and whose content was guarded like diamonds. When on occasion the down needed to be cleaned or the cover renewed, like the ladies who went to Tiffany's to have their pearls restrung, my mother would take her quilt to the refurbisher and watch every step of the process to make sure that *her* down, and only her down, was returned to the new covering. Having stripped geese herself, she was a connoisseur in these matters and would sometimes squeeze a doubtful pillow between her fingers to test whether the little spines were still there. This *perene* was her sole tangible connection to home. The older immigrants, the married couples or those already betrothed, arrived better prepared, with their silver candlesticks wrapped in their down quilt, or even with a silver samovar. But beyond the essential comforter, the young ones, like my mother, came without possessions, ready and even anxious to furnish their lives with the goods of the New World.

What was perhaps unexpected was their hunger for splendor, coming as they did from villages where benches were more common than chairs. Unlike the settlement house workers, who saw morality in straight lines and recommended plain deal furniture for immigrant homes, my parents and their neighbors invested in curves, high finishes, ornate carvings, and elaborately patterned linoleum "rugs." I spent many hours of my childhood hanging head down from our couch, tracing the palmettes and stylized flowers of the linoleum on the floor with my finger, and it was not until I was nine or ten that I first understood that there were soft woven carpets on which our replica was based. This discovery came in the living room of a school friend who lived in the neighborhood, but whose father occupied a highly respected place in our little world. He was the neighborhood pharmacist, which practically made him a doctor, which was as far as one's imagination could stretch. Unless it was to a "professor." In dire medical cases, the victim was sometimes operated on by a "professor," a sign of both privilege and despair.

Although he lived in our neighborhood, our pharmacist was clearly much more prosperous than we were, and his apartment had not only a soft and splendid Chinese rug but looming over it (since that was my perspective) a baby grand piano played in what seemed to me a dazzling style by my classmate's older sister. In my imagination the two flowed together, the piano and the rug, conveying as an ensemble warmth, culture, and luxury. I don't know if my parents really believed what they said when they criticized the rug's unhygienic nature—how it retained dust, polluting the air and one's lungs. Linoleum, on the other hand, could always be scrubbed, its shining surface a guarantee of its health-giving properties.

This dismissive attitude was not entirely convincing to me when I thought about the pharmacist's world—the softness, the grandness, the cosmopolitanism of it all. The piano-playing sister eventually married a German refugee and moved to Pittsburgh—all elements of unthinkable foreignness and distance given our tightly held circle. Of course our family and their friends and *landslayt* also came from Europe. But they were known quantities to me, speaking to one another in the comforting vernacular of Yiddish. But Germany? That was another world.

As for doctors and pharmacists, my parents' attitude toward these professionals was at the very least one of profound respect. It was a respect based on the same bewilderment that shaped their way of managing in the world. The university and medical education were beyond their imagining. It was not clear to them how or where one entered the ladder to such an accomplishment. But there was no doubt that these were men at the apex of humanity who could and did live on the Grand Concourse in the Bronx. This splendid avenue, a miniature Champs-Elysées, with its green center meridian and its handsome Art Deco apartment houses, was the culminating point of anyone's aspirations. It even ran along a ridge making it literally the high point of the Bronx, dividing east and west, and like the Champs-Elysées was a favorite promenade ground on weekends and holidays. Here not only the apartments but even the lobbies, attended by uniformed doormen, were of course carpeted in precious Oriental rugs weighted down by dark, heavily carved Renaissance tables with man-high Chinese vases guarding cavernous corners.

Once, when I had broken my arm, I had the occasion to visit one of these buildings for several Sundays running, to see the doctor who had set it and was checking on my progress. I would come in the morning, first passing through the hushed lobby, and then taking the elevator to his apartment. Here I would sometimes see the son of the family—about my age—vanishing down a hallway in what seemed like illimitable space having just picked up the newspaper that had been *delivered* to the door. It was this whiff of another life that made me think not only of the carpets but of the life, the kind of life that was lived with Oriental rugs underfoot and with the sort of service that brought a newspaper to the door on a snowy morning. These glimpses, however brief, showed me a life different from what I knew.

I endowed this family with everything that I longed for and found missing at home: the order, repose, and regularity of people who knew their way, who knew how to command the world as my parents did not, who knew, in fact, how to live. Very early I saw my parents as plainly adrift, confident enough at home but easily intimidated by officials, authority. My father, who was accustomed to tyrannize over a family of women, could be reduced to silence and submission by a word from a policeman or a government form letter, while my mother, as if arming us for an inevitable struggle, said, "You know who you are, no matter what people say." What went on in the glorious spaces on the Grand Concourse, by contrast, was an existence where people spoke softly, their desires cosseted, their senses indulged. It was something to mull over.

The only carpet that I ever saw that had been brought from the Old Country belonged to a Romanian family. Roughly woven, it did not speak of repose and luxury, but it added depth to the history of the family for whom it was a prized possession. It was large and giddily colored, with a pattern of red and pink roses on a green ground, and hung on the wall over their couch, not to be profaned by being trodden upon. It made the Romanians—already unique in a Polish-Russian enclave—seem even more exotic that they had this substantial talisman from home, as if it held them closer to the old ways than we who traveled with so little baggage.

Despite my parents' acceptance of their linoleum rug, I began to think, secretly, that they were missing something. Did they not know or care about the originals on which this poor cold thing was based? What I did not realize until much later was that this was a perfect example of how they managed the hand that life dealt them. Whatever they had or achieved was good and excellent, a testimony to their industry and prudence. Beyond that was excess, showiness, waste. My father could still remember vividly the hunger of his orphaned childhood, and my mother from her early teens knew the precarious life of a wage earner. A steady job—especially as the Depression deepened—was the utmost limit of one's dreams. It made a linoleum rug an excellent floor covering.

# 2

# Laughter

*"Narele, vus lakhste?*—Little fool, why are you laughing?" I heard this often as a child. It was a common formula, and told me that laughter was dangerous: It tempted the malign fates to intervene and snatch our happiness away, and then, too, it was silly, frivolous, not dignified. Dignity could be extended even to children, but its condition was sobriety and a rejection of fantasy, an insistence on the utility of every action. My parents rejected, for example, the possibility of sending me to kindergarten. What was the point of going to school just to play? Surely by five I was beyond such childish things.

Such an estimation flattered me, but it also gave me a pang as I wondered sometimes about what went on in those bright kindergarten rooms with their low tables and chairs. But I was mostly conscious of the importance bestowed on me by being treated as a serious person. This meant, I learned early, being aware of the layering that separated one's deepest, innermost core, which was inextricably tied up with being Jewish, and the public self that accommodated the transient mores of the transient world in which one happened to live. My parents, I am sure, never heard of the Hebraist and poet Judah Leib Gordon and his famous slogan, "Be a Jew at home, and a man in the street," yet I sometimes wonder whether Gordon in coining that watchword was not so much original as giving voice to the prevailing sentiment of his time. It remained true as well for my parents, for whom being Jewish was both sacred and private, and in their long perspective they perceived themselves as only the newest link in that eternal chain of Jewish history and suffering. There are well-known comparatives for the duration of time in Yiddish that express these ideas—"as long as the Jewish exile— *so lang vi dos yiddishen goles,*" or alternatively, "as long as Jewish troubles—*so lang vi di yiddishen tsores.*" And yet even I, born in a fortunate hour, in a Golden Land, was also part of that succession.

So there we were in Exile, in *goles,* the descendants of kings and martyrs, with a history of incomparable length and nobility, with laws to match, all of which were beyond the weak comprehension of the uninitiated but became the lifelong study of those born as Jews. All of this secret and ancient knowledge, in two arcane languages, formed the inner core of our identity. But one was surrounded by unseen forces both good and evil, and by the time I reached thirteen—the age from which I legally bore the responsibility for my own sins—I was well prepared to join the complex dance between these powers.

Good Jews know that they are responsible for the observance of 613 commandments, of which 365 are negative and 248 are positive. I never added up the commandments as I was taught them in the course of my childhood, but one phrase remains fixed in my mind. When I was forbidden to do something and asked why, the answer was always simply and finally, *"Me tor nit*—We are not allowed." Perhaps the most convincing part of that message was the "we"— because with that word one was joined through history and in extension into the present to all the Jews who ever lived, who also knew that *"me tor nit."*

Sholem Aleichem's Tevye, the Job of modern Yiddish literature, ends his long series of letters and conversations with "Mr. Sholem Aleichem" at the moment when he has been notified that he is being expelled from his village—the village in which his ancestors and his wife are buried, and where he himself spent his life as a dairyman and raised seven daughters. But he does not pause to mourn. He ends with a paean of praise to God for having made him a Jew, the servant of the Law and the lifelong student of the sacred writings. That unshakable sense of superiority that even the humblest Jew felt was the source of his stability amid the endemic anti-Semitism of Eastern Europe. He knew who he was, as we did, and it was incomparably the best, giving him (and us) the strength to brush away the slights, the low regard that the very fact of being Jewish brought in its wake. It would have been a surprise to Tevye's mockers and revilers to know what he thought of them.

The evils of anti-Semitism, pogroms, or expulsion were only the temporal manifestations of the good and evil spirits that floated in the air and could be tempted into action by an incautious word or deed. To this day, I am made slightly nervous by the idea of a baby shower. And as for laying on a whole nursery, I find that most imprudent. But one was not entirely helpless. There were, after all, counterspells to the evil eye, propitiatory rites or a red ribbon tied at just the right place and time for a newborn child. Foolishly, in a fit of rationalism at the age of twelve, I refused to learn these useful charms when my mother offered to teach them to me.

We also knew that the forces for good could be summoned in moments of need by the pure in heart. We were raised on the story of my grandfather who, when traveling in a forest during a summer thunderstorm, averted a bolt of lightning by calling out just in time, *"Shema Yisroel,"* the first words of the fundamental Jewish statement of belief in one God. And what were our good deeds, if not a shield that went before us to protect us on that final day of reckoning? As my father explained to me, the accounting was meticulous. Each night, as we slept, our souls flew up to heaven to enter into the Great Ledger our good and bad deeds. And on that final day a simple addition would quickly determine how our accounts stood.

These account books, it seems, were also available to Satan himself, as I. L. Peretz tells us in his story "A Pinch of Tobacco," about the last days of the rabbi of Chelm. When Satan discovers, to his outrage, that the debit side of the rabbi's account is blank, he strikes one of his famous bargains with the Lord, receiving permission to tempt the rabbi under the usual condition that he not harm him. The title of the story tells us what leads the rabbi finally into sin. Not beautiful women, jewels, money, or fiery horses, all of which are brought out to seduce him. As one of the apprentice devils reflects at the end, "One does not stumble over a mountain. It is the pebble in the road that causes our fall." And since the lightest transgression could tip the balance at the end, all of this induced a certain watchfulness.

But the danger was not only from within. The real world also had its evil elements. One of the earliest words that I heard was *sonim*, "enemies." By the nature of things, by their place in the world, in history, Jews were surrounded by enemies, and the political scene in particular was always being carefully scrutinized for *sonim*. Of course anti-Semitism in the United States was less violent than at home, but nonetheless it existed embedded in the social fabric, limiting immigration, determining policy in the public schools, placing invisible barriers around neighborhoods, careers, university education, restaurants, or resorts. When, in the 1930s, my father applied for jobs and was told that various of these companies didn't hire Jews, then anti-Semitism did the sort of damage that mere taunts and epithets never could. Against these, my father and his generation had been schooled and armored (as I was) from their earliest years. To combat economic discrimination required not defense but an outflanking course of action.

In the 1920s and 1930s, many young aspiring Jewish doctors who had been turned away by medical schools in the United States went off to Switzerland or Scotland for their professional education. This was an exercise not without its perils, as in the cautionary tale of my cousin Anna's friend Augusta. Her betrothed had gone off, like other medical students, his tuition paid by Augusta's parents and, as the saga went, even outfitted by them with two made-to-order suits. But as he came to the end of his studies, he revealed a bitter truth: He had found another love and was not returning home. (Or perhaps he *was* returning home, but not to Augusta. It no longer mattered.) It was a hard and heartbreaking world. In the tradition of Jewish storytelling where every anecdote carried its moral, we could measure and denounce the perfidious young man—his deceit, his betrayal. But we had no words for Augusta's feelings. Somehow Augusta's suffering was accepted with a mute resignation that a later generation would have made central.

Those with more modest ambitions stayed at home. For my older cousins in the late twenties and thirties, the great bridge between their ambition and reality was the Civil Service examination. This was the one route to a professional career that bypassed the anti-Semitism they expected and took for granted with an unblinking objectivity. The exclusions from restaurants, clubs, or even neighborhoods raised questions of civil liberties so removed and remote from any realistic aspiration that they were of no concern to my cousins. What mattered, desperately, was a *job*.

It was probably the occupational restrictions that the American-born generation found most galling. When anti-Semitism functioned as an economic barrier limiting Jewish access to employment or education, then the image of America was tarnished. No one cared about eating in a restaurant with *sonim*, but one needed a university degree to practice law or medicine. Matters darkened for second-generation Jews during the 1930s when the Depression heightened the already constricting effects of exclusionary practices. During that time, I remember an almost fatalistic acceptance by older cousins of the constraints placed upon them. Yet there was also a simmering indignation at the unfairness of a system that required them to go abroad for an education, that forced them to compress their talents, that deprived them of their dreams.

My cousins in that generation who aimed to be professionals limited their ambitions to becoming civil servants or accountants; optometrists rather than ophthalmologists; pharmacists rather than doctors. One painter manqué turned to picture-framing. At the pinnacle, for many, was a job as a teacher in the New York City public school system. At one stroke it combined an intellectual occupation with the steadiness and security of permanent, *government* employment. In a world where one was helpless against malice and irrationality, the Civil Service examination was the great leveler. There, certainty prevailed. A written examination ended in a score and it did not matter that your name was Rabinowitz. If you made high marks, you were entitled to a job in the vast and commodious government service—unless you wanted to be a teacher. Then there was a diabolical obstacle: the oral exam. Needless to say, only those with stellar results on the written even made it to this final ordeal. And here, as my cousins told their stories, real despair would come into their voices. A dentalized "t," an incorrect diphthong, an inappropriate glottal stop—real or imaginary—was enough to banish them forever from the paradise of teaching in the New York school system. Those who were turned away by the flaming sword of failure forever afterwards believed that these linguistic variants were only excuses seized upon by anti-Semites to limit the advancement of young Jews.

By the time I was twelve and enrolled in Hunter College High School—also achieved by competitive examination—I could nod my head sagely as I listened to their stories. Almost the first class at "Hunta High" (as we called it) was "Speech." Here we were gravely apprised of our lamentable habits and informed that all further progress in the world hung upon our changing our linguistic style. But even then in 1935, when students were perceived as passive receptacles, we were permitted to air our anxieties on the consequences of change. We feared being ostracized, being seen as outsiders, as people showing off, pretending to be better than family and neighbors. The price of difference was enormous, as it came tumbling out of us before those clear-eyed, gracious, cultivated women who were our teachers. But there was no help for it. We learned to tame our sibilants, to elide those final "gs" and level the singsong of our speech. We never *did* sound like the Miss Griffins and Miss Fields who so patiently taught us. Instead, we developed a distinctive hybrid speech that still touches my heart when I hear it on the radio occasionally as a social worker or teacher replies earnestly to an interviewer about inner-city problems. When I hear them, I think I know their biographies as intimately as my own.

For the immigrants, their early instruction at home—not even instruction, but a kind of atmosphere that even children breathed in—made it possible for them to look at the world gravely but warily, accepting the anti-Semitism they met as part of the inevitable weakness of mind and character of the "others." It confirmed them, too, in their low expectations of the others, dividing the world very early into good and bad. For the older generation of immigrants, the world had shadings of experience, with names to them, that were as yet invisible to the young. A man who had acted honorably, kindly, was spoken of respectfully, with wonderment, as *a fayner Christ*, "a fine Christian," and not with the customary and pejorative *goy*, which meant literally "a nation" and came to mean a member of *other* nations. More drily physiological, and rarely used in the New World, was *orl*—"the uncircumcised one." Many names for many aspects of the "others."

In the decades before World War II, it was not clear to the immigrant generation and their children how far "civil rights" took them. They had the right to vote, to express an opinion, the all-important right to strike. They could move and travel without reporting to the police. But beyond that, matters grew blurry. Did we object to Bible reading in school at the beginning of assemblies; to singing Christmas songs? I remember singing along cheerfully enough about "Dashing through the snow" and the "one-horse open sleigh." It was part of the magical, mythical America, just as reading about Dick and Jane and Spot and Grandmother's house was hardly different from reading a fairy tale. My own grandmother, who had borne eleven children and buried three husbands, was finally brought to America by her children in her old age—sixty? But she and I were separated by a chasm of time and place. This wrinkled, bewigged old woman would kiss me tremulously, tragically, as we stared wordlessly at one another. My bobe was surely not the grandmother of the beaming countenance, the polka-dot apron and steaming pies, of Dick and Jane. When I was learning to read Dick and Jane, in fact, I had not as yet even seen a pie.

Christmas, then, was all part of the fantasy lives of *yenem*, the "others"—those others who shaped and created the world in which we lived, and to which I secretly and passionately aspired. But at the word "Jesus," a word literally never pronounced at home, I remember feeling paralyzed and mute. Here I fell silent. On the last day before the Christmas vacation, the teacher distributed little cardboard boxes filled with brightly colored, hard Christmas candies—and these were given out impartially to every single child in the class. I liked that sense of inclusion in this vast event that was going on around us, but which was simply not ours. Its very ubiquitousness made me all the more aware that we were living in a Christian country.

Perhaps this was the beginning of the fine balancing act that preoccupied my generation, the first generation born in the Golden Land. We were both Americans and yet not, not quite. In school we were told that having been born here, we were Americans, and all Americans were equal. We accepted and delighted in this principle, as did our parents. But we knew—and they expected—that there would be a difference between us and those others, the Christian Americans who could pronounce the name "Jesus" without their lips trembling. We knew, and for a very long time accepted, that being a Jew was not "equal" but "other," but we were also persuaded that compared to the malign fate that had driven my parents and nearly 3 million fellow Jews out of their homes in search of safety, the exclusions that plagued our generation were mere bagatelles.

Did the members of the Union Club not have the right to exclude "Hebrew gentlemen" from their premises? It was ugly, to be sure, but compared to cruel years of service in the Tsar's army, or transportation to Siberia for the indiscreet expression of a political opinion, it was a regrettable imperfection. To my generation, this was the behavior that we had been taught to believe was inevitable. Our preoccupation was discovering how to make a living in a land where everything stood *almost* open.

What we asked ourselves was: were we Americans or were we some kind of hybrid? Quite apart from the question of rights, the definition seemed to elude neat answers. Citizenship was not taken lightly by the immigrant generation, who cherished and valued it with an emotion approaching reverence. Few immigrants ever got over a sense of gratitude to America for taking them in. They all had their stories of what had happened at Ellis Island—often humiliating stories where names had been changed, sometimes tragic stories of families parted as a member was sent back. But these and other painful memories could not obliterate their satisfaction at having arrived and made a place for themselves in the New World. Yet it was never home.

Half a century later, still hardly speaking a word of English, my father-in-law would say, with a sigh, *in der heym*—"at home"—as he made a comparison, not to the advantage of America. *In der heym*, the fruit and vegetables had taste. *In der heym*, he had enjoyed the delicious freedom of life in the orchards in the summer. *In der heym*, he had enjoyed a glass of hot tea. It was not until I acquired a samovar, and let some of the hissing hot water into his glass, that he finally nodded his head in approval—at last a glass of tea that was, as he put it, "warm."

It was not easy to convey a language and a culture with so much imperfect knowledge on both sides. The early life of our parents had taken place in a world with artifacts that simply did not exist in the Bronx—and since the immigrants' English was so incomplete, we often ran into terrible difficulties about simple objects. I remember the first time I heard the word *kayshel* from my mother-in-law. Since she did not know the word "basket," we began a kind of hilarious guessing game, in which she offered one description after another of the many uses to which a *kayshel* might be put, while I made wilder and wilder stabs at the meaning to her immense amusement at my inability to name such a simple object. It was indispensable, she said, for carrying chickens to market—a cage? Or if you were going on a journey it could be used to pack your clothes— a valise? Or again if you were collecting apples in an orchard—a sack? I've forgotten how we finally, explosively, came upon the real meaning of the word, but it was no wonder that Yiddish translated so imperfectly into the urban world of the Bronx.

How were we to understand the meaning of the saying, "He is so poor that he doesn't even have money for the water over his kasha"? For us, water flowed out of a faucet, free. We had to be told that water in the little villages of Eastern Europe was bought by the bucketful from the water carrier. Did we ever even learn the word for the yoke on which he carried the buckets or for all those other aspects of life that did not match ours? Once, when they were quite old ladies, my mother's elder sister came to visit her in New York. I took them to the American Wing of the Metropolitan Museum of Art, where we saw the homely implements of the early settlers. My mother and aunt were amazed and delighted. And for each of these strange objects that they had not seen in half a century—the combs for flax, the spinning wheels, the carding spindles—for each of these they had words, Yiddish words that I had never heard and which they had never even tried to teach me. How could they, when their landscape was so different from mine?

And the converse was true, too. One afternoon at my mother-in-law's house, one of her sons tried to explain the much despised game of baseball to her—which she translated along into Yiddish. The difficulty was that Yiddish had not yet caught up with some aspects of American culture. First he told her about the bases, which she rendered, from their appearance, as *kishelach*—little pillows. He was equally at a loss when it came to the bat, but demonstrating the swings vigorously in the living room, he conveyed the idea that it was a *shtekn*—a stick that was employed for this operation. The absurdity of the game was not diminished as she retold it later in Yiddish, a saga about a grown man swinging a stick at a ball and then running toward a little pillow.

Among this generation of immigrants, parents and children divided early—the parents lost in a language that did not fit the world to which they had come. It was a well that began drying up early, and for all but the staunchest Yiddishist, it became a kind of embarrassment. Faced with the splendors and apparatus of English in night school, Yiddish became for most of them a "jargon"— a private language in which they dreamed and remembered. But as the Yiddish newspapers and theaters faded, as English invaded their waking world, took over their children, Yiddish became a part of that past that they hid, that embarrassed them. In his old age, whenever my father was about to utter a Yiddish sentence, he always prefaced it with "Do you understand French?" and would then offer, for example, the traditional farewell: *"Fur gesunt un kum gesunt*—Travel in good health and return in good health." He could not resist the invocation which the occasion demanded, but he was self-conscious about it. The language and its formulations were powerfully part of his natural response, yet in time he became uncertain as to whether it still belonged in the waking world.

The immigrants never thought to make life in the "shtetl" picturesque. That would come later at the hands of the sentimentalists. But they knew that their world was primitive—without paved streets or sewers, without running water—and it made them ashamed. They were not quick to admit that they had started young to work for little wages and lived poorly. They did not think that such memories would bring them honor, but on the contrary would diminish them in the eyes of their delicately raised American children. They spoke circumspectly of the past, sometimes admitting that they went barefoot. We know now from photographs, from memoirs, and from literature not only how poor but also how hopeless their situation was in those villages.

They drank tea and ate herring because that was the diet of the poor—but Sholem Aleichem tells us how coffee with a buttered roll seemed to them the epitome of earthly bliss. And this same buttered roll, after all, is at the climax of Peretz's story *Bontshe Shvayg*, about the poor man who discovers that he is a saint when he dies and is received with hallelujahs by the angels in Paradise. When he is asked what he wants as his eternal reward for a life of noble, silent suffering, he replies, with a little smile of anticipation: "Every morning a hot roll with fresh butter." And, adds Peretz, "the angels lowered their heads in shame." In America, many of the Bontshe Shvaygs felt the shame themselves as they reveled in what seemed to them success beyond their wildest dreams. How could they explain to their children the satisfaction they felt in the fact that they lived in a warm apartment, with soft beds, and had a fresh roll for breakfast?

No one was better aware of the irony of their position than the immigrants themselves. There in the isolation of their communities in Eastern Europe, their lives and language had been one. The wholeness of the world out of which they had come and the language that described it were never reproduced in America. In the early stages of the immigration, when Yiddish was still all-pervasive in the immigrant settlements, American terms were imported into the language. In his *Adventures of Motl Peyse*, Sholem Aleichem uses the persona of a rather fiery young woman, "Branche," to comment sardonically on the way English sweeps like wildfire through the Yiddish of the immigrants replacing simple old words—"vinde" (window) for *fenster*, "spoon" for *leffel*. Yet as even Branche would have had to agree, some English words were brought in not as substitutes but to describe the New World—"shop," "payday" (used to mean wages), and "operator" (for anyone who used a sewing machine). Any new Yiddish formulation would only have been cumbersome and artificial. How many Yiddish-speaking house painters, for example, ever knew that the little round brush that they used for painting window frames—the "seshtl"—was actually a rendering of "sash tool"?

When Abraham Cahan took over the Yiddish newspaper the *Forverts*, in 1902, he recognized the inevitable and scandalized the educated Jewish world by not only permitting but actually encouraging such Americanisms in its columns, all transcribed into Hebrew letters, of course. He wanted a written Yiddish that matched the way people spoke. The other daily newspapers insisted on an elevated, Germanified, literary Yiddish, which, as time went on, could not help but become more and more at variance with everyday speech.

To a degree, in the early decades of this century, the geography of Europe was replicated in the big cities where sheer numbers and dense settlement permitted immigrants to reproduce the life they knew. The Little Italys, the Chinatowns, as well as the Jewish settlements, marked the various stages of the immigrants' odyssey in America. I lived in such a settlement in the Bronx, a few blocks east of the Grand Concourse, where the Jews bought their meat at the kosher butcher, their poultry at the slaughterer's where the still-feathered chickens were flung into open bins, and found their kind of bread at Friedhoffer's bakery where it was made on the premises several times a day. Strictly speaking, the Bronx was actually a second stage or even third stage of settlement. Before World War I, immigrants came to their relatives or *landslayt*, who lived on the Lower East Side or Brooklyn. The Bronx came later, when families had established themselves and could afford the more up-to-date living quarters available there.

The Italians, who were a minority in our neighborhood, had their own array of butchers, bakers, and greengrocers, which seemed reasonable and logical since they cooked and ate other foods. The Jewish families were all more or less kosher, coming out of a traditional world where it took a violent wrench to live differently. But I was very surprised to discover, when my uncle Chaim— my father's oldest brother—came to visit from Chicago, that there were degrees of kashruth. To my mother's outrage and humiliation, he made it plain that he would drink no more than a glass of tea in our house, implying serious doubt as to the quality of the kashruth in our kitchen. It was a kind of one-upmanship that could only leave ill-feeling in its wake, and it was a game all too often played. My mother's strained relationship with my father's family was not improved by this encounter.

As soon as I went to school, I discovered that there was something that I called privately "American food": white bread, tomato juice, slices of square yellow cheese, mayonnaise—strange and unknown tastes and textures. When I was five, my mother was taken to the hospital with a miscarriage and I was allowed to visit her as she lay very still and pale in her bed. In this frightening situation, the nurses were kind and brought me a glass of milk with a bread and butter sandwich—made with *white* bread and cut into dainty fingers. To this day, I can taste the coldness and delectable softness of my first encounter with American food.

The haunting question of what made one American was one that troubled the thoughts of the generation born in the United States. For the older generation, it was easier. They were forever immigrants who spoke English more or less badly, but who had

achieved American citizenship and had American children—
accomplishments of which they were equally proud.

For us, it was more muddled. To a degree, I always felt I spoke
a foreign language. As a child I had not, of course, heard nursery
rhymes, folk sayings, proverbs in English. "Snow meal, snow a
deal. Snow feather, sunny weather," said one of my daughters'
nursery school teachers on a dark winter day as the first flakes began
to fall. Such homely verses would sting me, well into my adult
years, as I realized how little the American voice was part of me. I
was more likely to have learned, in Yiddish, of course, "If you
laugh in the morning, you will cry before night."

Nor did I know the names in English of common flowers, trees,
or birds, or even of the spices in everyday use in our house. I had
to learn that what was commonplace to me was unknown to people who ate white bread. It was years before I found out that *kim-
mel,* the seed so liberally sprinkled in and on the rye bread that we
ate every day, was, in English, caraway seed. Sometimes I did not
know the names of common things either in English or in Yiddish.
Once, walking with a New England friend in a meadow on the
Vermont farm that my husband and I had bought in the sixties, I
listened with amazement and dismay as she identified the flowers,
and found myself wondering whether I was worthy of owning a
property when I could not even recognize its plant life.

"In our district, in the winter," said my father, "we often heard
of werewolves ... " and instantly a snowy landscape with dark pine
forests would unfold before my eyes. The stories that I heard when
I was growing up had to do with King Solomon (Shloyme
hameylekh) and how he tested the inevitability of one's chosen
mate by sending his daughter away to be raised in an impregnable
fortress, or the cunning of Alexander the Great, who for his own
safety had been disguised as a girl as a child and then. ... Or there
were the tales of Moyshe rabeynu (Moses Our Teacher), and the
one about the girl who knitted garments of nettles to free her broth-

ers from enchantment—all part of the landscape where werewolves roamed. And wonders occurred if one knew the right formula, like my grandfather, who knew when to shout, *"Shema Yisroel."* My mother had other formulas and knew of different kinds of magic.

School of course was the place where all these stories and injunctions came unraveled. In school, I was given the power of naming things. There I heard again the story of the girl who, maintaining perfect silence for seven years, had knit seven sweaters of nettles for her seven brothers who had been changed into swans. I learned that this was a fairy tale; that the stories about Shloyme hameylekh or Moyshe rabeynu or Alexander were legends, and that they were neither truth nor history. Until then they had all swum together in my head in a mythical, snowy landscape with mysterious forests in which ghosts and unwholesome spirits *(sheydim)* were as common as trees. Or there were the sandy wastes evoked by my mother's dark threats of *Mitsrayim* or Egypt as the place to which my sister would be dragged if she didn't stand still to have her hair curled. As for my mother's spells, and the evil eye and the mermaids who inhabited her seas, as well as the miraculous cures by old peasant women—all of that was simply superstition.

Now this knowledge, this secret knowledge, was really very difficult. On the one hand, it was dazzling to discover that events occurred in a discernible and orderly sequence; that they happened in the context of the rise and fall of empires, in places which could be fixed on a map. The wicked Pharaoh of the Passover Haggadah, the noble Maccabees who were responsible for the Hanukkah lights, were all part of *history*. It was also clear, on the contrary, that the poor girl who had to knit all those scratchy sweaters never existed. And I now even knew where to find books that had more such stories.

The problem was that there was no way to convey these new

truths at home. Could I set myself up as knowing more than my parents? With a choleric father who found it expedient to end disagreements with shouts or blows, it hardly seemed worth the risk. Yet what I learned in school was transparently and irrefutably true and it was also deliciously comforting. It made sense of the world— certainly better sense than the world where a man might be a wolf or a girl a fish. These names were the beginning of freedom and strength. The world began to take on a new rationality.

But laughter remained in short supply. The foibles and absurdities of human nature formed perhaps the best target for humor, and my mother-in-law was expert in capturing such moments and relating them at home. She could tell these stories on herself as well as on others. One of her set pieces about an outing to Coney Island—an hour and a half on the subway, with a half-dozen children, laden with the requisite picnic of borsht and hard-boiled eggs—was a saga that was begged for at family gatherings as the misadventures and mishaps grew from telling to telling.

What this story evoked was neither self-pity nor a sense of affliction. Rather, it brought out her high comical style—as she portrayed her efforts to keep track of her six younger children during the hazards of changing trains on the long, convoluted route out to Coney Island. Her eldest son, of course, was by this time engaged in more serious enterprises. This excursion, which required a certain commitment of funds—round-trip carfare for seven plus 25 cents for the rental of a locker—was an indulgence not to be contemplated more than once a year. All food and drink was taken along from home, because of restraints of both kashruth and economy. As my father-in-law was fond of saying: "A poor man always knows exactly how much money he has in his pocket."

The arrival at Coney Island only opened the second act of the drama. With the locker rented, the street clothes stashed, the next dilemma was the search for a bit of space on a beach crowded with humanity—a place to spread out a blanket and set up a base for the day. Then began the inevitable crises of lost and found children, vanished shoes, bathing caps, keys. While all of this figured largely in my mother-in-law's telling, the children remembered the cold, crashing waves, where they paddled and jumped rather than swam; the delicious sensation of ease when they were finally summoned out of the water; the cool, sweet-and-sour taste of the borsht; and the heat of the day subsiding into the late afternoon shadows as the tide of humanity also gradually withdrew, leaving more and more of the beach exposed, making possible more elaborate games, larger sandcastles, even ball playing.

At this sweetest time of day, however, the long return trip home had to be faced, as damp blankets and sandy shoes were gathered up from the beach, and finally in the locker room wet bathing suits were rolled into towels and street clothes pulled over damp bodies. On one memorable occasion when my mother-in-law had cannily rented a corner of someone's garage for her 25 cents instead of the usual cramped locker, she returned to find that her corset had fallen into a bucket of water, since, of course, even if she were going to Coney Island, she would be fully dressed in a corset for the long train ride. This event with its wretched consequence—having to wear the wet corset home—was the climax of her saga. In her telling, she was the lightning rod as well as the narrator of all the worries and mishaps that marked the day, while the children, un-conscious of the surrounding drama, could laugh as they recalled only the pleasures of the flashing water, the welcome coolness in the midst of New York's sticky heat, the adventure of the journey. In other stories, her tragical style had other rhythms—where at cer-tain intervals she would pause significantly, sigh, and say, *"Nu, Got hot geholfen* . . . Well, God helped," and then we knew there was about to be a *real* disaster.

Later, when I was old enough to have my own adventures, I found myself making stories of what I had seen—discovering drama in the gap between expectation and reality. My angle of vision had been shaped for me so long ago that I saw the world with a kind of double vision. The stories were in another language now, but I could hear the cadence, the turns of speech, the pauses of the old Jewish storytellers.

# 3

# Chairs

When my uncle Shloyme came home from work in the evening, he sat down on his favorite chair in the kitchen to read the paper. The kitchen was the first, the largest, and the best room in the apartment—on Washington Avenue in the Bronx. Next to the kitchen was a dark, rarely disturbed room completely filled with an equally dark mahogany table, baronial chairs, and their matching china closet and credenza. Off the dining room came two more rooms—a little one that opened onto an air shaft, also dark, where my cousin Abie slept, and then the front room, which had two windows and light, and faced the street. This was my uncle and aunt's bedroom. But most visitors rarely got beyond the kitchen with its porcelain-topped table and its wooden chairs. Unlike my mother, who cooked according to abstract and very high moral standards—no garlic, no spices, yes to chicken fat but no to butter—my Tante Necha-Leah cooked for taste, and there was always something delicious simmering on her stove.

Tante Necha-Leah was one of those legendary Jewish house-keepers whose pale linoleum shone, whose glass-fronted kitchen cabinets were polished relentlessly, and whose organdy curtains could stand by themselves after they had been through their weekly starching and ironing. In this brightly lit setting, my uncle Shloyme would settle down with his paper—*Der Tog*, a conservative newspaper, but not so religious as the Orthodox *Morgen-Zhurnal*, and spiced with luridly written crime stories, a serialized novel, poetry, and mildly Zionist views. From time to time, he paused in his reading to summarize what interested him or to read aloud from particularly telling passages.

After a day in "the shop"—the clothing factory where he worked—this was his time of restoration. I would see him arriving exhausted and bent. Then, as he opened the paper and leaned back in his chair, a new air of refreshment came over him, and with a sense of command he would require us to listen to this or that morsel that he had found. My aunt, however, was not at all intimidated by his authority, and as she swept the kitchen would knock loudly against his chair with her broom to demonstrate that this was *her* kitchen. Even as a child, I could see that there was something touching and vulnerable about him; perhaps it was the paleness of his coloring— hair that had once been red and was now an indeterminate straw color, pale blue eyes, and the fine, slightly freckled skin of the fair- haired. But his hands especially caught my attention—soft, smooth, and seemingly boneless from a lifetime of indoor work, sitting over a machine, guiding fabric through a throbbing needle. These were the hands of someone helpless. The hands of the women whom I knew were roughened with housework and laundry and exposure. But his were as delicate as a child's.

Tante Necha-Leah by contrast was little, dark and intense, with her luxuriant hair pulled back into a severe bun. While my uncle Shloyme was considered the dreamer, it was she who confronted the world, who made decisions, who counseled the children. It was she who, after the couple's two daughters were married, chose to move from their cold-water flat on the Lower East Side to the warmth and comfort of Washington Avenue. Uncle Shloyme ac- quiesced when he discovered there was a little *shul*, not one of your grand synagogues for the rich, but one for workingmen like himself, right at the corner. And Saturday morning, when he descended for the services, was Tante Necha-Leah's time for herself. The house was at peace; no work was permitted and Uncle Shloyme was away.

That was her moment to count up her resources and to dream. Of course it was forbidden to handle money on the Sabbath. But this wasn't really "handling," it was more like observing it. Like every Jewish housewife of her day, Tante Necha-Leah had her *knippel*, her "little knot" of money that she put by: little sums out of the housekeeping money, little extras that might come her way or presents of cash. Some women literally kept their money tied up in a knot in a handkerchief. Tante Necha-Leah's *knippel* was more substantial, and she kept it in the top drawer of her dresser. On Saturday mornings, standing at the dresser, she liked to fan out the bills and stack the silver—very quietly, very gently. And then, after contemplating it for a while, she quickly put it all away.

Tante Necha-Leah knew how to savor life, but it mostly occurred in uncle Shloyme's absence. Sometimes, in the morning, after he had breakfasted and gone, she allowed herself an indulgence. What she liked best was a thin, glazed *pletzel*—a soft, onion-tinged, poppy-seed–covered roll—lightly buttered and then layered with fresh farmer cheese. Biting into this, she felt strengthened for the work ahead.

Supper was, of course, the climax of Tante Necha-Leah's day as it was for Uncle Shloyme. In that neighborhood when women met on the street, they would ask, "What are you cooking for supper tonight?" It was, in any case, not a very large repertoire, and whatever was named received a nod of recognition. At Tante Necha-Leah's house, they followed the Old World pattern: first a large plate of filling soup—a barley and mushroom, or a dried pea or bean soup—and then a very small piece of soup meat or chicken and some potato. For dessert there was "compôte"—cooked dried fruit; perhaps a few cookies; and, of course, a large glass of tea. By this time, my uncle Shloyme was feeling quite genial, leaning back in his chair, being served by Tante Necha-Leah and oblivious to her noisy intimations that he might be in the way.

Occasionally I ventured into the dining room—another domain—just to look around. It was colder, of course, than the kitchen and filled with mysterious objects. Central, and occupying almost all the space, was the massive table surrounded by high-backed, ornately carved chairs with velvet seats. At the head of the table was the single chair with arms, the place of authority, the place reserved for my uncle Shloyme. I certainly never sat on one of those velvet chairs, but I loved inching around them to get to the china closet with its treasures: some Japanese cups and saucers, all the rage at the time, in a luster-brown glaze with a blue rim, enameled with tiny, flowering branches in high relief. Meant for display, of course, and not for drinking. A set (six) of colored tall stemmed wineglasses, also never used; and then, most baffling of all, a chrome cocktail shaker with stemmed chrome martini glasses.

With all this emphasis on alcohol, one would think that drinking was part of my aunt and uncle's way of life. And not only theirs—because that cocktail shaker appeared and reappeared in countless china closets. I think its arrival coincided with the discovery by designers that chrome looked, almost, like silver. And, even better, it did not need to be polished and was much cheaper. Suddenly the hardware stores in the Bronx were filled with ornamental chrome vessels modeled on their silver prototypes: butter dishes, fruit bowls, bread baskets, and, of course, the cocktail set.

Actually, Jewish drinking in the New York of the twenties and thirties was highly stylized, tied to an event—the Friday night Kiddush, a *bris* (circumcision), a Bar Mitzvah, a wedding—and to what was appropriate according to one's age, sex, and stage in life. It was a tidily divided world. Men liked (or were supposed to like) *gezalt-*

*senes*—salty, spicy snacks. Women were supposed to have a weakness for sweets.

What the men drank was the equivalent of their European *bronfen*, a rye whiskey, served in small shot glasses, gulped in a single swallow, accompanied by a loud *"L'Chaim*—To Life," and followed up with a bit of herring. On special occasions, there might be slivovitz (a plum brandy), savored more slowly and worthy of comment. Women sipped seltzer or fruit-flavored sodawaters, except at Passover where everyone drank the customary sweet thick wine. Shapiro's, a local winemaker on the Lower East Side, used to advertise on large billboards around New York with the slogan: "The wine you can cut with a knife," and leaving nothing to the imagination showed a sturdy breadknife.

Mr. Shapiro, whom I once interviewed, told me that the family came from Hungary and that they had been winemakers for generations. When I asked him how long he aged his wines, he looked at me with indignation, and announced that "every drop is fresh!" After that he showed me around his cellars, where the casks were marked "X," "XX," or "XXX" to indicate the level of sweetness. For Passover, of course, wine was bought in quantity, and many residents of the Bronx traveled to the Lower East Side to purchase their supplies for the two Seders when their twenty or so guests per evening were each expected to drink four cups.

The Prohibition era brought a real crisis into Jewish life since it was hardly worth the trouble to find a bootlegger for the relatively minute quantities a family might consume in the course of a year. The law, however, had a humane clause that permitted individuals to make wine or spirits for their own consumption. My father was one of the many who plunged into winemaking—buying bushels of Concord grapes in September; after a lengthy process of fermenting, squeezing, and scientifically measuring the alcoholic content with a hydrometer, he finally produced a very creditable, thick, sweet wine that would have won the approval of Mr. Shapiro.

Across the street, our Italian neighbors were doing the same thing. But they grew their own grapes. The backyards of single-family houses in the Bronx, particularly the North Bronx, were given over to pergolas covered with grapevines. In summer the family took out the kitchen table and chairs, sat in the shade of their vine, and ate their meals there when the weather was fine. In September, they harvested the grapes and made a very different kind of wine from my father's—a thin, sour wine that we tasted politely, as they tasted ours.

We, too, sat out in summer, but not under a pergola. The backyards of the tenements where we lived were deserts of concrete, with only a scrap of sky overhead. But the neighbors in our building knew how to make themselves comfortable. They took out their wooden folding chairs and sat together in little clusters on the sidewalk in front of the building, waiting for the heat to subside, talking together, softly, ruminatively, long into the night.

In summer, these apartments which were warm and bright in the winter became stifling as the temperature rose. And no room was more oppressive than the dining room, with its heavy furniture and its velvet chairs. It took a holiday like Passover or the New Year for this room to come into its own. Then the table was extended to its fullest, spread with a white tablecloth, and set with the special Passover wineglasses and dishes, not used from one end of the year to the next, until the holiday came around again. At Passover, Uncle Shloyme sat enthroned at the head of his table in the armchair, reclining against pillows, as the Haggadah prescribed, while Tante Necha-Leah, as a latter-day Salome, brought him a pitcher of water and a basin, with her best linen handtowel, so that he might ceremoniously "Lave," as our old bi-lingual Haggadah said.

A state visit, which was defined as strangers from afar, also meant that we sat in the dining room. On family visits, of course, we all sat in the kitchen. But state visits were ceremonious; they elicited tea and cake, and long interrogations of the visitor. He (it was generally a man) was someone, often unknown, who arrived from a far place and brought *"a lebedike gris—a* living greeting" from a relative or a landsman. These visits occurred long before any of us had telephones, and on any afternoon or evening, a stranger could suddenly appear at the door. The purpose of his visit ascertained at the threshold, he was invited in, plied with refreshments, and questioned closely—and not only about, say, Cousin Dvora, the initiator of his visit. He was asked for every possible morsel of information about her town, the circumstances of her life, other relatives, close friends left behind, neighbors, how the situation was for Jews . . . and on and on in ever-widening circles. Decades later, I learned about Benjamin of Tudela, who had traveled around the inhabited world in the twelfth century visiting Jewish communities and making just such inquiries wherever he came. (His work remains the best census of the Jewish world for the Middle Ages.) And to this day when friends come back even from a vacation in the Cayman Islands, I find myself following the old pattern of inquiry: And how many Jews live there, and is their community well established, and is the government well disposed toward them . . . ? I have to catch myself, knowing that I should be asking about—what? The tennis courts, the surf, the beaches, the best restaurants?

My Tante Anna's dining room was different from Tanta Necha-Leah's. It was not in the Bronx but in Brooklyn. The furniture was also mahogany, but lighter and warmer in color. The table was smaller, the chairs had lower backs, and this room contained not only the usual china closet and credenza but also my uncle Philip's wind-up Victrola, as well as a minute grand piano on which my two cousins practiced. The china closet with its mirrored back was a Garden of Delights for me. I would stand in front of it admiring the fanciful silver dishes—some pierced, some chased—the slender silver vases, the elaborately decorated china cups, and ever present and even brought out from time to time, a silver dish with nonpareils.

Since my uncle Philip was a great lover of popular Yiddish songs, and a connoisseur of cantorial singing—which was treated as an art form—he was always playing some new hit that he had just brought home, and humming along. We were allowed to lounge on the dining-room chairs, and the room—which also opened out from the kitchen—was brightly lit, the music filling the whole apartment. On one memorable occasion, his love for the latest popular songs caught my parents out on the day when they returned from City Hall, having just been secretly married in a civil ceremony. As they entered the dining room, Uncle Philip was playing his latest favorite: "Let's all kiss one another. / Mother may as well know / that we've gotten married . . . *Lomir sich zerkishen, / di mama meg shoyn vissen.* . . , "thus eliciting an embarrassed confession from the pair.

My uncle Philip was a window washer in Brooklyn, and, I always thought, something of a bon vivant, with his rosy complexion, his bald head, and his cigars. He was a member of the local synagogue, where he put his familiarity with cantorial styles to practical use, standing up and singing loudly in the intervals when the cantor was silent and the congregation prayed aloud. My father was always somewhat annoyed at this display since it quite eclipsed his own rapid and fluent reading, of which he was very proud. But since he didn't know the tropes, he couldn't compete with Uncle Philip. Quite oblivious to my father's displeasure, my uncle Philip enjoyed his Saturday mornings at the synagogue, where at last he could sing full voice the melodies that he hummed all week. This was his club, where he met his friends, shaking hands all around as he entered, and enjoying a glass of *bronfen* and the conviviality of the Kiddush after the services.

On his tiny income, he and Tante Anna managed to convey an atmosphere of sumptuous pleasure. They clearly thrived on those occasions during the year when they went out in splendid style, dressing up in their best clothes, my aunt even treating my uncle to a home-style manicure in preparation. But she also knew how to convert more prosaic moments into festivities. One winter, the grocery downstairs introduced frozen strawberries, preserved in a dense sugar syrup. Tante Anna in a grand gesture bought a carton of this luxury, and we all savored the extraordinary taste and sweetness of strawberries in December with sour cream.

In my parents' apartment there were no chairs in the living room; there was no dining-room set. There was no furniture at all, just an empty room, and hanging from the ceiling a dark blue silk, tasseled lampshade. It had come with the apartment and implied the table that was to go under it, but the table never appeared while we lived there. During the first five years of my life, my parents had been busy running a stationery store in the Bronx and had bought furniture for their bedroom, a kitchen table and chairs, and a bed for me. Shortly after my sister was born, my father's business failed and we moved to Brooklyn, not far from Tante Anna.

Into their new apartment, my parents moved their bedroom set, the kitchen table and chairs, my bed, a chest of drawers, and the baby's crib. But what should have been the dining room remained bare, a reminder of failure or hope, illuminated by the eerie bluish light of the hanging lampshade. These were the first horrifying years of the Depression as my father tried his hand at one failing business enterprise after another until he finally found work, the fabled "steady job," and we moved back to the Bronx. Uncle Philip, too, could no longer support his family in New York and moved to Ohio, where several cousins and *landslayt* already established there promised that life would be better.

In the few years before they left, just before the Depression struck, it seemed that all my older cousins got married—one after the other. For these events, for which I was just the right age and size to be a flower girl, I was outfitted with a drop-waisted, tiered, ruffled, pink silk dress, and even in the dead of winter was permitted to wear *short* pink silk socks with patent leather shoes. The delicious slippery coldness that came with sliding into those shoes always sent a tingle of anticipation through me as I thought of the festivities to come. I should explain that from October to May, I lived encased in "combinations" whose heavy, ribbed cotton fabric surrounded me like a second—and wrinkled—skin. When I could discard this oppressive weight for delicate silk, I felt that I had taken wing. How delicious to feel the cold!

The best, the most lavish weddings took place in the Second Avenue halls specially designed for the purpose, and the most exciting of these featured a faceted glass ball that hung from the ceiling, rotating slowly for the dancing. In the dimmed room, this threw a constant shower of prismatic light over the dancers, the walls, and the onlookers. But that came late in the evening. First there was the ceremony, then a magnificent dinner, kosher of course, while between courses and after dinner, there was dancing.

And here I need to murmur something about how that generation perceived their Orthodoxy. At first it was taken for granted that the enclosed life they had known in Eastern Europe would simply be transported and set down anew in America. In the synagogue, the men still sat separately from the women; only the men counted in the congregation and only a man could perform the duties of a cantor or rabbi. And, of course, these immigrants observed all the rituals of kashruth in their homes, circumcised their sons, and observed the Sabbath (when they could).

In their social life, however, Americanization made its way, insidiously, it seemed. The immigrants' stories stress how important appearance was to them. They didn't want to look as if they were just off the ship, and as soon after arriving as possible the young people especially dressed themselves in American clothes. Mary Antin, who came from the town of Plotsk in Russia, wrote in her best-selling autobiography, *The Promised Land*, published in 1912, that her father sent a strict reminder to her mother that she was to discard her marriage wig before she set out for America.

These attitudes had begun to reach even into the interior of Galicia, into the tiny town on the Bug River where my mother grew up. Her eldest sister, my Tante Elke, had managed the household since her mother died young, and she had grown into a forceful, forthright young woman. She was also striking-looking, with long red hair, and when the time came to entertain offers of marriage, my grandfather chose for her an amiable but rather quiet young man. Tante Elke accepted this choice largely because he, as well as she, wanted to go to America, and he was ready to leave as soon as they were married. On her wedding day, when the old women of the village wanted to shave her head, she rebelled. She was going to America, and she did not have to abide by the antiquated rules of the backward shtetl. To the scandal of the community, she prevailed. Later she even broke the taboo of kashruth. But that is another story.

The New World stood for the opportunity to start afresh, to right what was wrong in the world in which they lived, and especially for the women it offered an independence that they could not have dreamed of in their villages. America offered the kind of personal freedom that they would never have known in their old, circumscribed, closely watched lives. What might have seemed daring at home was merely conventional in the strange new land. Hardly noticing, they began to bend the rules.

The wedding was one of the first institutions to show how the Old World could be remade in the image of the New, and produce a vigorous hybrid. One of the most important features of an Old World wedding had been the "seating of the bride," accompanied by the playing of special music. As she sat in her wedding finery surrounded by her friends, the *badkhen* or bard recited the traditional mournful verses, sure to reduce her to tears, telling her of all the difficulties that lay before her. In America, the bride still sat enthroned as the guests arrived, but on Second Avenue it was only to receive their compliments and good wishes. The jester versemaker was transformed into a genial master of ceremonies, who during dinner read the congratulatory telegrams from absent friends and relatives. The inevitable fictional message: "As you start on the road to *martial* happiness . . . ," set the tone of hilarity for the evening.

Whereas in the Old Country the men and women would have been apart, and danced separately, here in America, mixed ballroom dancing had become the rage, and at weddings we saw the waltz and the fox-trot alternating with the traditional wedding dances from Eastern Europe. Without a word being lost on the subject, by common agreement the young immigrants abandoned one of the basic tenets of the traditional society that insisted on the segregation of the sexes. In America, men and women danced together, held one another close, and responded to the rush of blood in their veins.

My uncle Jake was my mother's favorite partner for the waltz, which they danced with great ceremony, he holding her off at arm's length through whirls and twirls. But then later in the evening, as the orchestra grew louder and faster and ever more Old Country, he would plunge into the "kazotske," a single dancer surrounded by clapping onlookers, whirling in lower and lower circles until he was down to the polished floor, throwing out his legs, his arms folded across his chest. Then it was the time for soloists—the sobbing of the violin, or the clarinetist draped in lights, who strolled among the tables coaxing an almost human wail out of his instrument.

At the banquet, then, men and women sat together, girls flirted, and matches were made. To our relief, the children were sent off to their own tables, grouped by age, and plied with unexpected service and wonders in the form of ices in midwinter. What made these banquet halls seem particularly magnificent were the chairs. First the throne on which the bride sat, and then the golden chairs with their red silk seats for the rest of us. That and my cold toes made me know that I was in the presence of splendor; also the way my aunts and uncles and cousins looked. With a powerful sense of occasion, they emerged from their everyday lives with all the glitter and color at their command. The men in their dark suits and with their elegant way of holding their cigarettes between their fingers hardly seemed like the work-worn figures we saw every day. Never mind that my mother's diamond engagement ring occasionally went into pawn to help tide us over a bad period. For this occasion she wore it, and her "lavalière," and, of course, the gold earrings that she had been given as a child.

For my parents' generation, there were only two styles in life, as in chairs: the kitchen chair, or the glory of the red silk–covered gold chair at the wedding hall. It was this hunger for the luxurious and the enjoyment of it at the great occasions of life—births, weddings, anniversaries—that gave meaning to the laborious days that they spent in the shops and on their jobs. For them, leisure meant dressing up in their best clothes, not in their oldest. For the occasion of the wedding, they lived a fantasy where they were all royalty, splendidly turned out and served by obsequious servitors. Well, maybe not so obsequious. But, at any rate, they sat in their chairs, were served the finest food that they could imagine, and could summon a waiter to bring them whatever their hearts desired.

It was a passionate society, a world reinventing itself, without support, without the safety net of indulgent and wealthy parents, but depending on neighbors, friends, *landslayt,* and the little self-help organizations that they created for the inevitable periods of unemployment—the dreaded "slack" of the garment industry. In times of sorrow, these friends and relatives formed a phalanx, shutting out common care and offering the devotion of nearness.

Yet soft words and gentle caresses were not the standard coinage of this society. The languishing looks and tender passages that they witnessed on the Yiddish stage were granted perhaps a brief season in their own lives. With a shyness that was in part a relic of that old segregated world they had left behind, or an incapacity that flowed from lack of example, husbands and wives demonstrated their affection for one another more symbolically than actually. They cared for one another devotedly in sickness, but rarely touched one another with a tender gesture in health.

When my uncle Philip grew old and fragile, Tante Anna said that she never begrudged a moment of the time that she spent caring for him. For her, every service was a pleasure. But they were an exceptional couple, always speaking affectionately to one another. It was not entirely customary. A more common mode of speech carried a somewhat ironic tone, a questioning inflection, a readiness to jab at a weakness. When my father found a misplaced fork in our kosher kitchen—a fork intended for dairy meals in the drawer with the meat cutlery—he didn't just remove it. He took the occasion to settle scores with my mother: *"Khassidishe tokhter!*—Daughter of a hasid!" he would say, reminding her of the oh so pious background that was sometimes *her* trump card. Children, too, may have been loved distractedly, but not tenderly. They were pinched and teased and yelled at and overprotected. But there were few moments of quiet affection or gentle conversation. Here, too, it was all by indirection, by signals and symbols, that tokens of love were exchanged.

There was very good precedent for this. The recital of the most passionate love poem in the Hebrew language, the Song of Songs, is reserved for the darkest and holiest moment in the Jewish year. After the completion of the Kol Nidrei service on Yom Kippur, after the other worshippers have left, it is read by those who are especially pious and spend the night in the synagogue. And then this most explicit and sensual of all love poems is read as an allegory of the love between God and Israel.

There was one ceremony from which chairs were banished, and that was during the period of mourning. Then the rules of observance required the mourners to sit on low, backless stools, their clothes ceremonially rent, and shoeless. We had few backless stools in the Bronx, and the customary substitutes were wooden milk cases which some neighbor would haul up from the nearby grocery store for the week of mourning. Amidst a continual coming and going, the family would sit, perched on their wooden boxes, in fulfillment of the ritual for the seven days. Neighbors cooked the meals; the men of the neighborhood and family members congregated in time to make up a *minyan* (quorum) for morning and evening services, and visitors came and went without greeting or saying goodbye—as we were taught. They sat with the bereaved family; they talked to one another and a comforting hubbub filled the room. The feeling of humanity. At parting the one formula uttered with great emotion by everyone was "May we meet only at *simkhes*—celebrations." It was meant as an embrace of life.

Many years later, the young sister of my friend Joseph died in an accident and the family gathered to mourn at his house. He was then a young man at the beginning of a brilliant career in publishing, whose parents had been immigrants from Poland, starting out in the "shops" and eventually making a fortune in the clothing business. They had made it early enough to enjoy it thoroughly, living in grand style on Park Avenue, driven about town in a chauffeured car, their table graced by eminent musicians and artists. The furniture and appointments for their fourteen rooms had been chosen by a fashionable decorator of cosmopolitan taste. But it was Western Europe that the decorator had invoked, not the East of her clients' origins. The dining room reproduced an eighteenth-century English setting worthy of Adam, and in the living room we were transported to pre-Revolutionary France. Amidst all this grandeur, they were still Izzie and Sadie, who spoke with the accents of their first years in this country.

But they were broken by the news of their daughter's death, and in the anguish following her funeral, they were brought to their son's apartment and surrounded by family. Following the old custom, throngs of friends who learned of the event came during the next week to console the parents, who seemed paralyzed in their grief. Joseph's wife was an eminent designer, and the apartment in which everyone congregated to sit "shivah" (the seven days of mourning) was uncompromisingly Bauhaus, its starkness in accord with the mood of the mourners. Adrift in the hubbub of visiting friends and relatives, the stricken parents had returned to some earlier state, oblivious to the world around them, bereft of ornament, their clothing slashed. Their only comfort or refuge was in the old rituals.

When I came to pay my respects, I found the mother and father of the dead girl shoeless, avoiding their usual places of honor. In their mourning, they were pursued by the luxury of the world they had created, which could not serve them in this moment of grief. Seeking the backless seats prescribed by law and custom, and far from the wooden milk cases of the Bronx, they sat perched instead, oddly and awkwardly, on the sumptuous black leather footstools of their son's Barcelona chairs.

# 4

# Awnings

The first signs of the change in season in the streets of the Bronx were not changes in climate, but a series of events. The earliest and surest harbinger of summer was the arrival of the "super" to put up the awnings. Once in place, with their orange background and multicolored stripes, these gave the street a rather celebratory quality, as of flags or banners waving in the wind. But what they gave me, alone in my bedroom, was a feeling of being in a protected, dimly lit cave. As I let the awning down with its smooth rope running through my hands, my bedroom, which had been in the glare of the sun, suddenly took on a shadowy feeling, the filtered light playing over the pale surfaces of bed and wall, bringing new nuances of color and shade. The awning seemed to cut off sound as well as light, making the room a kind of secret place. Only the rooms facing the street were given awnings. The others looking into the airshaft hardly saw the sun from one end of the year to the next, and so the super was spared the labor, the landlord the expense.

Summer started, too, when we were allowed to shed our "combinations," those undergarments that in the fevered imaginations of Jewish mothers were the guarantor of our health throughout the winter. The fear of catching cold was so acute among the immigrant generation that we children were always bundled up before we could defend ourselves in scarves, hats, galoshes, at the slightest hint of rain or snow. In our youthful confidence, we pooh-poohed their fears. But they knew better. In the Old World, people were carried off from one day to the next, seemingly for no reason. A little cough, a chill, and who knew to what fatal consequences it might lead. They all had their stories to tell. My mother above all, whose own mother had died as a consequence of a cold contracted on a business trip, never got over this loss, which left her orphaned when she was three years old. My grandfather had been a grain merchant, but in the time-honored way of the shtetl, he had devoted himself to study while his wife devoted herself to the business. One day, traveling home in an open wagon from a transaction in a neighboring city, she had been overtaken by a rainstorm, had caught a cold, which had turned into pneumonia, and led, not surprisingly, to her death within a very short time.

Every family harbored a similar story of the unpredictable and savage course of a simple chill—*farkilung*. In one of the most touching and surreal songs of the modern Yiddish repertoire, a parable by Itzik Manger on the escape of the young from the shtetl, a boy leaves home to become a bird and live in a tree. His mother comes to visit him as the leaves fall and winter is coming on. She can understand his leaving but, she urges, "at least take a scarf against the winter cold and some galoshes." For Sholem Asch, too, the scarf was the magic talisman of love. In a little story in which a husband, as is his right, divorces his wife after ten years of marriage because she is unable to bear a child, the last scene takes place outside the house of the rabbi where the papers of divorce have just been written and given to the wife. As they leave the house and the husband prepares to get into his wagon, the divorced wife begins to call out to him to put on his scarf—and then catches herself for the sin of speaking to a strange man.

In the Bronx the spring would drag on, the days would grow

lighter and warmer, and we would still be in our combinations. I finally developed the theory that my mother waited for some secret courier who would tell her when the ice had broken on the Dnieper, and only then could we be safely released from our winter bondage. Then came the delicious lightness of being freed of winter weights and the winter smells made up of wet wool and stale clothes. With summer came the smell of starch in cotton dresses, and the soft scent of breezes in the schoolroom as the windows were opened for the first time. When I was in second grade, I once witnessed how a teacher understood the necessity for change and made it happen. One of the little girls in the class was clearly poorer than any of us. She came to school every day wearing a heavy woolen dress. It was not just any wool dress, but clearly one that had been made at home out of some discarded coat. As the spring wore on, that dark wool dress seemed darker and heavier every day. And the little girl's face grew redder as she perspired under its weight. One day at lunchtime we saw the teacher take our classmate by the hand and leave the classroom with her. When we came back at one o'clock, there she was, but wearing a light, white cotton dress printed with lively colored balloons whose buoyancy expressed the relief that we all felt at seeing her released from her wintry prison.

As the season grew warmer, the schooldays seemed longer, while we spent the last weeks of June watching our teacher laboriously complete her records as we sat fettered to our seats. A few favored ones were allowed to move about—to wash the blackboards or empty the inkwells. Then finally with the distribution of the report cards and the assignment to next year's class, school was over and we were free for a whole summer on the streets.

I ask myself now how we passed the summer. There were no "programs" set up for us. The concrete expanses of the schoolyard were open, sometimes, but basketball had not yet come into its own as the after-school sport. We did not know about the country. We had, of course, heard of rich children who went to "camp." But this was all part of the mythical America that others inhabited. Our reality was bound up with our very own streets and backyards.

We made good use of them. Summer as well as winter we were given 15 cents on Saturdays to go to the movies. These were totally absorbing and very long afternoons—a newsreel, a cartoon, "Coming Attractions," and then two features. We lived off those features all week because we all but memorized every gesture and every line of the dialogue, and would then re-enact the movies faithfully roaming over backyard staircases, crashing through cellar doors as improvised (and secret) stage sets. They had to be secret, of course, because any exercise of fantasy or imagination was regarded by our parents with contempt, as absurd. Without any discussion amongst ourselves, we knew that we had to hide these enthralling re-enactments. We knew that such ventures into passion and feeling were not acceptable in our world. It did not stop us, of course, and in the usual way, the forbidden became all the more delicious.

I should add that this was a segregated world. The boys spent their summers differently from us; they were in any case a mysterious breed for me. While they played handball, we played jacks. They played stickball in the street; we skipped rope on the sidewalk. We also took the sidewalk for our rhyming ball games and chalked it over for "potsy," while they commandeered the street for ring-a-levio. So we rarely competed for territory, but occupied different parts of the block, contentedly hearing one another's sounds and knowing that this was summer.

The only thing that drew us together was the arrival of the iceman, who appeared every day with his dripping wagon filled with stacks of rectangular blocks of ice. These he would cut, rapidly and expertly, with his ice pick into the ten- or fifteen-cent sizes on his order sheet, lift them with his tongs to the hemp sack that protected his shoulder, and climb up to his customer's apartment. That was the moment we waited for, as we abandoned our games and scrambled onto his wagon, searching out delicious splinters of ice to suck on.

There was also the library. How many passages of autobiography have been dedicated by New York denizens to the old Carnegie libraries so generously salted around the city? Every neighborhood had one of these great glass-fronted buildings—deliberately designed by Andrew Carnegie to provide an enticing view from the street of the book stacks within. But those huge two-story windows also provided light, and the sturdy oak furniture offered a sense of indestructible permanence. More than a recreation, the library offered an entering wedge into that baffling, totally desirable and necessary world of the "other." Our parents might pretend scorn and distance from this "other," but we knew we needed to understand and come to terms with it. And after a while we came to love it.

To begin with, it entertained us. We read, even in first grade, with our first library cards, delightful illustrated books—meant to amuse us. The books told us stories, they pleaded for our attention, they flattered us and drew us in with beautiful pictures, coaxing us to read the text, and leading us to believe that the authors felt themselves rewarded if we were pleased. Where else were we treated so well? At home, we were expected to "behave." That meant silence and obedience. A complaint of boredom would lead my father to an indignant response (in Yiddish): "Go beat your head against the wall and shout 'Bravo!' " Such a recommendation did not lead to trusting confidences. My boredom, he was telling me, was clearly my problem, and neither he nor my mother felt any obligation to amuse me. Apart from entertainment, I had also discovered very early that there was no reliance to be put on my parents' answers to my questions. I was asking, after all, about a world that they themselves did not understand. My best friends, then, were these charming, patient, and friendly books.

They took us to faraway places; they took us to epochs in history that were totally unfathomable and utterly absorbing. In surprising ways, they sometimes answered our questions. We knew about period dramas from our Saturday afternoon movies, so Shakespeare, Dumas, the *Count of Monte Cristo* and *War and Peace*, the Crusades all ran together in our heads in a whirl of grand and dangerous living. Our problem, of course, was that we could not separate fantasy from reality—so we understood everything with an equal earnestness. It was from the Count of Monte Cristo that I learned that it was a merit to be on time. It was his habit, I read, to arrive precisely as the clock was striking. From *Little Women* I learned, further, that one ought to be unfailingly cheerful and kind. From *Gone with the Wind* I discovered that it was admirable to sit up straight with one's back never touching the chair. And, of course, firmness, bravery, and unflagging resoluteness were part of all the travel narratives that I read incessantly.

Since these habits received such approval from the authors, I thought they must surely be worth emulating. Even during the most exciting episodes, these hints on manners and morals caught my attention, and I added them to my growing list of how "people" behaved. One day, I too would meet "people," those who lived by the code in these books, and then I wanted to be prepared.

The library was, however, more than a repository for books. It was also a sample of what I thought of as the real America. The librarians had their system; they were not particularly cordial, but they were just. There was one law, and it was equally true for all, a principle that I found deeply satisfying in my chaotic universe. I learned this in first grade, during my first week as a borrower. When I came racing back to the library one Saturday afternoon, having finished the single book that I had taken out that morning, I was told firmly that I could have no more books that day. "The rules were" that a borrower could check out books only once a day. I was sad; I had nothing new to read until Monday but *Wags and Woofie* over and over again. Yet these rules were not directed against me, and just the sense that I had not been singled out was in itself a consolation. As for the next time, I had learned. I had to take out lots and lots of books—as many as were allowed—so as not to suffer the effects of a drought. Here too there were rules: four fiction, four non-fiction. What a glorious load one could carry home.

And we all read and read. In the afternoons when the sun was high and the streets baked, I would lie on my bed in the room shaded by the awning and read. Then I went down to the street taking a chair and read some more. And if it were totally absorbing, I would read early in the morning as soon as it was light to find out what happened next in these breathless adventures.

More than that, I felt that the library and the librarians gave me a tiny view into the interior of the "others' " lives. They spoke quietly to one another. They were tidy in their movements. They had beautifully clean hands. Above all, they had little vases with flowers on their desks. This was nothing short of miraculous. I could not even begin to imagine what the interiors of their homes must have looked like.

"Nature" was otherwise in very short supply in the Bronx. It is true that we had "Nature Study" as part of our curriculum, but it seemed more like an extension of "Geography" than anything else. In Geography, we learned the exports and imports of foreign countries, the names of their capitals, their rivers or mountains, and their boundaries. In Nature Study we learned, also by rote, the names of trees, where they grew and to what heights. I learned, for instance, just as they were beginning to die out, that elm trees grew to a height of 158 feet, but I had never seen so much as a picture of an elm tree. It never occurred to me—or to our teachers—to ask the names of the trees that grew in the neighboring streets.

On our block one of the apartment houses had a green hedge in front of it, securely surrounded by an iron fence. Every spring this hedge put out leaves, and at some point there emerged wonderful, tender pink flowers that I would pick, even though they quickly wilted in my hand. Did these flowers have a name? I knew better than to ask, but over the years I have thought about them. What could they have been? Now, with my tiny store of acquired horticultural knowledge, I sometimes think they were azaleas. But it didn't matter. Nature was only one part of the large world that I looked at with speechless wonder. I was not the only one, although I did not know it at the time. The great tri-lingual dictionary of Alexander Harkavy published in 1904 also surrendered on the point of natural history: the Yiddish names of various flowers and birds were rendered in English simply as "a kind of flower . . . a kind of bird." To this day, the far more sophisticated *Modern English-Yiddish Dictionary* edited by Uriel Weinreich still blithely translates "daffodil" and "narcissus" by the same word, *nartsis*. The natural world, it must be admitted, is not the strong suit of Yiddish.

It was quite clear to us that what we learned in the classroom and what we experienced on the streets existed in two entirely separate universes. It never occurred to us that learning could be useful. It seemed a mandarin game played for its own sake and it achieved its purest form for us, for example, in the spelling bee. Our education had its own internal patterns and symmetries, with the reward of high marks on tests or on the next report card as its goal. Even the ostensibly "useful" classes in cooking for the girls or shop for the boys fit that pattern of abstraction. In cooking we learned about dishes that we had never tasted and saw no reason to want after we had made them. White sauce? Custard? It was all totally alien and vaguely disgusting. It did not occur to us that we were being uplifted. The boys worked laboriously all term to make a wooden stool or a picture frame which they brought home generally as a present for their mother. These works were received with thanks and amazement, but once again, the wider lesson that this was to acquaint tenement boys with the use of tools never occurred to us.

Many years later, when the first of my friends married and bought a house, he invited us all out to visit him in his new glory. This was beyond the prosaic limits of the subway. We had to take the Long Island Railroad and were transported from the station by *car* to an amazing phenomenon—a freestanding house, owned by one of us. Finally, when we could bear it no longer, one of us asked: "But, Marty, what happens when something goes wrong? Here you can't just call the super." Marty was ready. Plumbing, he informed us, and other domestic disorders were no more intractable than the printed page. We had only to apply the same powers of observation to the physical world that we applied to our intellectual questions, and we would see that they were just as susceptible to solution. We shook our heads in disbelief. We didn't have fathers who had spent most of Saturday afternoons under cars. How did one even know where to look? Marty was adamant and, as I later discovered, he was right.

At the end of eighth grade, however, we were given an opportunity to apply education directly to life. The boys could go to a vocational high school and learn a trade, while the girls could enter a commercial course equipping them to become a secretary or bookkeeper. *There* what happened in the classroom led immediately to the world and work. To those of us whose parents were willing or could afford to send us to an academic high school, it was clear that we were evading our responsibility to earn money, that we were shirking; and yet it was equally clear that the "academic" course had higher status. We were destined for greater things, although for many years before us our friends in the commercial course would be in the working world, in the real world, and self-supporting.

Sometime in the early thirties a letter came from school with a remarkable offer—to send my younger sister to camp for two weeks at no cost to my parents. This generated a tremendous amount of excitement and concern in the family. The excitement was all on the side of the young, who saw this as an unexpected opportunity to taste America. The concern was my mother's. She knew about the country, she intimated to us, in ways that we, cosseted innocents that we were, could not even imagine. More, she knew about its dangers. The country meant impure water, and impure water meant typhoid fever—and for the sake of a few games was she to risk the life and health of her child and send her off with these unwitting Americans into the depths of the country? We argued. We adduced statistics—anecdotal, to be sure—indicating that the children whom we knew who went to camp all came back and even seemed healthier for it. But as they used to say in Yiddish, "Talk to her and talk to the wall." My mother knew what she knew, and her fears were based on different anecdotal evidence. So my sister didn't go to camp.

But in America, disease did not lurk only in the country. There was something new abroad, which affected the rich as well as the poor: polio. Even our president had been felled by it, and in the newspapers one saw repeatedly the bravely smiling faces of victims confined to their iron lungs. My mother, and her neighbors, had an old remedy against such evils, a cake of camphor. I don't know if they also spoke spells over it. But all of us ran around during the summer with our cakes of camphor sewn into little cloth bags bobbing around our necks. In time we got used to the trailing odor we generated, and hardly noticed that when we all sat together sometimes in earnest conclave, we smelled collectively like the inside of a storage closet.

Camphor was a very large ingredient, in general, in the transition from winter to summer. Everything in the house that was made of wool had to be protected from moths. The first step consisted of hanging all the woolens that we had used during the winter out in the sun on the fire escape. The sun was, in general, seen as the great purifier. Then pungent-smelling paper garment bags, striped to look like cedar, were hung in the closets to accommodate our winter coats. After their exposure to air and light, smaller items such as sweaters, scarves, woolen gloves, woolen dresses were carefully lay-ered in drawers with camphor flakes. In these small apartments one of the first smells of summer was the smell of camphor that seeped out from the drawers and closets where it was meant to do its work.

In richer houses than ours, even more extensive transformations took place. Woolen carpets were taken up, sent into storage, and replaced with druggets; the heavy winter portieres and draperies came down in favor of printed cotton hangings, and the upholstery was slip-covered—also in cotton—in order to provide its cooling comfort against the skin during the sticky summer months ahead. Summer was taken seriously since most of us were not going any-where, even those rich enough to have rugs and brocade draperies.

It was only gradually that the Catskills emerged as the summer playground of New York's Jewish population—its boarding houses turning into hotels and its facilities for families evolving into bun-galow colonies. In the first decades of this century, there were already modest hotels in the Catskills, especially for the young workers who had their week or two of vacation during the summer. Abraham Cahan writes about this in *The Rise of David Levinsky*. And my mother went there in the years just after the end of World War I on her vacations from the factory. She took her best clothes and her needlework, spending hours on the veranda poetically hold-ing her embroidery hoop and enjoying this intermission in her life. Was she hoping to meet the man of her dreams? She didn't say. But it was certainly meant as a period of rest and indulgence after long hours and days in the shop.

After she was married, these interludes became rare. A few sum-mers we went to Rockaway Beach—then a neighborhood of single-family houses along the streets leading to the ocean. Many of these homeowners rented out rooms in their houses for the summer; a few, willing to accommodate children, even equipped the rooms with rudimentary kitchens, making them very attractive to working-class families such as ours. This meant that my father lived at home

during the month or so that we were away, and came out to Rockaway by the Long Island Railroad only for the weekends.

The children in the neighborhood soon found one another, and
as in the city we lived our independent lives, exploring the beach,
paddling in the water, since few of us knew how to swim. In the
evening, we were dressed decorously and walked on the boardwalk,
gawking at the shops and especially the auction houses with their
gaudy and immensely desirable objects d'art: glorious rosebud-
encrusted Capodimonte vases, Chinese jade figurines, mother-of-
pearl inlaid tables, brass mocca sets on their ornate salvers, heroic
bronzes—all the exotica to which every working-class household
at that time aspired. I was, of course, hypnotized by the auctioneer's
patter, which was mainly to convince us that the object before us
was to be had nowhere else on earth, or, if it were to be found, then
only at distant, unattainable downtown department stores, or even
more extravagantly at Tiffany's, where, of course, we would not
dream of going. But here, and only here, these treasures were within
our reach. How could we let this opportunity slip by? We had only
to say the word and this rare treasure was ours. How desirable suddenly those china cockatoos, those painted velvet wall hangings,
those gold-rimmed tea sets became. All from places impossibly far
away.

On the beach, our ignorance of fauna and flora left us with no alternative but to invent names for what we saw before us. A kind of
seaweed that had lumps at regular intervals we called "shark's eggs."
(And, of course, to this day I don't know what that seaweed is
called.) We stared in amazement and pleasure at the nameless shells
at our feet and collected them passionately for their color and shape
in wooden cigar boxes, to the irritation of our mothers. We only
dimly divined that these had once been the homes of living creatures. I think we knew what the gulls were called, but the other birds
that occasionally skittered across the sand were nameless visitors.
Nonetheless, we were not there like Adam in Paradise with the re-

sponsibility to find names for what we saw. It was a time for pure physical pleasure—different from our life in the city streets. Here we spent hours in the water leaping and turning, allowing ourselves to be carried by the waves, until blue with cold we would be summoned out by our mothers to the warm beach. I think we lived in those summers on hard-boiled eggs. What else was so efficiently wrapped—impervious to the sand—in its own shell until the very moment when it was wanted?

Those few weeks in Rockaway were like time lifted out of the calendar, and we would come back to the streets of the Bronx, to reality, as if we had been on another planet. It took a little while to adjust again to the rigid grid of streets and houses. I missed the salt air and the walks on the boardwalk at night, hearing the ocean pounding against the sand, out of sight and yet the audible heartbeat of Rockaway. Nonetheless, I would fold back into the urban rhythms and urban ways.

In summer we ate differently from the winter world of meat and potatoes. Suddenly our diet was all white and light, the world of *milchiks* . . . dairy—light soups, noodle dishes, delicate blintzes, fresh cheeses, and lots of fruit and sour cream. Two soups—borsht and schav—were the staples of the summer, both with the bitter tang that spelled refreshment. Borsht, among its other properties, was also a test of character. The clear summer borsht, eaten cold with a hot boiled potato and sour cream, could be enriched with a beaten egg. But this required a pure and resolute soul. *"Untershlogn a borsht*—beating an egg into a borsht" was not to be undertaken lightly. Here was where my mother's ethical approach to cookery reached its apogee. The slightest moral disturbance, and the egg would curdle.

Schav was even more work than borsht, if not as fraught with danger. And of course it was decades before I learned that sorrel— its English name—was an exquisite delicacy in French haute cuisine. Sorrel has become, in fact, such a great delicacy that it is now sold in supermarkets in tiny half-ounce packages as an herb. In the working-class Bronx of the thirties it was still sold by the pound as "sour grass." The cheapness of its price was in inverse proportion to its laborious preparation since, to begin with, the sandy leaves required repeated washings. The spines then had to be stripped, the leaves chopped, then finally cooked in broth or water and seasoned with lemon before the soup was served later in the day, cold and tangy, with wedges of hard-boiled egg. This was the ascetic version. A richer variant called for the addition of beaten eggs and sour cream—none of which we, as children, appreciated, as we longed to rush back to the street, to our friends and our interrupted games.

It was a cuisine that survived intact for decades before suffering the exaggeration and invasion of other cultures and other standards. Now it is in tatters, with a few shreds surviving in oddly distorted form: a pastrami sandwich with melted cheese? But then it was still whole. One ate either meat or dairy, and one knew what to expect at every season of the year.

There is no doubt that it took expertise in shopping, and even greater expertise in cooking, to put supper on the table. Before the era of machines, it also took strength of character and a powerful right arm to beat a dozen egg whites for even something so simple as a sponge cake. While at this long distance we tend to romanticize what went on in those kitchens, the truth is it was an intensely laborious life. The kitchen tables of the 1920s were enamel-topped and were designed with a built-in noodle board that pulled out like a drawer from underneath the top of the table, and fitted, of course, right over it. This design was both very practical and an indication of the expectations of the time. These noodle boards were used weekly as a matter of course. But such expectations did not end with noodles. Some of the heaviest laundry may have been sent out to the "wet wash" and returned damp in net bags to be hung out on the line. But much of it was done at home on a galvanized-tin washboard, the clothing scrubbed and rinsed and blued and hung out on those movable lines above the yard. It was no wonder that our mothers' hands grew rough and hard, just as the endless labor turned many of the women into drudges.

The amazing exceptions were the "Americans" who lived in the same apartments, did the same work, and yet looked so different. They were invariably fresh and neatly turned out even in the midst of their housework. With the crash of the stock market, a few of these families had suddenly appeared in our midst. It was clear that they had formerly lived in grander circumstances but were now reduced to the tenements in the Bronx. One woman, who told us that her husband had been a banker, particularly excited my admiration. What immediately differentiated her from the others was that she was slender. The regulars—the European-born ladies—were all round, which we assumed was the standard shape of mothers, who then laced themselves into respectability and a certain firmness of outline with their all-in-one corsets. But the American ladies did this without corsets. They wore trimly fitting little dresses, moved with a light step, and sported thin, delicate shoes rather than the heavy, laced oxfords preferred or needed by our mothers with their painful varicose veins.

My mother, who perhaps still dreamed of her unmarried days and her elegant, made-to-order clothes, took a cautionary line on these coarsened bodies and rough hands. This was what came of marrying and staying home, she said, flying in the face of the common wisdom—which she also advocated, sometimes—that a girl's principal aim in life was to get married. In fact, when I fell and skinned my knee or suffered some other superficial bruise, I would be dismissed with the Yiddish saying: *"Es vet nisht shatn tsum khasene—* It won't interfere with your getting married." The message about marriage was not entirely positive, but the Americans at least seemed to have a more graceful way of going about it.

The banker's wife immediately won a place in the hearts of her new neighbors by complaining about her husband—how he never picked up after himself, left wet towels on the floor of the bathroom, and so on. "It's not as if we have maids any more," she would add, at one stroke intimating the past glories of her former life and yet conveying that she herself was not too proud to pick up the wet towel. It was a story told and received with great satisfaction all around.

The consequence of this ambivalence about housekeeping played itself out in a variety of ways in the next generation. There were those who applied the "American" principles of rationality, energy, and organization, and invented new ways of running their houses. They may not have repudiated the standards of the old house-keepers, but they had no patience with martyrdom as the way of achieving it. Others were so horrified by what they saw that they would not ever after, as they used to say in Yiddish, even "dip a hand into cold water." Long before the advent of prepared foods, these dissidents had ways of putting a meal on the table without cooking, of tidying up without cleaning—and as soon as there was a little money to spare, while the rest of us were still wrestling with social qualms and our shyness, they quickly hired household help.

We always knew that summer was coming to an end on the day we were asked to submit our white summer shoes for examination. If they were found to be in sound condition, they were sent to the shoe-maker to be dyed so that they could be pressed into another season of wear. They came back black or brown and nicely polished, it is true, but with the old creases, and somehow it turned the beginning of school into a sadness. Everything else was so fresh: the smell of new paint in the hallways, the smell of the oilcloth with which we covered our schoolbooks, the new pencils and notebooks. And then the old shoes. Well, they would not last forever.

The end of summer was more than the end of a season. It was the end of a time of irresponsibility. All the rest of the year we, like our parents, were in harness to the world of work and obligation.

We took school seriously, were terrified when we arrived late, feared our principal like a god, and rose on command when he or another visitor entered our schoolroom. We learned early about rank and deference, and found it natural to accord respect to those who inhabited a superior world.

Except for the library and the movies, the territory of our explorations was very narrow. Physically, we covered no more than the few blocks that our legs could carry us in a radius around our home base. But we knew that there were other worlds and other ways beyond that radius. Someday we would encounter those worlds; and in the meanwhile, we divined, our school was going to prepare us, however indirectly, for that encounter.

# 5

# Hats

By the late 1920s, when my father-in-law and his companions—his *hevra layt*—had been in this country for some two decades, they felt themselves settled in the New World. They had their trades and their hard-won unions. They were householders, fathers of families, and they had amassed a little competence and comfort. At that point, one of their number resolved that the time had come to take a trip back to the Old Country. This was an important event not only for him but for his whole circle of friends, who decided to make a holiday of his departure by accompanying him to the ship to see him off. There was one difficulty: The ship sailed on a Saturday and none of them, of course, would violate the Sabbath by traveling to the pier on that day. There was a way around this difficulty, however. They would go downtown on Friday, spend the night with friends and relatives, give themselves an outing in Manhattan the next day, all on foot, of course, and then see the traveler off in the evening when the ship sailed.

On Saturday morning they met for morning services, and out of curiosity, for a lark, they decided that they would go to Temple Emanuel—the splendid citadel of German Jewish Reform on Fifth Avenue—known to be frequented by the rich and the great in New

York. Who could tell? A Schiff or a Warburg might just happen to be there. Our little group entered, took seats in the quiet under-populated sanctuary, put on their prayer shawls, and expertly turned to the appropriate place in the prayer book. Suddenly one of the Temple officials came down the aisle and spoke to them. "You," he said, addressing them collectively. "Here we take off our hats in the sanctuary." They were dumbfounded. They remonstrated. They cited Talmudic law. They cited custom: they always wore their hats, not only in the synagogue but on the street, at work and, of course, at home. The official was unmoved. He was master in his house, and insisted that they comply with the rules. With aching hearts, they were about to bare their heads when suddenly their tor-mentor pointed to the one member of the group who had a beard. "All right. This one," he said magnanimously, "he can wear his hat."

This was a story that gained in the retelling over the years. Now it was the theme of the friends, their camaraderie and their loyalty to one another that was stressed. Sometimes it was the arrogance of the official and unkind reflections on German Jews. Sometimes it was a meditation on the difference between Reform Judaism and their own traditional *authentic* Judaism. But as the years wore on, and they saw their sons go bareheaded, heard of synagogues where men and women sat together, saw the *tefilim* (phylacteries) that they had bought with so much care for their sons' Bar Mitzvahs fall into disuse, the point of the story shifted. They—the daring, ad-venturous young men who had crossed the Atlantic, who had en-gaged in untold scrapes and escapades—were suddenly the old guard, holding fast to customs that were ignored or were falling into disuse in modern America.

Yet they could do no other. Abroad they wore hats, modern American hats, and most favored was the snap-brim fedora. At home, however, they were most comfortable in a black silk yarmulke that was as much a part of indoor dress as their felt slippers. This was what a Jew did. And, of course, it was this perfect acceptance and adherence to the custom that led to one of the kinder jokes told by the next generation in a mock Talmudic question-and-answer session:

*Q:* How do we know that Abraham wore a head covering when he received the three angels?

*A:* Well, it says right here in the Bible: "And Abraham hastened into the tent unto Sarah, and said, Make ready quickly three measures of fine meal, knead it, and make cakes. . . . "

*Q:* I don't see how that proves anything. It doesn't say anything about his wearing a head covering.

*A:* How can you be so obtuse? Would Abraham go into his tent without a head covering?

Those gray fedora hats, the conventional, unobtrusive, omnipresent hats of the first decade of this century, visible in every photograph of the crowds on Fifth Avenue, also had their expressive side among the Jewish immigrants. Here in America, they no longer felt marked and looked down upon because of the caps that were the customary headgear of the workingman. In the Jewish villages of Eastern Europe, wealth and status were immediately visible. Rich men, and even their young sons, wore the impressive fur-trimmed *streimel*—sometimes close-fitting, sometimes broad, but always edged in fur. The very rich and the great rabbis might even have it trimmed in sable. In America, however, where all were equal, even the laborer could wear a hat when he chose. And he *chose* to wear it, particularly on his days of rest. Felt in winter and straw in the summer.

Now, at the end of the twentieth century, when jogging outfits are displacing conventional suits on all but the most elevated occasions, it is hard to imagine how formal dress was once embraced. But the workingman who had labored all week in his oldest clothes,

essentially in cast-offs, wanted to celebrate the Sabbath and his freedom in something fine—in a good suit and a white shirt. The Sabbath peace was heightened as he felt the smoothly ironed broadcloth
against his skin. For a day—and later, even two days—his week in
a noisy, dirty factory fell away and he could be the equal of any man.
The weekend was the time for leisure and for family visits, of course
in a suit and tie and with his hat at a *balebatish*—a respectable angle
on his head.

Women, no less than men, found the hat a powerful symbol, in
their case made even more intense by the struggle in the New World
over the marriage wig. This inescapable symbol of her status
awaited every traditional Jewish bride as soon as her head was
shaved on her wedding day. In the villages, women wore scarves
over their heads—a *tikhl*—and in winter thick woolen shawls. Rich
women wore headbands over their wigs embroidered with pearls
or other jewels. But in the greater universe of cities and boulevards,
hats were the prerogative of the rich and worldly, and it was one of
the wonders of the Industrial Revolution that made imitations of
these elaborate confections available inexpensively to the lower orders. In fact, that was part of the attraction of city life, where, on
her afternoon off, a ladies' maid might look almost like a duchess.

Dress, then, was a code, a sign language that revealed how much
money one had, one's place of origin, and even one's beliefs and aspirations. Among the Hasidim, the adherents of the various sects
distinguished themselves by dress, some even retaining the knee
breeches and long white stockings of the eighteenth century. The
*Maskilim*, the adherents of the Enlightenment and of Western
ideals, of course in principle adopted Western clothing, while the
tiny number of Jewish gymnasial and university students wore the
uniforms of their schools. A man stood, therefore, dressed in his
convictions, identifiable by a dozen signifiers before he had even said
a word.

In the memoirs of one immigrant, Rose Gallup Cohen, who arrived in New York in 1892 from her "small Russian village," we read how vividly even small variations registered. At the age of twelve she had been sent ahead of the rest of her family to join her father. When she finally recognized him on her arrival, she knew that she was in the presence of cataclysmic change. The details were not lost on a child who had come out of a closely regulated society. On "the first of July," she writes, "Aunt Masha and I stood in Castle Garden. With fluttering hearts yet patiently we stood scanning the faces of a group of Americans divided from us by iron gates. 'My father could never be among those wonderfully dressed people,' I thought." Then she sees him,

> that man in the light tan suit, smiling and waving . . . I felt a thrill. "Am I really in America at last?" . . . Father was so changed. I hardly expected to find him in his black long tailed coat in which he left home. But of course yet with his same full grown beard and earlocks. Now instead I saw a young man with a closely cut beard and no sign of earlocks. As I looked at him I could scarcely believe my eyes. Father had been the most pious Jew in our neighborhood. I wondered was it true then . . . that in America one at once became a libertine?

A few weeks later, she is horrified to see her father handle money on the Sabbath as he offers to buy her a treat. She then remembers the prophecy of a neighbor in the Old Country: " 'The first thing men do in America,' she had said, 'is cut off their beards and the first thing the women do is to leave off their wigs. And you,' she had said, turning to me venomously, 'you who will not break a thread on the Sabbath now, will eat swine in America.' "

America, then, was the land of frightening possibility because the rules and cohesion of enclosed Jewish life were lifted. In a sense there was nothing more orderly than the Jewish world, with its ever-repeating rhythms anchored by the weekly observance of the Sabbath and the procession of holidays through the year. Many an immigrant arrived at Ellis Island knowing only that he or she had been born "three days before Purim," or "on the seventh night of Hanukkah," but with not a clue as to the month or year according to the Gregorian calendar.

There should have been tranquility in a life in which there were no surprises. But by the end of the nineteenth century, the scaffold of tradition had become confining rather than consoling. It had taken the better part of a century for the Enlightenment of the West—the *Haskalah*—to reach the Jewish communities of Eastern Europe. And when it arrived, it introduced more than philosophical ideas into the East; it also brought with it a new basis for daily life, and new premises for relationships between people.

Shalom Jacob Abromowitsch, who used the pen name Mendele Mokher Seforim, Mendele the Bookseller, was both a pioneer in creating modern Yiddish literature and an unsparing critic of traditional Jewish life. In his wicked novel *The Little Man*, published in 1864, Mendele does more than expose the hypocrisy of conventional shtetl types. He also has a lyrical chapter describing the household of a "German," i.e., a member of the *Haskalah* movement. Herr Gutman (the eponymous Good Man) lives in a little house at the edge of town and accepts the fact that he is "frequently insulted and persecuted" by the townspeople. The protagonist of the novel, as an orphaned apprentice, is taken in for a time as a servant in this Enlightened but impoverished household. Here the poor abused servant-child for the first time experiences the pleasures of a well-regulated home, and even more significantly, the humane and gentle way that the members of the family treat him as well as one another. This was meant as an undisguised criticism of the chaotic lives and the often brutal human relations that were more characteristic of Jewish life than modern mythmaking would have us believe.

"He was very poor," the narrator says of his master,

> But in his home, poverty was not manifested by filth, slovenliness, sloth or any of the other ugly signs of poverty which may be seen

in most poor homes, especially those of the Jewish poor. The house was clean, everything had its place. Every last corner shone and sparkled. Madame, his wife . . . was continually cooking, baking, cleaning, sewing, mending clothes—all of which makes some women as wild as beasts, but she was always calm and quiet with a pleasant countenance. . . . No matter how busy she was, she managed to spare some time to sit down with a book in order to find out what was going on in the world. . . . I felt instinctively that Gutman and his wife were somehow a different kind of people, not, for example, like . . . the rich owner of the general store and his fat, strapping wife—an Amazon with a tireless tongue—who wore a string of real pearls and a dress of real silk but who was encrusted with filth nevertheless. I saw only that this was a different kind of house, that the children were not the usual bedraggled and uncouth Jewish brats.

The rationality exemplified in this household, this new way of ordering the world, this new way of thinking attracted, however, only a minority of Jews in Eastern Europe. And even these were largely drawn from the small pool who were well read and well educated in European languages as well as in the traditional learning. What the *Haskalah* attempted was a revolutionary break with the inertia of centuries. The *Maskilim* had to struggle not only against an entrenched mode of belief but also against the entire social organization that supported both the belief and the way of life that went with it. It was too hard, as Mendele showed in his portrait of Gutman, to be forced to live as an outcast in the settled, tightly organized communities of Eastern Europe.

But in America, these powerful, watchful, deeply intertwined communities dissolved, and the young immigrants who came to make a new life were ready to rethink many practices that had been inevitable in the Old World and seemed almost absurd in the New. In America they inevitably formed new *shtetlach*, but these were for use and not for authority. They wanted the intimacy of "home," those heart-warming, intensely close feelings toward family and friends; but they also wanted something more, something that they were sure they would find in the West.

Many of these young travelers could not even name what they were seeking. But they recognized it when they met it. During a five-hour stopover in Berlin in 1882, Isidore Kopeloff, the twenty-three-year-old from Bobruisk, surreptitiously leaves his train, which is crossing Europe to take him to his ship in Hamburg. What he finds as he explores the city puts him in a state of euphoria:

In my eyes, the radiant world had never seemed so wonderfully beautiful, lovely and grand. And without even wishing it, suddenly Bobruisk, my mother, my father and our poor house appeared before my eyes; the streets alone, muddy up to your neck, made a striking contrast with the well-tended, paved streets here before me; the yellow, gloomy faces, the peculiar gestures and mannerisms suddenly seemed strange and ugly in contrast with the smoothly shaven, fresh faces of the Germans. The elegant hats happened to remind me of the hat with its ear flaps that Nahum Itshe, the town crier, had worn winter and summer for easily the last fourteen years, and that looked as if it had melted into place on him.

Before my eyes there arose the gray figures of the women of Bobruisk, with their thick padded jackets and kerchiefs, standing behind their little warming stoves in the market; the young girls who looked away ashamed when they encountered a man's glance. And I compared them with the women of Berlin. Oh, what tasteful clothes these women were wearing, and what a graceful and elegant way they had of moving.

Of course his ruminations come to a sudden and ugly end when he is accosted by an anti-Semitic policeman. But for a boy from Bobruisk, this was nothing new.

The hat, which caught Kopeloff's imagination in Berlin, was no less a powerful symbol in America. Elegantly trimmed fantasies for the women, worn over their own natural hair, together with straw boaters for the men, became demonstrations of a new, free, and debonair way to live. Here the individual had desires and wishes outside the tightly constrained world of tradition. In his novel *Yekl*, Abraham Cahan makes the hat or its absence the central emblem of his novel. When the hero, Yekl—now Jake—who has preceded his wife to America, sees her after three years as she arrives at Ellis Island, his "joyous anticipation" gives way to disgust and shame. He first glimpses her behind the barrier with "her hair concealed under a voluminous wig of a pitch-black hue. . . . The wig made her seem stouter. . . . It also added at least five years to her looks." With that glimpse, he "averted his face, as if loth to rest his eyes on her . . . and vaguely wished that her release were delayed indefinitely."

Later, when the illicit dancing partner of his bachelor days appears at his apartment before his dowdy, work-worn wife, her assurance is conveyed in a few images, culminating in her hat. "The door flew open, and in came Mamie, preceded by a cloud of cologne odours . . . she was powdered and straight-laced and resplendent in a waist of blazing red, gaudily trimmed and with puff sleeves, each wider than the vast expanse of white straw, surmounted with a whole forest of ostrich feathers, which adorned her head." As the novel proceeds toward the inevitable divorce, Gitl, the immigrant wife, both fascinated and ashamed, secretly tries on the hat and corset, the symbols of Americanization, which her husband has bought for her.

Cahan fixes on the episode where she abandons her wig as her moment of self-assertion and the moment of her husband's defeat. On the day of the divorce proceedings, she appears at the rabbi's room wearing a fashionable hat over her own hair for the first time in her life. The change in her appearance, "her general Americanized make-up, and, above all, that broad-brimmed rather fussy hat of hers, nettled him. It seemed to defy him, and as if devised for that express purpose."

Was it simply vanity that moved these young women (and men)

to violate a custom that had almost the force of law? The answer lies with the sea. The voyage to the New World carried with it the implicit reasoning that everything was now in question and the world was awaiting reinvention. Even the fundamental institution of marriage took on a new dimension. Jewish young women, many of whom lived alone or with distant relations, were freed, as they had never been before, to decide their own fates; to pick their own husbands. They no longer required a matchmaker to find a spouse, nor did they need the elaborate financial prenuptial arrangement that, in the Old World, often turned on the number of years that the bride's parents would support the young couple. Above all, women were freed of the need for a dowry as the indispensable precondition for marriage. And while they worked, they were the sole administrators of the money they earned.

By the turn of the century, working and earning money had become a matter of course for young unmarried girls. As a count by the U.S. Bureau of the Census showed, nearly 90 percent of women workers in the United States were unmarried, almost half under the age of twenty-five. In New York, with its myriad of small factories requiring only a little dexterity and application, even country girls with no training could find a place. By 1911 Jewish women, largely immigrants, made up 60 percent of the work force in the ladies' garment industry. In the artificial flower and feather factories, in the clothing shops, in the millinery lofts, in the cigar and paper box factories, wherever they earned their wages, they planned lives different from what they knew in their villages. And they spent their hard-earned money according to new standards and tastes. To the scandal of their Italian co-workers, the Jewish girls seemed to waste it all on hats and gloves, unlike the Italians who were still closely constrained within a tight family system.

One of the best demonstrations of the truth of this charge can be seen in a famous photograph taken from the balcony of the Cooper Union auditorium in New York in 1908 during a strike meeting of the Waist Makers' Union. Far and wide across the balcony, the camera looks down on a sea of modish, cartwheel-sized hats elaborately trimmed in gauze and silks and feathers. Most of these were undoubtedly sewn by their wearers, girls handy with a needle, who could pick up a hat body in one place, the ribbons and flowers in another, and create a delicious concoction. This longing for both "bread and roses," as the women in the textile mills in New England put it, indicated the poetry in all those young people who labored and hoped for a better life.

My mother was one of those who loved gloves, kid gloves, another of the vices of the working girl. They could be short or long, loose at the wrist or fastened with tiny pearl buttons, but they had to be fine and thin and hug the hand. She had very particular notions as to how one should dress to go out in the evening. What she admired most of all was a black velvet coat and, of course, black kid gloves. As she confided to me once, "Velvet is so warm!" In later years, in her most expansive moments, she would let me accompany her as she went to buy gloves, which turned out to be as fine an art as buying a hat.

Sizing in kid gloves, it seemed, was somewhat unreliable, so that one of them would have to be pulled onto the hand to see whether the fingers were actually long enough, whether there was room enough at the joints. For this operation a little velvet pad was placed on the counter, the seated customer placed her elbow on the pad holding her hand up, and the glove was then carefully pulled on, fingers first, thumb last. Then the moment of anxious testing. When the fingers were just a little tight, the saleswoman had a delicate wooden device that could be inserted into the offending part and opened a notch so that it applied just enough pressure to stretch the glove. Again, it seemed to me that the processes of choosing, fitting, adjusting were as much a part of the mystique of the kid gloves as the glove itself. Invisible tightnesses, invisible wrinkles perceived only by the discerning eye of the fitter, were smoothed away. There was a powerful implication of gentility here that made the buyer feel she had not only bought gloves but also her way into some other system of being. They brought my mother an immense satisfaction in their fit, their soothing softness against her hands, and their intrinsic excellence. There was something satisfying about pulling each glove on the hand and fumbling for an instant with the buttons. It was the finishing touch to a perfect costume. When she took out her gloves preparatory to a state visit, one knew that my mother was ready for every contingency.

All of these seemingly frivolous but actually heart-stabbing changes to the older generation could not really affect the younger generation's essential commitment to *Yidishkeyt*—to Jewish life. What the old rabbis viewed as doom was actually the freedom to make Jewish life thrive and flourish in a new way, through new secular forms: the theater, music, dance, literature, and a proliferation of political groups.

Contradictions thrived as well. There were committed Socialists and union men who would never miss a morning *minyan* (religious service), just as there was the Hebraist-Zionist who subscribed to all the Hebrew journals but had no intention of moving any further than to Borough Park in Brooklyn. *Yidishkeyt* took many forms in the immigrant generation, but it needed no definition since it was only in the world of their peers that these immigrants were truly at home, pushing at the old boundaries, creating new ones, but with a powerful sense of the centrality of their shared history and language.

When they left their villages, they moved to the most advanced industrial cities in Europe and America, but also away from an atmosphere of medieval thought. They found a world where many of the ideas they had brought with them could not stand up to scrutiny. And on important matters, they began to be silent and watchful. In the Old World, women had learned to accept that only half their children would survive. A serious illness was a physical catastrophe whose cure, as everyone knew, lay in God's will. A prayer, a spell, in dark moments, a vow might in some way mitigate a terrible fate. But it all lay outside human hands. The political world was no less mysterious. Outside the penumbra of the Tsar were other heads of state, other governments. And in some, it was said, a Jew might live a peaceful, undisturbed existence: Argentina, Canada, England—these were names to conjure with. Yet even the astonishing physical combination of lights, steam, and power that drove them across the Atlantic in ten days could hardly prepare them for the new Industrial Age of elevated railways, street lights, sewage disposal, safe drinking water available at the turn of a tap. In crossing the Atlantic they had made a leap of centuries in time.

What is cleanliness in a little Galician village, with its tumble-down houses, without running water or electricity, with privies in the backyard? Once a year, at Passover, chairs, tables, and cupboards were carried outside for a thorough scrubbing, the floor given a new coat of clay and spread with sand. Not only cleanliness, but the very acts of living meant arduous work. In the Galician villages, water, brought on the shoulders of the town water carrier, was used carefully and more than once. Wood for the stove had to be cut in the forest, bundled, and carried to the village on someone's back, then stacked and sheltered from the weather, a product of strenuous labor and expense.

What was cleanliness in the Lithuanian villages as they were described in 1897 by the official Russian census takers? In a confidential report to the Tsarist government, the enumerators were not diffident about expressing the prejudices with which they had started on their scientific mission. Yet their findings ran counter to every stereotype on which they had been nourished. "They had been accustomed from childhood on," the census takers wrote of themselves,

to see an exploiter in every Jew. But they were surprised when they saw with their own eyes in what kind of conditions the majority of the Jews lived. Frightful crowding, misery, a mass of beggars, people without any definite occupation. . . . In one room, there are often ten people living, and seldom fewer than six or eight; a whole family has only one bed, on which naturally only a few can sleep, while the others simply lie on the floor. A family of four or five people will subsist for an entire day on a four-pound loaf of bread and a single herring. They all go barefoot and in rags. The children are skinny, listless, with evidence of tuberculosis and malnourishment.

What was at stake here was neither aesthetics nor hygiene but pure naked survival.

My father often described how he ran barefoot, even over the stubble of the fields, from Passover to Yom Kippur, but in his depiction he made it seem an act of freedom and bravado. With these little hints, we were told and yet not told about what it meant to be poor in the Old Country. Occasionally, a story, an incident would surface, but it required close attention to decipher it at the moment of its telling when the narrator felt that he was putting a shameful part of his past up for public viewing, and turned and twisted it to make it acceptable to an American listener. In telling us with a certain flourish that he went barefoot, my father thought he was hiding the fact that his mother had been too poor to buy him shoes, and emphasized instead his own toughness in running free in every climate, over every terrain.

But in the Bronx, another kind of effort, another standard was used to measure comportment, cleanliness, to produce order out of the chaos of daily life. In this our parents were as ignorant as we, but we had our daily lessons from our Irish schoolteachers. We all had to learn, sometimes to our shame, what were the requirements of another culture. When we had slept in our underwear a few nights too long, our teachers were not shy about telling us to change. Just as they insisted on morning inspection where they examined our fingernails, our necks, and looked behind our ears. That we also had to produce a clean handkerchief was an exoticism that some-times was beyond the understanding of our mothers.

Our teachers reached even further into our lives and homes, charging us to tell our mothers that it was unhygienic for the entire family to use a single towel and that each person in the family should have one for his or her exclusive use. This finally was too much for my mother, who at once complied and made a mockery of the long arm of America that had presumed to intrude into her home. The next day there was no longer the single fluffy Turkish towel, but four thin, limp cotton dishtowels—one for each of us. I could decide which route I preferred.

I used to listen with a bemused fascination to my "American" classmates as they complained about their mothers' irritation because they hadn't cleaned up the mess in their bureaus. I assured anyone who would listen that my mess was equally noteworthy, but privately I tried to imagine the way of life implied by these complaints. Each of these children had a whole bureau to himself. In addition, they had enough clothing to fill it, and also so many clothes that they themselves no longer knew what they had. In our family, there was a single bureau for a family of four. It contained all the family linens and all of our underwear, slips, socks, handkerchiefs, pajamas. My mother was the chatelaine of this central item of furniture, and only she had the knowledge or authority to open it to redeem the item that might be needed.

Was there perhaps an echo of Mendele and the *Maskilim* here in our search for order in some part of our lives? Many of the young Jewish women writers in America also found that it had a redemptive quality. A room of one's own, above all a clean room, served the same purpose in New York as in Virginia Woolf's London. Anzia Yezierska describes her search for a place to live on the Lower East Side in New York. At one stop she is offered "a little coffin of a room, dark as the grave. 'I got three girls sleeping here already,' says the landlady. 'And there's yet a place for a fourth in the bed.' "

When Yezierska declares that she wants a room "all alone to my-self," the landlady says fiercely, "This is a decent house. I'm a re-spectable woman." But Yezierska continues her search. "For the first time in my life," she writes, "I saw what a luxury it was for a poor girl to want to be alone in a room." When she is finally offered a filthy room, she takes it." " 'This is just the thing for me,' I cried. 'I'll clean it up like a palace.' "

Not a lot of the young girls who were in the Ladies Waist Mak-ers' Union aspired to literary careers or even to a room of their own. But they aspired to a new place for themselves in the world.

Among the men very few, like my father, took the extraordinary step of joining the U.S. Army as a gesture of freedom. What greater way of showing his distance from the Old Country, where men maimed themselves rather than be called up? He had arrived in this country at the age of sixteen, with little education but bursting with energy and ambition. His first workplace had been the clothing-shop floor where his brother and other family members were employed. He was a good learner, and quickly worked his way into the rhythm of the shop, making a place for himself among the other immi-grants. But once into the life, watching his friends and relatives, his anxiety grew. He was horrified at what the hours bent over a sewing machine did to the spirits and bodies of the young men around him, and he knew that he would have to leave for something different. It was only a matter of time and opportunity. And indeed one spring day, a year after his arrival in the United States, the lure of a re-cruiting sergeant captured his imagination and his signature. Now it was his family's turn to be horrified: to *volunteer*?

My father served for a full four-year term, mostly stationed in Texas, contemplated enlisting for a second "hitch," but decided that the time had come to return to civilian life. Although he spoke eagerly and often about his army experiences, I never heard him say one negative word about his four years as a young foreigner in a tough military setting. Being in the army taught him to swear loudly and violently, improved his English, and gave him a powerful respect for the usefulness of a disciplined, orderly life. Ever after in family photographs we were always arranged neatly by size. In the kitchen, to my mother's exasperation, he was always reorganizing jars on shelves and dishes in a rank order quite unrelated to their function or frequency of use. But the experience stood him in good stead in later years when he ran a business and understood the principles of inventory control long before the concept became commonplace.

For the Jewish immigrant men in America, however humble their status may have seemed from an American perspective or from their children's perspective, they were experiencing what they never could have hoped for in Europe—a freedom of choice, a freedom of motion. Above all, however, was the freedom from fear in public places. They, too, like real Americans took their cramped bodies off to Coney Island, donned gaudy and humorous bathing suits, and cavorted with others in the surf. They went off to the mountains to breathe the air and stroll in the woods. In keeping with their sense of astonishment at their new pastimes, there was a story that was told with a glint of self-mockery about two men sauntering along a dirt road in the Catskills enjoying the experience of the countryside. One of them notices a patch of bright flowers and asks his friend if he knows their names. "How should I know?" answers the friend. "Am I in the millinery business?" Despite such setbacks, they went on with their explorations.

They learned to dance and went to the dance halls that were the popular Saturday night entertainment on the Lower East Side. They went to vaudeville and cabaret. They strolled along Second Avenue and Houston Street and stopped at the crowded cafés to see and be seen. In short, they learned how to have a good time, a category that did not play a big part in shtetl life. One of the memorable photographs in our family album showed three couples enjoying themselves in an afternoon in the park: the girls in little black flapper dresses, with tightly fitted cloches, looking roguishly into the camera; the gentlemen, including my less than romantic uncle Jake, holding their indispensable and jaunty straw hats.

Sometime after this outing, Uncle Jake married and together with his bride opened a candy store in the Bronx. These little neighborhood businesses were a fate that many of the young immigrants took upon themselves once they had acquired a few hundred dollars in capital. The neighborhoods of the Bronx and Brooklyn were lined with little shops minutely divided by specialization, each one just barely supporting a family by offering an indispensable service or selling necessary goods. All but the most ambitious housewives, for example, sent their lace curtains out to be washed professionally. In front of these laundries on any fine day, some eight or ten wooden frames could be seen propped up on the sidewalk with delicate curtains pinned to them so that the panels would dry to their original size. The laundries were not alone in regarding the sidewalk as an extension of their space. Groceries ranged open sacks of beans and spices under a carefully lowered awning, the stationery store put a wooden newsstand outside the door for the latest editions, and, of course, the fruit and vegetables were arrayed in boxes on the sidewalk until the first frost.

Many households began tentatively, anxiously, by living in the little space in the back of the store, improvising cooking and sanitary facilities so as not to incur an extra expense until it was clear that the business would succeed. In the novel *Call It Sleep* by Henry Roth (first published in 1934), an engaged couple planning to open a candy store when they marry discuss their situation with the bride's sister.

"If we live somewhere else," said Mr. Sternowitz [the prospective groom], "there go half the profits. Why throw away money on rent when you can get it free? A place to sleep in is all we need—and a place to eat a breakfast and a supper."

"I don't care where we live," said Aunt Bertha [the bride] "as long as we make money. Money, cursed money! What if it is a little uncomfortable. . . . Later when we've sold the store and made a little money, we'll talk again. . . . A little while we'll struggle; we'll pee in the dark. And then we'll have a home. And when we'll have a home we'll have a decent home. Thick furniture with red legs such as I see in the store windows. Everything covered with glass. Handsome chandeliers! A phonograph! We'll work our way up! 'Stimm hitt' [steam heat] like bosses! What bliss to wake up in the morning without chilling the marrow! A white sink! A toilet inside! A bath-tub! A genuine bath-tub for my suffering hide in July! . . . Not that radish grate there," she pointed to the washtub in the kitchen.

My uncle Jake began further up the ladder, and although he and his wife put in long hours six and a half days a week, they were prosperous enough to enjoy a comfortable apartment. When they first moved in, we were all summoned to admire the parquet floors, the new furniture, the painted black velvet hanging over the sofa. My Tante Lena was, in any case, one who knew how to appreciate the moment. Once, we had all gone out to the movies together and returned after the show to have a snack in the kitchen. As we sat about bathed in the afterglow of the Hollywood experience, Tante Lena exclaimed: "Right now, I wouldn't change places with the Queen of England! Would she be so comfortable sitting in a kitchen and eating what she likes?" As usual, this started a hare in my poor muddled childish brain. Was there a way to compare the pleasures of the Queen of England and Tante Lena? Were the Queen's necessarily greater because she was the Queen, or were Tante Lena's greater, as she implied, because they were truer and more intensely felt? We did not lack for philosophy in the Bronx.

But Tante Lena's capacity to enjoy life was sorely tried by Uncle Jake, who, having married Tante Lena and fathered three sons, seemed to spend most of his remaining time as a dormouse sleeping, unless roused by his wife or one of his sons. He took the early

morning shift at the candy store, which meant meeting the newspaper trucks at 6:00 A.M. when they made their deliveries, sorting
and arranging the papers for the first customers, and setting up the
store for the day. By midmorning, when Tante Lena had sent the
boys off to school, done the housework, and cooked dinner, he was
ready for a nap. He would return eventually, but sometime in the
afternoon there would be another nap while Tante Lena managed
the store, balanced the books, and made the decisions that Uncle
Jake was always putting off. She never complained, but she consoled
herself at the milliner's.

She would settle into a little chair at a shallow mirrored table,
in which she could barely see her face in the attractively shaded
lighting. "I need something to wear on weekdays," she would
say, sighing. "Something cheerful." Neither she nor the milliner
were to be hurried. They knew that there was something larger at
stake. And as the milliner reached for the first candidate, a little
bit of Tante Lena's story would begin to come out. Nor would she
need to fill in too many details. After all, they were all neighbors.
They knew one another's lives and bank accounts intimately.
Tante Lena just needed to talk. The milliner smoothed her hair,
tried one hat and then another; she listened and nodded and com-
plimented Tante Lena on her fine profile, her beautiful coloring.
With her looks, said the milliner, she didn't need to wear the sort
of ordinary hat that everybody wore. She could try something interesting, daring. Finally, when the milliner offered her a hand mirror so that Tante Lena could see the effect from the back, she
gradually grew calmer, more cheerful. She even began to pay attention to the hats.

I don't know if Uncle Jake ever noticed Tante Lena's hats. But
they were part of a women's conspiracy, a signal at our house.
When Tante Lena appeared for a visit in one of her dashing new
hats, my mother took it as a hint. After she had admired it out loud
and at length, the two of them would disappear into a bedroom for

a heart-to-heart colloquy on the torments of the soul that can be stilled, for a while at least, by hats.

Men had other consolations. Among that old guild of tailors, whatever their later occupations, there was nothing that could arouse a flush of passion like a fine piece of worsted. And they were fanatical about fit. A collar had to hit the back without the slightest shadow of a wrinkle and there was never to be a tug across the shoulders or a bunching under the arms. If the sleeve did not exactly hit the first knuckle of the thumb, then one might just have to take apart the entire jacket. As soon as there was a little money, they would have a suit made to order, which, carefully preserved in camphor, would be expected to last the better part of a lifetime. When these paragons of tailoring were produced for the *simkhes* that dotted the years, their owners eyed one another narrowly. They could catch at a glance the mismatched stripes at the shoulder, the buttons that tugged, the swell under the arm of the suit with a badly cut interlining. It added to their enjoyment of their own that fitted, as they liked to say, *"vi gegosn*—as though poured on." At such moments their sensual delight in the very best cloth, in the perfect weight and hang of the suit as it slid over the body, quite outweighed even their *Schadenfreude*. They knew how to count their pleasures.

They had come a long way from the *kapotes*—the gaberdines of their fathers. The rhythm of the Jewish week impinged now only lightly on work-ridden lives, yet *Yidishkeyt* lived on among them. According to legend, every Jew then born and the soul of every Jew to be born in later ages stood with Moses at Sinai to accept the covenant of the Law. The *Yidishkeyt* among these young Jewish immigrants, however, was less theological than historical. It was an identification with every past epoch and with every wrong done to a Jew since Moyshe rabeynu—Moses Our Teacher—had shown them their path. From Haman to Chmielnicki to the Kishinev massacres, the path of Jewish history had been a path of tears and suffering. Yet there was an art to survival as well, knowing when to resist and when to escape. Wherever they went, Jews carried with them that long memory of ancestors in far places who remained immediate in their consciousness because at any moment, that fate might be theirs.

Then in America, *Yidishkeyt* became less tragic, less a sorrowful remembrance and more of an affirmation. *Yidishkeyt* meant remembering the past that had only just slipped around the corner, forgiving it, gilding it a little. It did not matter to these young Jews that they had drifted from the beliefs and practices they had brought from home, that new rituals were gradually remaking the old holidays and the old traditions. What counted was that irreducible sense of community, the expressiveness of their own language and the power of their own literature as it spoke to them, the tug at the heartstrings of the music. There was center and periphery, but for them there was no doubt in their minds as to where the center was. *"A yid,"* they said, *"blaybt a yid—*A Jew remains a Jew." And in that tenacity of memory and being they planted the old life on the new continent.

# 6

# Papers

When did we begin to laugh? It was only then, I think, that American *Yidishkeyt* began to define itself. As the comedians found targets in newly minted Jewish types, as Yiddish newspapers described distinctively American scenes—flirtations in Second Avenue dance halls, in the hotels in the Catskills, quarrels among housewives in the *kokhaleyns* (the vacation bungalow colonies where everyone shared a kitchen), the perpetual card games. These jokes established the new types: the "all-rightnik," the *yente* (the vulgar busybody), the *kokhlefel* (the energetic organizer), the kibitzer, and the obsessive garment manufacturer. I sometimes think that if our two men on the country road had gone on with their conversation, it might have included the following passage:

"Tell me, have you heard from Max lately?"

"Then you didn't hear? Max died suddenly last week."

"What? At the height of the season!"

Once we had assembled our cast of characters, it was easy to go on. We had abandoned the old East European types—the rabbi's wife, the ignoramus, the wagon drivers, the rich man, and that motherlode that began, "Two Jews went to Paris . . . " These jokes now took on a slightly musty air as we developed our own targets.

The first indigenous American comic character was the boarder: the ubiquitous bachelor who was both a source of income for the wife and a source of worry for the husband as he considered the dangers of harboring a strange young man in his household. That the boarder was worrying in fact, as well as in fantasy, is demonstrated in the countless letters to the *Forward* advice column. In a final absurdity, the culmination of his career is celebrated in Aaron Lebedeff's song *"Ikh bin a border bay mayn vayb*—I'm a boarder at my wife's house." Here the married man finds the best of all possible worlds by divorcing his wife and continuing to live in his home as a boarder. "Men!" he urges, "I recommend this to you. What a marvelous thing! She cares for me, but she can't nag or scold me when I come home and lie down on the sofa to read the newspaper."

As life for the immigrants in the Bronx began to take form, as they drifted from their Yiddish newspapers, there was no better mirror for their preoccupations and aspirations than the *New York Post*, New York City's oldest daily. It had inevitably gone through many metamorphoses since its founding in 1801, but perhaps the strangest was the transformation in the 1930s when it discovered its Jewish reading public. Newspaper reading was a serious avocation in the immigrant Jewish community. People bought two a day, one on the way to work in the morning and another on the way home. The morning paper was read on the train, during lunch hour, and provided the basis for the conversation that occupied the workshops. The evening paper had a more leisurely, more discursive atmosphere, where it was less the news than the opinions that were so gripping. Evening papers were associated with the idea of an unhurried perusal, as our boarder testified, lying on the couch where the recovery from the efforts of the day was somehow connected with the canvass of opinion on the state of the world.

These straphangers were avid readers not only of newspapers but also of literature. As Irving Howe observes in his autobiography, "The culture of New York was then still a culture of the word. . . .

A high-school graduate would have read at least a novel by Dickens and a play by Shakespeare." Understanding this, the *Post* began to build readership by offering the complete works of great authors. Ultimately the list included Hugo, Balzac, Dumas, Shakespeare, De Maupassant, Fenimore Cooper, Joseph Conrad, Dickens, and Mark Twain. The appeals were various. From Victor Hugo, the *Post* offered "Thrills-Thrills and More Thrills." Dickens was going to "add a vital touch of beauty, dignity and distinction to your home." In the case of Mark Twain, the approach was more fundamentally moral: "You MUST not deny yourself or your family of [sic] so deep and extraordinary a pleasure. These illustrious books are yours PRACTICALLY AS A GIFT." And that was certainly true.

Even in the thirties, these editions were bargains. They were offered in sets of three volumes at a time, at 93 cents for each set. Balzac, the most wordy, appeared in thirty-six volumes in the *Post* edition, while Mark Twain and Shakespeare each came in at a mere eighteen. The only condition imposed on the reader was that with the 93 cents the purchaser also had to present twenty-four differently numbered coupons that were printed, one each day, in the paper. At such a price, every home could be decorated with these icons of culture, and there was hardly a household in the Bronx that didn't have its set of Dickens or Twain, the two most popular authors. The books were so successful that the *Post* went on to present a portfolio of prints by Van Gogh, and later even classical recordings, all against a combination of cash and daily coupons.

In the end, the *Post* not only responded to its readers but with its cultural suggestions molded the taste of an entire generation. The painting portfolio, wisely chosen for its audience, was secular. No Madonnas, no Nativities, no Depositions from the Cross. Someone had made a bold choice. All of modern art was presented simply and solely through the work of Vincent Van Gogh, "the immortal torch bearer of a New Art." "Eight paintings and Giant Portfolio," the description continued. "The finest paintings in a ten million dollar collection," guaranteed "to add beauty and dignity to your home." The *Sunflowers,* the *Berceuse,* his views of vegetable gardens became the indispensable wall ornaments of Bronx apartments when a mere $1.19 plus forty-five coupons bought the collector a portfolio of "Duplaix Duplicates." No young couple's new home was complete without one of these prints, carefully chosen out of the portfolio and framed. They taught us about color, harmony, boldness, and prepared us for our next encounters with what the *Post* called New Art. The immigrant generation was perhaps less interested in the cultural context, but it also seized on the Van Gogh works as representing America. Milton Klonsky, who grew up in Brighton Beach, remembered how his grandfather's picture was displaced. "His picture in a gilt frame," he wrote, "was first hung in the parlor; but after a few years we found it didn't look 'nice' with the new furniture, and so *zeda* [grandfather] was relegated to the bedroom. A Van Gogh print was put in his place."

In a somewhat more didactic vein than the promotion of the picture portfolio, the music series offered to "enrich your home with these 10 complete symphonies." The selections moved steadily and uncompromisingly from two Bach Brandenburg Concertos through the Mozart Jupiter Symphony, the Beethoven Fifth, Schubert, Tchaikovsky, and ended with César Franck. Wagner was included as well with overtures to *Die Meistersinger* and *Parsifal.* As an introduction to classical music it could not have been better chosen. What is amazing as we contemplate this list is how the *Post* did not condescend to its readers. It did not offer "The Top of the Pops," a few Strauss waltzes, Sousa marches, or "entertaining" musical novelties, but plunged directly into the heart of the tradition.

Classical music was not easy to find on the radio in the 1930s. Station WNYC—the non-profit municipal station—had a "Sunrise Symphony" program at 6:00 A.M. and another hour of classical music in the evening. The Metropolitan Opera was broadcast on

Saturday afternoons, and the Philharmonic Orchestra on Sundays. It took very careful management, therefore, to catch what was available. Only gradually as I heard some of these works repeated and listened closely to the comments of Deems Taylor, who talked during intermissions of the Philharmonic program on Sundays, did I begin to understand where the main lines of Western musical composition were drawn.

Meanwhile the opera was identified for me with the husky voice of Milton Cross, who, for decades, narrated the plots, gossiped about the celebrities, and heroically filled all the intermissions with tales of the composers, the history of opera, and the biographies of the singers. In fact, so hypnotic was his telling that when I finally got to the Metropolitan, the actual experience seemed somehow less vivid without his voice in my ear than my Saturday afternoons in front of the radio. That first time was a performance of *Madame Butterfly*, and my main feelings were of dismay and disappointment. Sitting close, I was able to see clearly the rather tawdry paper umbrellas twirled by Suzuki's companions as they sang their opening chorus. The painted backdrop did not compare with the mysterious cloud-wreathed mountains behind Suzuki's little house as described by Cross. And where was the glittering harbor that she watched so constantly from her garden? No, the Metropolitan stage was a poor wooden thing compared to the rich pictures conjured up by that mellifluous voice. And at the curtain calls his melting descriptions of the costumes awakened a kind of longing for an elusive, make-believe grandeur that could not be matched by mere cloth and paste jewels.

On Saturday afternoons, as soon as the name of the next week's opera was announced, I rushed to the library to take out the libretto, anxious to get there before what I was sure would be the stampede of opera lovers looking for the same volume. But it never occurred to me that there were more reliable ways of hearing the music than the happenstance of radio. The *Post* impresarios, however, recognized the basic fact that most of their readers did not have turntables on which to play the records they were selling. They offered, therefore, to supply one: a minimal ten-inch turntable that could be hooked up to any radio. For a five-dollar deposit, the affluent could acquire this turntable with their first symphony, the money to be refunded when they had bought their last. Those without ready cash had to wait until they had completed the series. Nor was this the age of convenience. Every day the *Post* printed on its second page a "Numbered certificate for the World's Greatest Music." The applicant had to "clip and save 24 of these certificates, each differently numbered, and bring them to the New York Post together with the Privilege Voucher and $1.93 and you will be immediately handed your first group of three double-faced, twelve-inch records." On the tenth trip, the subscriber would be handed the record player "Absolutely Free!"

After my tenth trip, I was indeed handed my record player, which opened the door to new problems as to how to connect it. At a stroke, the *Post* had opened up the whole world of do-it-yourselfism. Having grown up in a household in which electricity was still feared, I was not prepared to command and tame the forces of two electrical machines at once. Shamelessly, I called on a friend who had spent most of his childhood taking apart toasters for fun. He came, ran wires under carpets, produced an array of pliers, electrical tape, quadruple plugs, and after some moments of silent, intense concentration glorious sound suddenly filled the living room. My parents came home that evening to find an ugly gray box on top of their shiny Stromberg-Carlson console and a tangle of wires behind it. They may have objected, but now, with other *Post* readers, I was on my way from being a mere listener to becoming a collector of classical music.

In summer, we enthusiasts congregated at Lewisohn Stadium—the open-air amphitheater at 138 Street and Amsterdam Avenue, in the neighborhood of City College—where the New York Philharmonic and illustrious solists played for an audience of fifteen thousand. For 25 cents we could sit on the stone steps and listen to an evening of music. People came from the shops right after work, students came, office workers and the elderly, and we all stood sociably in line, holding places for one another until the evening dimmed and finally the ticket sales began. To this day, there are certain compositions, Lewisohn Stadium favorites such as the Mendelssohn Violin Concerto, that seem lacking in substance without the light drone of airplanes overhead.

Spread out on the field before us were rows of wooden chairs, and at the very front several dozen round tables with a ticket price of $1.50 per person. At these sat gentlemen in Palm Beach suits and ladies in little pastel silk dresses, sipping iced drinks. We were separated from them by far more than the few hundred feet between our perches and their comfortable chairs. This was that other world that we glimpsed so often and did not yet understand. But Minnie Guggenheim, the chief benefactor of the Stadium concerts, never intimidated us. With her familiar, homely name and her hearty manner, she always made us feel as if the concerts had been organized for us alone. When she came out on the stage—a block away—once or twice a season to say a few friendly words, we felt that she was talking to us and we cheered her with wild enthusiasm. *She* knew how we felt about those concerts.

Quite apart from the *Post* premiums, largely of interest to the younger generation with their well-known thirst for culture, what the *Post* reflected in its presentation of the news, in its columnists, even in its advertisements were the habits and dreams of the immigrant generation—now Americans, but with a difference. And it was just this margin of difference that gave the Jewish settlement in the Bronx its coloring and established the code by which it lived.

The *Post* writers offered more support than they knew to the tabernacle of Bronx *Yidishkeyt* as they dealt with the political, social, and moral problems that so occupied the immigrant generation.

Jewish readers in the Bronx were intent on the state of the world. They followed each columnist's pronouncements closely, debating the political positions and reading the news with a degree of personal engagement that others reserve for family letters. Roosevelt was the idol of the Jewish working class, who saw him as the great intercessor between the uncertainties of their own lives and the malign forces that could take away what little they had. And then there was the outspoken Eleanor. Times were hard, but in the Bronx, we felt we had defenders in high places.

During the thirties, the Hitler regime began to throw its dark shadow across the Bronx, as his followers in the German American Bund demonstrated in Yorkville and Father Coughlin preached his brand of anti-Semitism in Sunday afternoon broadcasts. The combination of hooligans in the street and rabble-rousing priests was all too familiar. And that it should be happening in America was incomprehensible. Suddenly there were German refugees in New York, and as the decade drew to a close, letters from Poland began to arrive from relatives who were afraid of what was happening and wanted help to leave. In fact, as it turned out, the European news in the *Post* became an extension of those family letters.

The politics of the younger generation was not nearly so concisely reasoned, nor so focused on the two or three issues that animated the immigrants. News from Europe, which so gripped our parents, agitated us less than our own American problems: our failing economy, our glaring social inequities, the dustbowl, the sharecroppers. Irving Howe has written eloquently in his *Margin of Hope* about the attraction of the Socialists and his own activities in the Young People's Socialist League—the YPSLs, as they were known colloquially. Even those of us who were less political than Howe could not help but brush against some of the leftist youth groups that were operating in the Bronx or in our schools, and which spoke to our sense that the world needed to be put right.

I was twice invited to meetings of the Young Communist League, and each time had the feeling that I was being drawn into a conspiracy. At the first, which was arranged by a high school classmate, a handful of us met in a room at the 92nd Street YMHA. There, a speaker from the Party addressed us on the urgent need for sanctions against Franco. As we left, he let us know that this was actually a clandestine meeting and that we should not discuss it in school. But we were supposed to write to our congressmen. My real problem was that I did not quite understand what people meant by "sanctions." My history teacher, Miss Griffin, an outspoken Catholic, was against them. The Party was for them, and the dictionary said that "to sanction" meant to approve of something. In this topsy-turvy world, it seemed that sanctions actually had to do with disapproving. It was all so confusing that I never went back to another meeting at the Y, although it seemed pretty exciting to be part of a secret group.

My second invitation was issued for a recruitment party in Brooklyn. What gave the invitation a particular twist was that the organizer was a rabbi's daughter, intimidatingly beautiful and expensively dressed. The connection between the rabbi's daughter and my friend Esther, who had invited me, was that Esther worked in the rabbi's wedding parlor on weekend afternoons and evenings to help support her desperately poor family. When we arrived, we discovered that the group (or was it a cell?) seemed to be made up exclusively of the rabbi's daughter and her boyfriend, Teddy. As the evening began, it was quite clear that it was Teddy who was the moving force in the enterprise. He proposed that we form a study group in which we would discover the usefulness and truth of Marxist teachings as we proceeded through all the fields of human learning, beginning alphabetically with anthropology.

As an example of its universal applicability, and to end the evening on a lighter note, he announced that he would play Prokofiev's *Peter and the Wolf* for us, first prefacing it with a Marxist analysis. He began with the grandfather, representing the unenlightened bourgeoisie, who forbids Peter to venture forth into the light of true understanding. The duck in the pond, with the "damned wantlessness of the poor," was the credulous worker who believes the blandishments and promises of capitalism, represented by the Wolf. Already in 1862, according to Teddy, the state Socialist Ferdinand Lassalle, traveling around Germany, had inveighed against the lack of working-class consciousness. As for the chirping bird in the tree, it clearly stood for Rosa Luxemburg exhorting and encouraging Peter, who was the symbol of the alert and active worker. But Peter by himself—i.e., the workers—could not defeat capitalism. Here Teddy reached the climax of his parable. For this victory, said Teddy, now quoting chapter and verse, as Lenin had so correctly stated in *What Is to Be Done?*, they needed the help of the avant-garde of the Communist Party, that is, the hunters, who arrive in time to capture the Wolf. This is accomplished without violence, it should be noted, but they take him off to the zoo, where he presumably spends a comfortable old age on display as an example of capitalist wickedness to the liberated proletariat.

We were all impressed not only with the cogency of the analysis of this seemingly innocent piece of music, but also with Teddy's erudition. After the meeting, as we walked to the subway, Esther and I took counsel with one another. Should we join? And here prudence triumphed over idealism. We both harbored as our dearest wish the hope of someday winning a place in the Civil Service— either in New York or Washington. It was a future that promised a living wage and would also shelter us from two of the uglier aspects of capitalism, anti-Semitism and unemployment. Now, it was true that the Communist Party was perfectly legal. They published a newspaper; their headquarters were listed in the phone book. Earl Browder in suit and tie, looking not unlike Thomas Dewey, made equally statesmanlike statements to the press and congressional committees. But how would it appear, we asked one another, if we had to write on some application form that we had been members of the Young Communist League? We agreed that it could not do us any good. With regret, therefore, we declined to join the rabbi's daughter's cell.

My next encounter with the Communist Party occurred a few years later (around 1938–39), when I was spending weekends working in my father's delicatessen store. A few doors away was a large grocery store owned by a man who was an avowed Communist, as was his clerk, Moyshe. On summer nights when our respective stores closed around midnight, we would stand out on the sidewalk in the warm air talking politics. Moyshe was a member of a Party branch on the Lower East Side and wanted to bring me into the group. He had found a very direct connection between his own history and the appeal of the Party.

He came from a poor, extremely observant family, and his father owned a small store on the Lower East Side. But as a pious Jew, he would close early on Friday and keep the business closed through the Sabbath. Moyshe bitterly blamed the family's misery on his father's stubbornness and unwillingness to adapt to modern life. Religion, as Marx had so correctly pointed out, said Moyshe, was the opium of the masses, and it was religion that had caused his family's suffering. I listened to Moyshe's story with tender sympathy. Moyshe had smoldering dark eyes and his intensity was very disturbing. But somehow I didn't get to his branch meetings.

His boss, on the other hand, spoke to my mind rather than to my heart as he painted the workers' paradise of the Soviet Union. He did not realize, however, that he was talking to a wily opponent. By then, I had joined Marxist reading groups and knew a little more than in the days when I did not yet understand sanctions. I had heard about the show trials, the suppression of free speech, that the country was ruled totally and inexorably by fiat from above, by the Party. One member of my study group was writing a dissertation on Soviet bureaucracy and as his work progressed he told us of his discoveries. We heard about the famine in the Ukraine of the twenties, about the inefficiencies of Socialist production, and especially about a corrupt and bloated bureaucracy. Moyshe's boss listened to my complaints with a tolerant smile, particularly to my criticism that a true democracy would permit other parties. He had what seemed to him an irrefutable answer. "Why," he asked, "why if you had finally achieved socialism in one country, would you even want another party?" He continued to read the *Daily Worker* and I the *New York Post*.

What drew me to the paper were the daily morality plays presided over by the psychologist Rose Franzblau, who typically began her responses by blaming all concerned. The letters to Rose Franzblau were in a different key from those anguished calls for help to the *Forward* letter column from abandoned wives or cheated business partners or daughters struggling to escape from home. They were about how to live, about standards of courtesy and respect. It is not irrelevant that the phrase for these qualities in Yiddish is *derekh erets*—literally, "the way of the land." Our friends and neighbors in the Bronx were seeking and inventing exactly that: new customs in the way of the land.

Language and manners were frank in the Bronx, although they had not yet caught up with the nuances of American, Emily Post–style *derekh erets*. Above all, one was required to communicate. "You could call an uncle once in a while; it wouldn't hurt. I don't say you have to visit, but at least ask how everybody is." This classical plaint was at the heart of relations between the two generations. The immigrants saw their children literally vanishing out of their reach, moving to other neighborhoods, even other cities, and entering lines of work that with the best will were not truly comprehensible. Rose Franzblau's columns were filled with the lament of parents who felt abandoned, bereft, somehow not taken seriously by their children, who were friendly enough in that breezy American way. But this was not the *derekh erets*, the respectful attitude toward parents that was their due. Rose Franzblau soothingly mediated, suggesting fewer phone calls and more invitations to dinner.

We, the American-born, had our own problems with American *derekh erets*. The codes of behavior in our two communities did not quite mesh, and one was at a disadvantage without knowing the American code. The *Daily News*, a newspaper with a more popular touch than the *Post*, spoke to this perplexity with a daily feature entitled "The Correct Thing." It generally showed two painfully neatly dressed young people learning to shake hands or to utter the correct formulas on arriving or leaving. When I reached high school, I thought it was time for a more systematic study of this culture and went to the library to find an etiquette book. Unfortunately, Hunter High School had been around a long time, and its etiquette books dated from the nineteenth century. With complete trust and absorption, I started at the beginning and was promptly defeated. The first chapter was devoted to the ritual of morning calls and the arcana of calling cards. I decided that direct observation would have to do.

For all its anxiety, the world I knew in the Bronx was of Jews who no longer lived at that desperate edge of their means that characterized the first immigrant years. There was a freedom and opportunity that grew out of their new, if moderate, prosperity, and new modes of decorum were required for it. Here was where Rose Franzblau became the sounding board for all the novelties that life suddenly offered. One of the inventions of the New World was the proliferation and enlargement of *simkhes*—the festivals and celebrations that dotted the landscape of Jewish life. Modest and rare in the Old Country, where they were fixed and stylized in content and form, these suddenly blossomed in the New World as people yearned for occasions to socialize and caterers obliged with the invention of "traditional" ceremonies. The changing form of the Bar Mitzvah celebration over the last half century, for example, is in itself practically a guide to the varying forms of Jewish acculturation in America.

These events did not come cheaply. They required festive dress and the appropriate, carefully calibrated gift. One of Franzblau's most distressed correspondents wrote on just this theme: The setting is the Bronx apartment house. The cast consists of two devoted neighbors. The writer has been the recipient of many invitations from her friend over the years and has on each occasion brought a lavish gift. At last the writer and her husband are themselves the hosts at a large anniversary party, and when the gifts are publicly opened, it turns out that the neighbor's offering is some trifle—to the consternation and humiliation of her friend. "Believe me," she writes in anguish to Rose Franzblau, "I don't need her presents!"

This was one of the ruling postures in the Bronx, a high-minded attitude toward money, which was regarded almost disdainfully as merely the instrument toward realizing some finer purpose. In the columns of the *Post*, the writers acknowledged the existence of monetary motivation in others, but for themselves they always acted out of principle. It was also out of principle that they patronized the discount houses, waited for sales before buying, went shopping at stores with low overhead and no fixtures. "It's not so much the money" (such a consideration showed a contemptible meanness of spirit), "but what's the point of spending more if you can spend less?"

So much time was occupied in spending less that it became a veritable art form, in fact a kind of mixed-media art. First there was the actual shopping expedition, and then there was the narration, which was the cathartic conclusion—as trophies were held aloft and the buyer explained how she found this amazing whatsis, how it took a real eye even to discern it in the jumble that surrounded her, but when she did find it, the price was scandalously low. Murmurs of admiration, reexamination of the whatsis, requests for the address of this treasure trove, and so on. What a satisfying conclusion to a day!

Many years after I had left New York, I returned briefly on one occasion to do some serious shopping. I stayed with friends, but as I learned to my cost, they were not natives of the Bronx. In the old tradition, when I returned late in the afternoon, I launched on the tale of my adventures, held my whatsis aloft, and asked the rhetorical question: "And do you know what I paid for it?" But before I could reach the climax, my host, a man with beautiful manners, stood up, very embarrassed, and said, "No," and he didn't think I ought to tell. We had to have a long talk after that while we canvassed the problems of cross-cultural contact.

My growing up in the Bronx had not prepared me, in fact, for the restfulness and reliability of his good manners. What dominated conversation there above all was a certain vehemence of expression and a frankness about the usual taboo subject of money that we later learned to curb. As these young immigrant couples for the first time had the opportunity of buying more than necessities, they fixed on what seemed to them durable goods: furniture, fine clothing, fur coats, or jewelry, and in so doing came to a very interesting consensus. Unlike Italians, who bought land and houses as soon as they had a little capital, Jews in the Bronx remained with the old European belief in portable riches. After that, the key phrases were "How often do you buy a bedroom set in a lifetime?" showing a certain foresighted prudence. Or "A coat like that you can wear on any occasion," as if at any moment one might be invited to Buckingham Palace. Whatever it was, it had to be "the best," as a justification for the expenditure. "The best" may not have been absolute, it may have only been "the best" in that particular store, but it provided the needed moral basis for these expenditures, making them seem much less frivolous. The durable bedroom set, the universally wearable fur coat, the intrinsically valuable gold watch became at once gratifying possessions and "investments."

The columns of the *Post* also charted the rhythm of the year, the pastimes, recreations, and favored vacation spots of those bound to their apartments for all but the longed-for two-week vacation. The first sign of spring and warmer weather in New York came as the windows were opened, at first cautiously, and then left wide to catch every breath of air. This soon had an unfortunate and audible consequence when apartment dwellers found something crunching underfoot. As the exhalations from nearby chimneys flew in and covered floors, sills, and every exposed surface with a fine layer of black grit, New Yorkers knew that summer was on its way. Max Lerner, in a memorable column, once described how he and his wife had decided to use only the mottled Russell Wright charcoal gray china on their terrace because it so beautifully camouflaged the fly ash.

Nonetheless, the summer vacation loomed, and the Catskills offered a tempting array of possibilities. In large and small print, somehow typographically suggesting their physical qualities on the page, the resorts announced their offerings. The clothing industry had only grudgingly acceded to the idea of a paid vacation and began with the first week in July, a solution that neatly disposed of the problem of absenteeism around the Fourth of July. This change greatly widened the population base of the vacationers. Despite the unsporting character of conventional Jewish recreation, there was a positive reverence, as we have seen, for fresh air and the country. Behind this lay a very simple logic. Just as the tenements bred weakness and disease, so the opposite—open spaces—must lead to good health, a belief that transcended class and education. Victor Erlich, grandson of the great Russian Jewish historian Simon Dubnow, tells of being taken for healthful walks in the 1920s by his grandfather in the woods outside of Berlin. At intervals, Dubnow would stop and say, "Breathe, Victor, breathe."

In the mythology of the Bronx, "the mountains," as the Catskills were called, had an edge over the seashore in promoting a sound body. With every turn of the road as it rose higher in the hills, the traveler would feel that the air was lighter, better, purer. Sending the wife and children to the country, therefore, was practically a moral obligation—even if only for a week or two. This was regarded as a period in which one soaked up good health and stored it for its later beneficial effects. For most of the immigrants, the arrangements in the Catskills, however, were far from the dachas of fictional Boiberik, the summer resort of Sholem Aleichem's Tevye stories. There, summer houses were taken for the season by well-to-do householders, who arrived with family and servants to continue the luxurious life to which they were accustomed, "with every dainty brought ready to their door." The Catskills were much more democratically organized, and even a workingman might send his wife and children to "Livingston Manor—Blue Bird bungs. by babbling brook. $12.50 a week." Like the first shy crocus, these modest two-line notices advertising equally modest accommodations appeared early in the spring in the *Post*. For the bungalows, one had to be canny and reserve early. It was not until nearly summer that the big hotels began to advertise, stressing the separate children's dining room. While life was not yet as highly organized as it later became, parents at least had the relief of not having to supervise their children during mealtimes.

The implicit key to these vacations was indulgence. After a long hard year at work, the vacationers looked forward to a week or two of fantasy in which they would be cossetted, cared for, and live *"vi Got in Frankraykh*—like God in France." For the women it meant that beds would be made, meals would be cooked, and their only responsibility was to enjoy themselves. Similarly for the men—it was the *release* from the rhythm of their work week that led them to stretch their arms, to swim in the nearby lake, to sink into afternoon-long card games. The absence of activity—rest—was the key word for vacations. And what better expression of indulgence than the lavish helpings of delectable, familiar food at every meal.

It was perhaps this emphasis on the vacation almost as a right, their assiduous sending of the family to the mountains or the seashore, that gave Jewish men a special reputation in the immigrant communities of New York. Jewish husbands, according to the stereotype, were generous, indulgent, and, above all, non-violent.

When the rare intermarriage occurred, generally between a Jewish man and a non-Jewish woman, this image was rather defensively invoked by the bride-to-be.

As the Depression eased, the watchword, in the special English of the Bronx, became "live a little." For people who had come from real deprivation, living a little was applied first and foremost to the fundamentals of life—food, shelter, and clothing. It meant the indulgence on Sunday mornings of fresh rolls, as well as a visit to the appetizing store to buy smoked fish and little black oil-cured olives—*maslines*. Tevye's musings on the pleasure of a fresh roll were not confined to Sholem Aleichem's fiction. What the next generation took for granted as Sunday morning ritual remained an exquisite extravagance for the immigrant generation, for whom the crisp yet tender poppy-seed rolls always remained a luxury.

Simultaneously, the advertisements that filled the tabloid-sized pages eloquently revealed the needs and aspirations of a community just beginning to have a little disposable income. For the living room, it meant plush upholstery and heavy draperies made to measure. When Tante Anna and Uncle Philip decided to replace their two daughters' ramshackle iron beds with a real bedroom set, they went out and bought something that was the envy of every other girl in the extended family. It was ornate; it was of wood; and it was painted a pale green with festoons of rosebuds nestled in shining leaves. In a similarly lavish moment my parents went out and bought a long-desired embroidered satin bedspread with matching pillow shams and a Kewpie doll. The whole ensemble was spread out on the bed only on the rare occasions when we had company. From my mother's pleasure in the texture of the satin, in the workmanship of the design, I understood that this was meant to last a lifetime. It was not to be used up frivolously by being put out every day. Only much later did I ask myself why she didn't give herself this pleasure more often. Then, however, I still shared the belief that pleasure was not to be taken lightly, but was to be savored in small and infrequent doses. In the end, therefore, these objects became not just furnishings but prizes, trophies in the struggle for life in America. Is it any wonder that they were watched over, tenderly cared for—the visible fruit of labor and accomplishment?

The advertisers in the *New York Post* were at one with their readers and talked about "quality" and "value." In later periods, the campaigns launched at the *"hi-geboyrene*—the American-born generation" featured the advertiser's "Rennaisance" (as it was spelled in the *Post*) furniture, or confided that he was offering "enchanting antiques from France and Italy, from Spain and England—treasures destined to become family heirlooms. All one of a kind. . . . " But the immigrant generation was done with Europe. They didn't want old furniture, or even new furniture that had been freshly "distressed." Neither "Rennaisance" nor Queen Anne nor Louis Quinze were words that moved them. They wanted something that would last; they wanted "the best." They wanted, finally, the sort of visible opulence that would take their breath away as they looked about them and thought of home.

It was not until after World War II that Jews from the Bronx actually began to buy their dwellings—cooperative apartments in the northern reaches of the borough or even houses in the suburbs. Until then, they had contented themselves with moving from a smaller to a larger apartment and filling it with treasures of the heart. But from the time that Abraham bought the cave at Machpelah to bury Sarah, there has been one kind of real estate that every Jew has bought, and that is a cemetery plot. When they first arrived in America, poor workingmen formed their landsmanshaft organizations which, as we have seen, as a first order of business bought a quadrant of land in a cemetery. Members paid their monthly dues to ensure being laid to rest in a decent grave amid their friends in the event of an untimely death. Set apart from the individual or family plots in the cemetery, the entrances to these areas are guarded sometimes by fine ironwork or by massive and ornamental granite pillars inscribed with the name of the organization, the date of its founding, and the names of its principal officers. The sociability requirement, however, remained uppermost even later as families bought their own private burial sites. The *New York Post* advertising columns spoke directly to the needs of that generation of independents who wanted to carve out their own eternity on new ground.

In the Old Country, people visited the cemetery to pour out their hearts, to take counsel, to implore the intercession of the dead at critical moments. In America, the cemeteries were far away, not easily available for an intimate confession, a whispered prayer, but people continued to go, even if at greater intervals. Visiting family graves was more than a pious duty for the immigrant generation. It was also a comfort. In addition to pilgrimages on the anniversary of the death, even non-religious Jews customarily visited relatives' graves in the weeks just preceding the Jewish New Year holidays. For my mother, therefore, it was an ever renewed source of sorrow that her parents were buried far, far away and that she did not have the solace of these annual pilgrimages. Alert for any opportunity for sociability, many people turned these visits into family get-togethers as relatives arranged to meet at the grave and afterwards convened to reminisce and talk at a nearby restaurant.

Cemeteries were not places for forgetting but for remembering. As Jews in America began to take hold of their fortunes a little more firmly, they began to wish for pleasanter, opener cemeteries than the crowded graveyards with man-high tombstones that characterized the old landsmanshaft enclaves. The advertisements in the *New York Post* soon responded to these feelings. They appealed to the *Post* readers' gregarious spirit, their love of refinement, their desire for "the best." The new cemeteries offered "dignified, exclusive, luxurious" accommodations, so that even death became a marketable commodity. One of the ads stresses the fact that the cemetery was only "23 minutes by subway from Times Square . . .

and only five minutes away from the following cemeteries where your next of kin may be resting." Thirteen cemeteries are then named: the list conjures up a vision of gregarious Jewish ghosts entertaining themselves through eternity by visits to their relatives, when not tooling over to Times Square by subway.

One cemetery ad with its eye firmly set on the here and now, however, makes the unmistakable point: "This cemetery," they proclaim, "is for the living," a theme promptly taken up by its rivals. "Reverence, serenity, beauty, inspiration" were the terms used in the *New York Post* ads to restore the cemetery to its former place in Jewish life as the culmination of all earthly desire. This was perhaps most succinctly expressed in one of those classic stories from Eastern Europe about two Jews who make a pilgrimage to Paris where, among other wonders, they hope to see the Rothschild mausoleum. When they arrive and are directed to the tomb, it is everything that they hoped in its splendor and grandeur. And we can hear an echo of their satisfaction as our visitors from the Bronx survey one of the newly laid out cemeteries, with its well-tended lawns and plantings, its discreet brass plaques embedded in the grass. "This," they say, in the words of those European forbears, "this is what you call living."

# 7

# Work

In 1690 Glückel von Hameln, the widow of a prosperous Jewish merchant of Hamburg, began to write in Yiddish a memoir of her life, in part as a remembrance of her late husband whom she had loved deeply, and in part as a work of moral instruction for her twelve children. She opens with the following story:

A bird once set out to cross a windy sea with three fledglings. The sea was so wide and the wind so strong, the father bird was forced to carry his young, one by one, in his strong claws. When he was halfway across with the first fledgling, he said, "My child, look at how I am struggling and risking my life in your behalf. When you are grown up, will you do as much for me and provide for my old age?" The fledgling replied, "Only bring me to safety, and when you are old I shall do everything you ask of me." Whereat the father bird dropped his child into the sea and it drowned, and he said, "So shall it be done to such a liar as you."

This is repeated a second time. When he asks the third fledgling the same question, under the same circumstances, the baby bird replies, "My dear father, it is true you are struggling mightily and risking your life on my behalf, and I shall be wrong not to repay you when you are old, but I cannot bind myself. This, though, I can promise: when I am grown up and have children of my own, I shall do as much for them as you have done for me." Whereupon the father bird said, "Well spoken my child, and wisely: for so much honesty, I will spare your life and carry you to shore in safety."

Two and a quarter centuries later, my father told me this very story in our living room in the Bronx. In his version, the bird was a stork, but his intent was the same as Glückel's, which was to demonstrate, as she said, that parents put themselves "to great pains for their children, for on this the world is built, yet we must understand that if children did as much for their parents, the children would quickly tire of it."

This was not a very pleasant story in the seventeenth century and it did not improve with age, for short of devoting the rest of his or her days to his parents, every child was cast immediately into the position of a lifelong ingrate. Yet I can hardly think of anything else that so sharply illuminates the everlasting perception of the immigrant generation that they had been set adrift in the world and their only salvation was their own unremitting labor. They had received no help from their parents and steeled themselves to expect none from their children. In his old age, as if resuming this ancient conversation, my father would repeat a saying that was current among his elderly neighbors in Florida: "One father," he would say, "can care for ten children, but ten children can't care for one father."

This was not a generation that waited for or expected help. Aside from the occasional sick benefit offered by their landsmanshaft organizations or their unions—to both of which they had, after all, paid their dues—they expected to earn their living with whatever strength or resources they could bring to the labor market. And unlike the Old Country, where occupations were graded by a strict ranking system, in America, they discovered, it did not matter what you did. What was important was that you "made a living." In the shtetl or in the big cities in Eastern Europe, synagogues were often organized by trade; the shoemakers prayed together, the butchers had their own synagogue, and the rich—whatever the source of their wealth—also had their place of worship, each decorated according to the taste and means of its members. In the pitiless hierarchy of the ghetto, the tailors' synagogue together with the shoemakers' were at the bottom of the scale. In crowded New York, the tailors and milliners and furriers accepted and perpetuated this distinction, forming synagogues in the districts where they worked, meeting in comradely fellowship for morning and evening prayer. But in America they enjoyed one another's company out of free choice, without the sense of stigma.

In one of Sholem Aleichem's stories, Tevye the milkman's youngest daughter sails for America with her husband when his immense business empire crashes. After a while she writes to her father, who reports to "Panye" Sholem Aleichem that his daughter and son-in-law are now well settled and "making a living." Not a word about what they do; nor does it matter. This fluidity of occupation fascinated Sholem Aleichem, who spent the last two years of his life in the Bronx, and used the voice of the orphan Motl who arrives in this country with his extended family to describe the process of Americanization. What captured Sholem Aleichem was how quickly and without preparation his unworldly characters—Motl's elder brother and his friend Pinye—move from one occupation to another. Neither they nor their employers expect them to know anything about what they are doing. After a quarter of an hour of practice on a piece of cloth, they are declared "operators" fit to work in a garment factory. Then they move on to become pressers. Later, still without speaking any English, Pinye becomes an insurance agent, knowing only that he is supposed to collect a quarter at every address on his list.

Sholem Aleichem was, of course, a humorist and drew his caricatures in broad strokes, but his mournful sense of the chaos that awaited his fellow Jews in the New World is inescapable. At a number of points, Motl's mother speaks with pride of how the family descends from a long line of cantors, but this is always protested by her sons and daughter-in-law as totally irrelevant in the New World. Eventually it is clear even to the mother that cantors are not what is wanted in America, and her boys, just as all the other new immigrants, will simply have to improvise. This contrasts with the sense that Sholem Aleichem conveys in his earlier stories of an intact, orderly society where Tevye is proud of the quality of his butter and cream and cheeses, and boasts that even the non-Jews seek him out to buy his products.

In Europe, for a while at least, Tevye was lucky. He had a trade, with a clientele and a steady rhythm of work caring for his cows, milking them, processing their milk—with the help of his family—and selling their products. The tailor and shoemakers, also, however low in the social scale, had their trade with their own workshops and the self-respect of men who were expert in their calling. These skills counted for little in mechanized, industrialized America, where the accomplished craftsman found only factory work. In America, only the very rich wanted or needed a fine pair of boots made to measure when they were available cheaper, and in greater variety, ready-made in the shoe store. Similarly, the tailor who had served years of apprenticeship learning his trade was now no better than the newest hand on the factory floor when he applied for a job in one of the shops. There what was needed was application and quickness at the repetitious task of sewing his part in the bundle of garments.

By the same token, what diminished the craftsman raised those multitudes of *Luftmentshen* who populated the shtetl. These paupers who "lived on air," who improvised from day to day at odd jobs, who had never been trained in a craft, who, as they said, starved to death three times a day, now could hope. Even they could find a place in America, where the factories and other enterprises swallowed "hands" into the maw of industrial society with no questions asked. At last these marginal men could find steady work and fit into the scheme of America.

In the end, however, whether skilled or unskilled, work in America was a lifelong sentence both for men and women. The unions in the garment industries, in the fur and millinery trades ameliorated that sentence, improving working conditions, stabilizing wages, controlling the arbitrary conditions of employment. But their goals were achieved at the cost of strikes and sometimes violence and death. The precarious and seasonal nature of the garment industry, the fierce competition which led to constant shaving of the worker's wages, converted everyday life into a struggle. A popular song about *"Motl der Apreyter*—Motl the [Machine] Operator" emphasizes that Motl wants "neither riches nor money." He wants only "bread for his wife and children." But Motl is killed by thugs who attack him on the picket line. The song expressed the helpless feelings of workers in an industry where being an "operator" was almost a guarantee of martyrdom.

Unions were, however, more than just an economic bulwark. In the immigrants' intense search for community, the unions provided yet another nodal point for activity. During the working day, the shop floors may have been the scene of acrimony and competition, but they also provided fellowship to young and lonesome new arrivals. With a little money in their pockets, they were eager to experience the world, and here were their ready-made companions. For very simple and practical reasons of language, the unions in New York divided into national sections, and there immigrant youth most naturally found their recreation with one another. My cousin Abie, a member of the chicken-pluckers' union, was a devoted member of their baseball team. The garment workers organized choruses, mandolin groups, put on plays, arranged picnics. And in the summer there were excursions and camps for longer stays.

I am not sure whether the unions were the promoters or simply the vehicle for a very powerful sense of class that marked these union groups. One of the ILGWU pieces of union propaganda showed a large cluster of bananas on a plain ground, with the slogan: "Stick to your bunch!" But that, I think, came after the fact. "We're plain people," my relatives would say, or, "We're working people," and there was an insistence on this plainness in which was mixed a good deal of pride. They boasted of what they did *not* have, those emblems of luxury—fur coats, jewels, cars. It did not matter that they did not have the means to buy these things in the first place. I think it was true that they did not have the appetite for what they saw as beyond their place in life. Nonetheless, in a grand gesture, they were renouncing them ahead of time. They believed, in fact, they insisted that these baubles brought only enmity and unhappiness into the world. They, however, advocated the eternal verities of simplicity, of not overreaching, of enjoying to the full what America made possible. This was not what Lassalle called the "damned wantlessness of the poor." Rather, it was the memory of the deprivation from which they had escaped as children, and that lasted them for the rest of their lives. They could not drop a piece of bread without picking it up quickly and guiltily. And when it snowed, they could still revel, albeit silently, in how wonderful it was to have thick boots and a warm coat. It made moderate comfort seem like luxury. Their children were perhaps unaware that the moral principles and social programs that figured so intensely in their parents' talk and in their politics grew directly out of a childhood of hardship that mostly lay camouflaged or hidden from view.

Their pleasures took on some of this coloring of being easily pleased. Those with a taste for classical music often spoke rapturously of their pleasure in it, and took it for granted that they would wait for an hour or two after work outside Lewisohn Stadium in order to sit on the stone amphitheater seats. They waited for more hours for standing-room places at the Metropolitan Opera, or entering by the side entrance on 39th Street, made the steep climb up uncarpeted steps to the Family Circle where one could sit for 55 cents.

But underneath it all, every worker knew that his health and his strength were all that stood between him and destitution. When Social Security legislation was passed in 1935 guaranteeing workers a *lifetime* income upon their retirement, it was more security than most had ever dreamed of. Small wonder that Roosevelt was regarded as only a little lower than Moses in the Jewish working-class community. All over New York, in workshops and store windows, a particularly dashing picture of him in a cloak was on display. In a hard world, he touched many hearts.

As I listened to the members of the immigrant generation tell the stories of their childhood in the Old Country, what I heard, again and again, were tales of want and fear. While work might have tempered want, there was no way to still the constant fear of sudden, irrational, capricious attacks by the peasants, by the military, by the forces of the lawfully constituted government. There was only flight. In 1906, when my father was ten years old, there was a pogrom in Bialystok, the city nearest his village, and as word spread through the countryside, it only confirmed the underlying apprehension in the neighboring Jewish hamlets. However daring or defiant the Jews may have felt, they also knew that as unarmed men they had no chance against a peasantry backed by a complaisant police and incited by a hostile clergy.

Five years later, in 1911, Mendel Beilis, the foreman of a brick factory in the neighborhood of Kiev, was arrested and charged with ritual murder. The prosecution of this case which had the enthusiastic encouragement of the Tsar further chilled the hearts of the Jewish population. It was a regime that they knew despised its Jewish subjects and by a combination of chicanery, discrimination, and outright persecution hoped to make them go away. But the Beilis

Case was too much for the outside world. International committees were formed. Prominent jurists protested the injustice, the sheer superstition of the accusation. After holding Beilis in jail for two years, the regime was finally forced to bring him to trial under the observation of an international audience. The government's case was so weak that even a jury of peasants found Beilis not guilty, and after his acquittal in 1913, he left with his family for Palestine.

In the same year, my father left for the United States, as had his brothers and sisters before him. By then, having started at eleven, he had had five years of apprenticeship to a tailor and felt himself equipped to earn his way in the New World. My father was lucky. He had only heard of the pogrom in Bialystok and the Beilis trial. Others who had experienced the violence themselves, or whose relatives had survived to tell of the looting, raping, and burning, were forever marked by their exposure to these horrors. Their memories left them with a fear of impending menace and a sense of apprehension that they carried with them to the New World and could never shake off.

The primitive condition of commerce and lack of opportunity in the tiny villages, or even in the bigger towns, were discouraging circumstances for the apprentices who had finished their training—a training bought dearly during years when they received no more than their subsistence. With no capital of their own, no resources to back them at home, they were turned loose on a world where there was little advancement and less pay. For older men with families to support, the chronic lack of steady employment was even worse. Others ran market stalls or tiny businesses that went nowhere, but were nonetheless subject to the caprices of local authorities. Least fortunate of all were those who struggled as day laborers for an uncertain income: as porters, carriers of wood and water, as workers at odd jobs. Is it any wonder that America beckoned?

The very small Polonized or Russified middle class did not, on the whole, join the great exodus to America. They had a different agenda in their lives, and they had reason to stay. The poor, Yiddish-speaking Jews lived in another universe, almost in a different time. But poverty was not the only force that moved them out of their villages. Equally disruptive were the death and disease among the poor that created orphans at a tender age, or left widowed mothers with a desperate responsibility for young children. Far too young, many of the immigrants had had to shoulder burdens that were beyond their strength—caring for siblings, attempting to earn money or barter services for food with the peasants as a way of adding to the family resources, or even leaving home so as to lessen the burden on those who remained. In one way or another, these child immigrants carried the mark of their early experiences into their American lives. And nowhere did their expectations and hopes emerge more fervently than in their work.

In America, it seemed, one could only fall upwards. What counted was not where one started or even what one did. Frequently, the making of a living became a family affair. Many Jewish couples opened little stores in the neighborhoods where they lived—groceries, dry goods, butchers, fish stores. Every member of the family was drawn into the vortex of these enterprises. Even in butcher shops, where the husband had special skills, the wives attended the cash register, wrapped packages, or made up the simpler orders. These little stores were open for long hours, and the children in the family had the choice of an empty apartment when they returned from school or a table in the back of the store. They or their parents generally settled for the table, where the children did their homework, were given their meals, and spent their hours until closing time or until they were taken home. In stores that were open seven days a week, family came and visited, sitting at that same table—sometimes set in the store itself and sometimes in a little room behind it.

The natural beginning for these enterprises was of course the local neighborhood, or one like it with an immigrant population where the storekeeper spoke the language of his customers and sold the products that he and they knew. Through bravery or accident, some ventured further out to neighborhoods of the "other." My uncle Harry, who was a baker, set himself up in a pastoral setting in Astoria, Queens, where he had his store and living quarters all in one house on a quiet residential street. In the basement was his bakery proper. On the ground floor was the store, with its show window displaying his wares to the public. Behind the shop was the kitchen and parlor, while the bedrooms were upstairs. Best of all, for us, as visiting children, was the large cobblestone yard that opened off the kitchen, where his chickens ran about and where he maintained the stable for his horse and wagon. Of course, his bakery production was closely calculated to account for the tastes of his clientele—largely of German and Irish origin—for whom he baked white bread, soda bread, meltingly sweet cookies and jelly doughnuts. For his own family, he baked poppy-seed cakes and rye bread. But the family bread had to ripen for half a day before we were permitted to eat it. It had no taste, he maintained, until it had aged. His son Moe, who had been trained as a kosher butcher, found a business opportunity in the Bedford-Stuyvesant part of Brooklyn, then as now a neighborhood largely inhabited by blacks. He quickly expanded his repertoire to include the hindquarters of animals he knew, as well as the anatomy of the pig which he didn't, building a successful business with his wife at his side.

My own parents at the end of the 1930s opened an unreconstructed Jewish delicatessen store at the end of the subway line in Queens, following the small middle-class Jewish population that had ventured out to that part of the world. In accord with the lessening strictness in the Jewish mores, as well as with his own anti-clerical prejudices, my father decided to operate a "kosher-style" rather than kosher delicatessen. This was a distinction that was more formal than actual, but permitted us to operate without troubling about a rabbinical supervisor. In addition to the usual delicatessen sandwiches with homemade potato salad or coleslaw, we also had a full-scale kitchen offering old-time Jewish specialties like gefilte fish or matzo ball soup, as well as the Americanized fare of hot roast beef sandwiches.

While my mother supervised the kitchen, the actual cooks came successively from a bewildering variety of national backgrounds. It seemed that you didn't have to be an observer of the 613 commandments to cook a Jewish meal. Our most exotic chef was Chinese, and I never did learn his real name. My mother listened carefully as he presented himself, and then called him "Yankel," which was as close as she could get to what he was saying. He didn't seem to mind, was extremely amiable, and taught me how to count to ten in Chinese. He also brought with him a mysterious and seemingly indispensable black-lacquered tin box with a finely painted pine branch on its front. It was filled with a white powder and he kept it handy on a shelf near the stove. He and my mother got along beautifully as he turned out all the specialties of the Jewish cuisine with an expert hand.

My mother's acquaintance with the languages of Central Europe came to better use with a Ukrainian cook with whom she spoke the particular dialect of her region. Both my parents had grown up with several languages, as did their fellow immigrants, but it was a talent mostly allowed to lapse in this country. Although both began with Yiddish as their home language, my mother spoke Polish as well. Living in a corner of the Austro-Hungarian Empire, she had also learned German in school, where she was called Marie, and had studied the poetry of Schiller and Goethe. Ever afterwards, acquaintance with German language and literature provided the touchstone by which she judged the cultural rank of new people who crossed her path.

But whether as a worker in a shop or in business for themselves, the members of my parents' generation—and then we ourselves—

knew that work was arduous, long, and exhausting. It was not just our fathers and mothers whom we saw engaged in a daily struggle. Every summer, the streets of New York would come alive, opened along a thousand seams by Italian ditch diggers who worked stripped to the waist laying pipes and cables or simply repairing the roads. On the hottest days, we saw them out there, with kerchiefs around their necks to absorb the sweat, their pickaxes rising and falling rhythmically several feet below street level. Even as children, we understood that this was *hard* labor. There was a lot of hard labor in the Bronx—by the men who delivered coal, dumping a ton on the sidewalk at the end of summer and then shoveling it by hand into the cellar so that it would be in place for the winter. We saw the Irish hod carriers with their loads of bricks climbing up precariously angled ladders, or carpenters lifting boards to an upper story from the street, hand over hand, up the scaffolding until they reached their destination. Everything was bought dearly in exertion. Everything had its price. We learned early to calculate how many weeks of labor it took to buy a winter coat.

Even academic work was realized only at the cost of immense struggle. Most of those who went to college paid their way by holding outside jobs. And then proud and somewhat bewildered parents would tell of finding their children asleep over their books at night, too exhausted by their double load to continue their studies. A college education came with a variety of prices. Sometimes it was only perpetual guilt. Many working-class families believed that a college education was wasted on girls, and those who prevailed were made to feel the favor that was being bestowed on them. When I wanted to go to college, it took a gathering of the entire clan before I was given permission. My parents were, accordingly, regarded as immensely indulgent and self-sacrificing, since they would be deprived of the income I might have earned had I gone to work directly from high school, as was expected. As was right! The most original route to a college education was one that was told quietly in the family because it eluded every moralizing cliché. It concerned a bargain struck between a young woman and a well-to-do older man of her acquaintance whom she had sought out. She would marry him, she said, if he would agree to put her through medical school. He agreed; she went to medical school; and by the time I heard the story, she was a well-established doctor and still married to her original benefactor.

The key to everything was work. One needed to work to exist. How much more so if one were ambitious and hoped for a profession or a business. Founded with a tiny capital that generally represented the total financial resources of the family, the little stores of the immigrants drew on every member's strength, from children to grandmothers. Whoever lived in the household became part of the enterprise. It was surprising how useful children and the old could be. At a time when I could not yet read, and my grandmother did not know the Roman alphabet, we were both able to sell newspapers from a stand in front of my father's stationery store. I had worked out my own mnemonic device for distinguishing the *News* from the *Mirror* when asked to hand up a copy. I don't know what my grandmother's method was.

Later, when my parents owned their delicatessen store and I was already in college, I was given the task of peeling and slicing tubs of boiled potatoes for potato salad. Since this could take an entire Saturday afternoon and I feared falling behind in my assignments, my twelve-year-old sister was pressed into service as a reader. Sitting across from me on a carton of canned peaches in the basement of my parents' store, she patiently read aloud my texts in history and philosophy as I prepared the potatoes.

During one fall semester when my sister read Plato's *Republic* over a series of Saturday afternoons, we discovered that we were definitely on the side of Glaucon. He asked the obvious, clear, commonsensical questions that we would have asked—only to be beaten down by a verbose but, we had to admit, convincing Socrates. During those long sessions, we were as dogged as Glaucon was, and we cheered him on each time he rebounded and made yet another of his sturdy observations. We could not help but notice, as time went on, how his replies grew weaker until eventually he was reduced to saying, "Yes, Socrates," or, "Of course, Socrates." Was he subdued by words, as we were, or was it the wine? Many years later my sister told me that when she had come to the passage about the cave, she had read it not as a parable, but as a fair representation of the dim and shadowy precincts in which she was confined.

It did not often seem to us that life should be otherwise, although early on those Saturdays as we came to work, we watched families go off on pleasure trips to New York and we sometimes wondered how this happened. We knew only that we were helping to make a living—that living that stood between all of us and the abyss of destitution. My sister and I very early took on the dread of our parents' generation of the penalty that awaited idleness. It tempered our choices and moderated our daring. It affected our definition of pleasure.

We never again, after our introduction to work, complained of boredom. The highest pleasure, it seemed to us, ever after, was rest, the absence of work. Work was that ever present, inescapable, deeply necessitous activity by which we earned our right to exist, but when it was finally done, we were free and accountable only to ourselves.

My mother managed to convey these ideas in her sibylline way when we were quite young. Once when my father reproached her for not enlisting me in some household task, she replied, *"Now* she doesn't need to. She'll work plenty in her life." It was both a prophecy and an admonition. When was "plenty" enough? Perhaps my parents' generation understood that distinction. We were more earnest, taking hints for principles, suggestions for laws.

What we didn't know about was pleasure, or that it was allowed. Somehow in our minds, work and pleasure were paired. With the one, one earned the other. And then, as we slowly discovered, our parents' pleasures were not transmittable. Their pleasures took place in the context of their world. Their theater spoke to them, in their language, about their preoccupations. It laughed with them about us or commiserated with them about our wretched behavior. It wallowed with them in nostalgia about their past or evoked the great figures in another literature. It saw the world through different lenses from ours. The annual banquet of the landsmanshaft organization was once again in their territory, however cordially we were invited to come. They were seeing *their* friends, reminiscing about a village that we had never seen. As a generation, they were intensely social and enjoyed themselves, always within a context that included other people. They went to hear readings by Sholem Asch or Sholem Aleichem. They went to lectures sponsored by their unions or their landsmanschaft organizations. They went to dances or card parties organized by one or another of their political or charitable organizations. And they went to political rallies as if they were entertainments. It was all delightful, as long as they were arm-in-arm with a friend.

It would not have occurred to them to go off to the woods alone. They founded camps and summer colonies, which featured concerts and lectures as well as swimming and boating. They went on picnics and daylong outings arranged by the Workmen's Circle. Even their summer vacations were often arranged under the auspices of Benevolent Associations or political groups. The Socialists had their Camp Tamiment, and the more informal Camp Mekhaya (Pleasure). The Communist Party organized a number of "Proletarian Camps": Nitgedayget (Unworried) in 1923; its companion children's camp, Kinderland, with Camp Unity and Winona for English speakers. "Followers of the Trail," a colony organized near Peekskill in 1929 largely by Russian Jewish immigrant workers with Communist sympathies, attracted new members, as one of its founders explained, "because of its communal life. We lived together, we were in the fresh air together. On the weekends, when we came, there was dancing Saturday nights, there were lectures on Sundays. And people who stayed here during the week didn't idle around either. There were cultural activities for those that stayed during the week. . . . "

For one dizzying afternoon, my family too entertained the idea of joining such a tent colony. A neighbor in the Bronx was proposing that several of the families on the block get together and rent a piece of land in the Catskills where we would put up tents and spend some weeks together during the summer. The children would have playmates; the families would have one another's company; and we would all have fresh air. I knew my parents too well even to raise my hopes. Communal pleasures could never prevail over my mother's fears and my father's thrift.

In this yearning for the country was a nostalgia for the landscape of the immigrants' youth. Although Jews are generally thought of as an urban people, it is often forgotten that millions lived in the Russian Pale in tiny villages with forest and pasture and farmland no more than a street away. They didn't own the land or till the soil, but they knew the countryside and experienced the seasons as no city dweller could. How many of them have reminisced happily over the summers they spent in their leased orchards, sleeping in makeshift shelters, enjoying the expansive life of the out-of-doors. In the mythology of Jewish immigrant thought, nature not only represented health but had certain redemptive, uplifting powers that they associated with many of their other recreations. There was a self-consciousness about their pleasures that we, in a freer age, find perhaps puzzling. But every pleasure had to be justified. One didn't just enjoy fresh air and a walk in the woods. It needed to be explained that such a walk brought spiritual thoughts as well as health, and that such thoughts separated man from beast.

Living so close to the margin, they assured themselves and one another that they were better than brutes because of their wisely chosen diversions. They read the newspaper, studied a page of a sacred text if they were pious, and from time to time went to the theater. When my mother-in-law recalled times when money was tight, she reported how she would divide her last 10 cents, spending 5 for rolls, 3 for soup greens, and the last 2 for the *Forward*. She knew very well that this was a grand gesture in the direction of civilization.

It took my generation a long time to discover what our pleasures were and that they would be different from our parents'. I think that we also approached pleasure with the same studious earnestness that we brought to everything else. First came the moment of discovery; then, if one were lucky enough, an opportunity to sample it; and then the far more difficult process of making it one's own. Cocktail parties, restaurants, nightclubs, the opera, concerts, sports—all were amusements in another key, another mode from what we knew. This was what we saw in the movies or pictured in glossy magazines, and it took practice to acclimate oneself and feel easy with experiences for which our past left us totally unprepared.

In my generation, our class-consciousness was not very strong, and our attachment to Yiddish, with its publications and theater, grew more and more distant. But the political issues that absorbed our parents, the cleavages between Zionist and non-Zionists, the hostility between the Socialists and the Communists, these caught us up in new incarnations. Our arenas were different. We no longer read the *Freiheit* and the *Forward*, but the issue of "social justice," as it was called in the thirties, aroused our most powerful passions. We joined groups; we signed petitions; we wrote urgent letters to Washington; we had firm opinions on Tom Mooney, the Scottsboro Boys, the Spanish Civil War, on the redemptive value of public housing, and on the perniciousness of capitalist greed. Naturally, all of these activities were undertaken in groups, large or small. While we had not found much in our cultural heritage that we were ready to claim, we could not escape the tradition of social consciousness.

As we reached college age, the rising fever in our blood was also not to be denied, but flirtation and romance were not within our everyday experience. The pattern that our parents used was still drawn from the Old Country, where Orthodoxy with its taboos and the professional matchmaker set the terms—terms to which every sensible person would have to agree. It was a careful matching game, and when all the elements had been balanced—money, looks, learning, profession, and family honor—the match *had* to be a success. And maybe some of them were.

Of course, by the time the immigrant generation left their villages, the matchmaker was becoming obsolete even in the Old Country. But for a long time he was not to be denied, and in the New World had learned to trick himself out in American fancy dress. We certainly would find our own partners, but discovered that we would have to present them to our parents under the old rubrics. We were shyer with one another than our "American" contemporaries. Despite the famous Jewish humor and wit, we had not learned how to be lighthearted, to be giddy, to be carefree. This was yet another part of America that took us by surprise, and we had to learn that too. It took us longer to learn to love.

# 8

# Food

While everyone has heard of the urban myth of the alligators in the sewers of New York, the grapevine seems to have missed the one that circulated and recirculated in the thirties in the Jewish Bronx. It was about a little boy who was very sick and whose parents were finally told by their doctor that the only thing that could save him was eating bacon. "It was a *medical* prescription," the storyteller would emphasize, and we would all shiver in horror and disgust at this possibility. Another urban myth, the companion piece to this story, is that observant Jews long for nothing more than to eat the forbidden foods. Of course, anyone who will believe that has never talked to an anthropologist or heard about the power of taboos.

Growing up in the Bronx, we learned from a very early age to regard the food of the "others" as not quite fit for human consumption. We all took our lunch to school in brown paper bags, and having paid our weekly milk money subscription were given every day a carton of almost room temperature milk halfway through the morning. Unrefrigerated for hours, there was no shock of the cold, but a furry fullness filling the mouth and reviving our flagging bodies. But to forget lunch spelled disaster. None of us ever had any money, and even if one could borrow money from a teacher, was the food in the lunch room permissible? Edible? All the smells were so strange, so repellent. It was a prospect that held out so many unpleasant complications that none of us could face it. We remembered to bring our lunch.

Living in a traditional Jewish household, a child learns very early what is permitted and what is not. It is simply another part of learning how to live in the world. Why does an Eskimo child think that wild blueberries and whale blubber are a treat? Why did I think that *schmalz*—rendered chicken fat—on rye bread was delicious? We were not only learning the rules of kashruth but also acquiring a palette of tastes, with its distinctive smells and textures. Anything outside that palette, at the beginning at least, turned my stomach. In my school there were a large number of Italian children whose families lived in attached brownstones, solidly built, shoulder to shoulder along one block and facing the tenements in which we lived. One afternoon, after school, I went to visit one of these classmates and naturally wound up in the kitchen where, for the first time, I smelled grated Italian cheese. It did not smell delicious to me. It smelled like rotten milk and I felt fortunate not to be asked to eat anything. It did not occur to me to wonder whether they would have found any of our delicacies equally unpalatable.

What neither my friend Theresa nor I realized was that we were each living in a completely enclosed system, and that it would take another generation for us to amalgamate our favorite dishes into an international cuisine. Every week my mother made noodles on her noodle board. After she had rolled the dough out into large circles, she hung them over the backs of the wooden kitchen chairs to dry—a little. But then they had to be taken up again at just the right moment while still soft enough to be pliable, quickly rolled up, cut into strips, thick and thin, and allowed to dry completely. Thus provisioned, for the rest of the week we had thin noodles to go into the chicken soup, while for a dish that was both main course and dessert, we had wide noodles tossed with butter and pot cheese and flavored with sugar and cinnamon. Tomato sauce on my mother's delicate broad noodles? It was simply outside her vocabulary.

In our densely Jewish neighborhood, we never even saw forbidden foods. Our fish store featured live carp swimming in a tank and the freshwater fish beloved in Central and Eastern Europe. (I am still not sure what *Hecht* is, but when I find it on the menu in Germany I always order it, knowing that forgotten tastes will be revived.) We never saw shrimp or any of the mollusks or lobster or crabs. When I finally did, they seemed like a gigantic form of vermin to me. Similarly, the dairy had only the fresh, white cheeses that were considered kosher, having barely emerged from their earlier incarnation as cream. Molded into loaves, they were called farmer cheese. Pressed though a fine sieve and with a little added cream, the product was cottage cheese; pressed through a coarser sieve and left dry, it was pot cheese, that indispensable ingredient for *lukshn mit kez*—noodles with cheese. And this word *lukshn* was the source of one of my earliest perplexities in moving from one language to another. *Lukshn* was so powerfully what it was, in its making, in its preparation, in the luscious and familiar dishes that it produced, that I was never quite sure whether "noodles" was the same thing. "Noodles" certainly had no resonance for me; but I learned to say it, strange as it was on the tongue, meaning all the while simple, heart-warming *lukshn*. The world of cheese posed a similar problem. Jewish cheese, kosher cheese, was never aged. If it aged, it turned rotten, and for a very long time all but the most sterile processed cheese seemed to smell bad, to have strange textures. In short, they seemed quite inedible.

With such a limited repertoire of cheeses, it is remarkable what an array of dairy dishes the Jewish cuisine could produce. In traditional Jewish life, meals are strictly divided. They are, of course, based either on dairy or meat. In each case, a separate set of pots and pans is used in their preparation, and a separate set of dishes and cutlery for eating. I always suspect Sholem Aleichem of having been a secret vegetarian because of the rapture with which he lists the dairy dishes customarily eaten on the holiday of Shavuot, in biblical times the celebration of the harvest of the first fruits. The combinations of dumplings, filled pancakes, puddings, and, of course, noodles and cheese produced a much longer list in Sholem Aleichem's Boiberik than we ever saw in the Bronx. But in our generation we could not long for what we did not know.

For many years, when my mother wanted milk, I was charged with taking a tin can with its own cover to the dairy where the milk was ladled into it with a dipper. Similarly, we brought jars or glasses to be filled with "a measure" (a half pint) of sour cream, just as butter was cut to order from great blocks, the salted and the sweet standing side by side in the perpetual chilliness of the dairies.

But all of this changed when Mr. Breakstone—the Kraft of the Jewish dairy business—began to package these requisites. No longer did we need to frame the ritual "Is it fresh?"—half accusation, half question. Now we could silently and somberly read the date on the carton. Only one vestige of the dairyman's art remained after Breakstone's newly invented gummy cream cheese. Much less fragile than the soft handmade cheese, it was put up in two-pound blocks in wooden boxes, with beautifully dowelled corners, where the cover slid magically in grooves across the top. These solid and durable white rectangles of cheese quickly drove out their more perishable ancestor and were then cut to order, quarter pound by quarter pound, by the dairyman.

What was happening to all of us born in America was that a vocabulary of tastes was being built which forever after would spell food. It is true that with the great spring forward that came after the end of World War II, many of us also leapt out of our universe of received ideas to taste and experiment in the world around us.

But the effect of *escargots*, which came late in our experience, was never the same on the palate and on that obscure cluster of brain cells that signal pleasure as the lox and cream cheese of our early years.

Not only did the immigrant generation fail to move on to *escargots*, it never really got over its amazement at having enough to eat. Many of the popular songs—sometimes sentimentally, sometimes comically—dwell on the themes of hunger and want. In one, a father comes home with a single loaf for his family of eight. The lyrics describe how the mother divides the bread carefully according to the size of each child; but when it is all gone, it is discovered that she "forgot" to give herself a piece. Another, dedicated to the potato—a kind of counting song—lists each day of the week, on each of which there are only potatoes. In a short story by Sholem Aleichem titled ironically *Di Fressers (The Gluttons)*, the husband in a desperately poor family catalogues rapturously all of his favorite dairy dishes. Meanwhile they count themselves fortunate if they have a single challah to divide among their children on Friday night.

For the immigrant generation, then, food in abundance was the first evidence of a blessed and bountiful life. In a culture in which bread was the measure of prosperity, the image of a basket of rolls on the table was the ultimate symbol of the good life. The most famous dairy restaurant on the Lower East Side, Ratner's, to this day has its waiters present a basket piled high with assorted rolls even before offering the menu. Rolls in the East European Jewish cuisine were not just miniature breads, but had qualities and textures of their own: the now famous and debased bagel; the *pletzel*, which was crisp, glazed, sprinkled with poppy seeds, and made the perfect foil for farmer cheese, as did the tough and chewy bialy with its whisper of fried onions. More delicate and most common was the unglazed poppy-seed roll, with its crackly, pinwheel crust and its soft interior. Then there were the richer, glazed egg rolls, soft whole wheat rolls, little braided rolls . . . The smell of a Bronx bakery in the morning was itself worth a visit. Just as unforgettable was the sound of a tray of rolls fresh out of the oven being spilled into a wire basket by the baker, still in his white undershirt and floury apron. It did not take great sophistication to know that a fresh roll with butter was simply and fundamentally good. Accompanied by hot coffee, it was food for angels.

In fact, it was not the food of the poor Jews in Eastern Europe. In the first story of Sholem Aleichem's Tevye cycle, Tevye tells of how he rescues two well-to-do ladies who have lost their way in the woods. It is late in the afternoon. They have been wandering about all day, and, as they complain to him, they have had nothing to eat since their breakfast of a buttered roll and coffee. Tevye does not feel sorry for them. Indeed, their mention of a *"buter bilke mit kave*—buttered roll and coffee" sends him off on a reverie trying to remember the time when he last had such a breakfast. He himself, it turns out, subsists on black bread and tea, eked out with a little herring. For the immigrant generation, the fresh buttered roll, the glass of coffee with cream, remained to the end of their days an inexpressible daily miracle.

For the next generation, life grew a little more complicated. Our schools existed not only to teach us but also to civilize us, something that we humbly acknowledged to be necessary. But sometimes the new civilization was more perplexing than useful. And I am thinking now of our cooking classes in Domestic Science. Fortunately, the schools in New York were too poor to provide meat for our experiments, an absence that resolved what would have been a major problem for the Jewish children from observant households. We began, bewilderingly enough, with the basic element in the American cuisine: white sauce. We watched with astonishment as milk was turned into glue before our eyes. We even learned how to do it ourselves, but it did not solve our confusion as to what one was supposed to do with it once it was made. There did not seem much point to bathing perfectly good vegetables or even tuna fish in this mixture. But it did have, it seemed, a higher purpose. Although our teacher could not demonstrate it, she told us about chicken à la king—seemingly a fundamental American dish, but unfortunately beyond our imaginations or palates.

What stopped us ultimately from taking into our daily lives the sauces, the soups, or the blancmange for dessert that our teachers taught us to make, was that these dishes simply had no relation to the food we knew at home. They had, as we said to one another, "no Jewish taste—*kayn yidishn tam.*" This was a judgment that it took a very long and arduous experience in the world to overcome. Hidden in our heads was that original tuning fork with its fundamental tones, its flavors, tastes, textures. In an international village, we have grown very wise. We have learned to discriminate among the varieties of Chinese cuisines; we are connoisseurs of sushi; we know our way through the intricacies of the regional cooking of the Indian subcontinent. European specialties, of course, have long been seamlessly blended into our everyday excursions to the supermarket. But the tuning fork remains humming, testing new tastes and old. It reasserts itself on a dark day in February just as we are recovering from the flu. Then we don't want sushi or coquilles St. Jacques or chicken burritos. What we want is something very fundamental: the comfort of noodles and cheese.

Immigrant food was poor people's food. But it did not appear so to them. When there was enough, there was nothing better. And the only thing that distinguished a wedding feast from a very good dinner at home was quantity: more courses, plates richly crowded with delicacies that were laborious to make. The menu was fixed: fish as a first course; then "the Golden Broth"; followed by roasted chicken with many little side dishes. The great wedding feasts of the twenties reveled not in exotic foods but in quantity.

And here, of course, immigrant Jewish society and America

parted company on the great and grand way to honor one's guests. Hearty eating and the groaning board, by the American standards of the twenties could only be described as vulgar. The conventional, stylized presentation of food that was "correct" at that time implied that people of high status were above actual consumption. Presented at parties in an ornamented, formalized way, the preferred dishes ran to molded aspics, soufflés, miniature vol-au-vents filled with creamed chicken, little finger sandwiches, petits fours. Every piece that was removed was instantly visible, disturbing the symmetry of the whole. The guests, who perfectly understood this culture, of course expected to take only token amounts. Thus the total quantity available was calculated to be close to what would actually be consumed. It would have been quite bad manners, i.e., lower class, on the part of the host to offer too much, as if he expected his guests to eat "vulgar" amounts. The descriptions of the food at high-status banquets, therefore, tend to use words that imply small quantities: exquisite, delicate, fine, refined, elegant.

At the grandest receptions, the formal presentation of food in relatively inaccessible forms—in molds, in elaborately designed platters, whole birds in plumage, or a huge roast requiring the services of a carver—made possible the presentation of very large quantities, although the emphasis was on form rather than content. It was expected, however, that a great part of these foods would remain intact. A run on the buffet table, the cleaning bare of the platters would have been inconceivable. In any case, only small amounts were available at any one time to the diner passing along the buffet line, who would be given a single slice of roast beef, but would have had explicitly to request it if he wanted more.

In drinking, these events would permit, even encourage, the consumption of substantial amounts of wine or liquor with long cocktail hours and many kinds of wine served at a seated dinner. But the key element here was control, knowing how "to put it away," so that a large amount was drunk but without any visible outward sign. Once again the premium was on control rather than gratification. In eating, control lay in not taking too much. In drinking, the point would be to have drunk "too much" and control the consequent behavior.

Jewish immigrant ideas of hospitality and celebration ran exactly counter to every principle of these banquets. Very simply, it was the responsibility of the host to provide great quantities of food and drink. In fact, in the Old Country a great wedding banquet would be expected to include enough for all the beggars and poor of the town. In America, the Jewish banquet was restricted to invited guests, but extravagant amounts were provided as an invitation to the guests to eat heartily and without shame. Since there was so much being presented, even a large appetite would make no discernible difference on the display of food. The "good guest" then was one who ate copiously, returned often to refill his or her plate, and praised the food. In one of the jokes of the period, an enthusiastic diner exclaims over the excellence of the gefilte fish. "It's so wonderful that I've been back three times already," he says. "Eat in good health," says his host, "who's counting? But it was four." Similarly, the wine or drink was expected to increase the celebratory mood, and all of this noisy enjoyment was demonstrably the direct consequence of the host's lavish hand.

Presented with the bountiful resources of America, the immigrant generation developed an exacting connoisseurship in the relatively narrow range of East European cooking. Every housewife knew that the excellence of her pot roast stood or fell according to her relations with butcher. She knew enough to avoid the "commission bakery" and walked the extra three blocks to where the bread was baked on the premises. Nor would she patronize the Wonder Bread Thrift Stores that dotted the Bronx, where day-old bread, gashed with a pattern of nails, was sold for half price. In fact, she wouldn't have bought it at any price when she could have the rye bread or corn bread available in the Jewish bakeries. (Jewish corn bread, incidentally, had no connection with the corn bread of the South. "Corn" was used here in the untranslated European sense of grain, and the result was a particularly heavy, moist, and crusty kind of rye bread.) And when our housewife dealt with the fruit and vegetable man, real expertise was at stake. "I want a melon for tonight," she would say warningly. "It should be ripe." But after a lifetime in the trade, he was not easily intimidated. "What time do you want it for?" he would ask, tossing one in his hand.

Although restricted in its scope, Jewish cooking required not a little art and a great deal of physical strength. Cakes made with many eggs—especially at Passover—necessitated a strong arm and a firm will. It was a cuisine that took the seasons into account, offering a different kind of piquancy from summer to winter. But a great deal depended on its being freshly prepared. Much of the bad reputation of Jewish cooking for leathery and sodden food has come from its commercialization, its standing long in steam tables before it is served at huge public banquets or in the gargantuan dining halls of the Catskill hotels.

When I was twelve, my mother took me and my little sister for our one and only excursion "to the mountains." We stayed at a farm run by a Jewish family, who also maintained a house for guests—perhaps twenty or thirty. This was an important cash crop. In those early days of the hotel industry, such a side occupation did not interfere with the farmwork that went on as before. People came to rest and to eat. For recreation there was a swing for four out on the front lawn, and one afternoon the children were taken out for a ride on top of the hay wagon. The great luxury that this farm offered to working-class women like my mother was that for this one week or so in the year, they would sit at a table and be served their meals. Their children would be fed separately at some "children's table," so that the burden of everyday life was totally and magically lifted from their shoulders. Shopping, carrying groceries, cooking, cleaning, even doing the laundry was no longer their responsibility. I think almost any kind of cooking would have been acceptable to them, but our little farm produced really excellent home-cooked meals. This was the familiar food that we knew in all its summer glory. We had a kind of salad for lunch, known as "Greek salad," then common and now a vanishing memory. It was based on a thinly sliced cabbage, chopped green peppers, shredded carrots and cucumbers, in a sweet and sour vinegar dressing, and then topped with slices of herring. This with slices of rye bread and sweet butter made the world a brighter place. Based on a dairy farm, the kitchen of course specialized in blintzes (cheese-filled pancakes) and lost no opportunity to serve vats of cottage cheese and sour cream as options at breakfast and lunch.

As far as I could tell, this was home cooking raised to some exponential level with none of the off days, the accidents of overdone chicken or burnt pot roast that were part of the drama of daily life. Even the delectable little dry cakes called mandelbrot that are the hallmark of Jewish pastries were available by the basketful at the end of dinner, when my mother lingered at the table drinking tea and talking with her neighbors, while we snatched a few surreptitiously and made off to the porch. To this day, my sister and I find a deep satisfaction in these dry, very lightly sugared, delicately flavored cakes. Again, they offer the ultimate comfort along with a glass of tea on that rainy February afternoon.

In the 1990s, Italian biscotti suddenly bloomed in up-scale coffee bars and other fashionable watering holes around America. These dry biscuits, the perfect accompaniment to a sweet Italian wine in a trattoria in Florence, have become the all-purpose substitute for cake for those who keep an eye on their calories. They permit the gesture without exacting the price. When my sister and I chanced upon them in a café one afternoon, we looked at one another significantly. These were none other than a dryer variant of the *mandelbrot* of our childhood, and in our opinion hardly as satisfying. As I realize that even the memory of these old recipes is passing, I feel an urgent wish to pass on to my faithful readers at least two out of the arsenal that we've discussed. Both require a certain willingness to experience a new taste. They do not seduce the palate, nor do they appeal to the hair-shirt mentality that makes consuming dry biscotti an acceptable outdoor sport. They are in quite another key from what is considered delectable even in contemporary America, which seeks out the exotic. In fact, there are only a tested few whom I would invite to lunch and offer what my mother called Greek salad.

The recipe that follows makes enough for twelve.

### Greek Salad

*Salad ingredients*

1 small green cabbage (about 2 lbs.), finely sliced

5 carrots, thinly sliced into rounds or grated

1 green pepper, cored and cut into small dice

1 small red onion, thinly sliced and separated into rings

2 cucumbers, thinly sliced

3 cloves garlic, peeled and thinly sliced

*The Dressing*

1 cup white vinegar

3/4 cup sugar

3/8 cup water

1 Tbs. coarse salt

4 Tbs. corn oil

Sprinkle the sliced cabbage with an extra tablespoon of coarse salt and allow to stand in a large bowl for about 1 hour. Pour off the accumulated liquid and squeeze the cabbage to remove the last water. Combine the drained cabbage with the remaining vegetables.

While the cabbage is soaking, combine the ingredients for the dressing in a saucepan and bring to a boil—just long enough to dissolve the sugar. Allow to cool. Pour the cooled dressing over the vegetables and allow to stand for at least 1 hour. This salad can be made as much as a day in advance and mixed often.

To serve: drain the marinade, toss the salad with ½ cup chopped parsley, and arrange on a platter. Top with slices of filleted matjes herring, which should be very young, very fresh, and hardly salty. (This will be the hardest part of the recipe to find.) Serve with a good rye bread and unsalted butter.

*Mandelbrot*

| | |
|---|---|
| 3 eggs | Rind and juice of 1 orange |
| 3/4 cup sugar | 6 Tbs. corn oil |
| 3 1/2 cups sifted flour | 1/2 cup almonds, blanched, |
| 3 tsp. baking powder | split, and toasted |
| Pinch of salt | 4 Tbs. dried cherries, cut up |
| 1 tsp. almond flavoring | |

Sift the flour with baking powder and salt, and set aside.

Beat eggs and sugar together until double in bulk and quite thick. Add the orange rind, juice, and almond flavoring. Then add half the flour mixture and combine thoroughly. Add the oil, and when it is incorporated, add the remaining flour. Then add the toasted almonds and cherries. Beat together until the mixture forms a ball and then put it into the refrigerator, tightly covered, to chill for at least 2 hours. (It can also be made a day in advance.)

When ready to bake, preheat oven to 350° F. and line a large baking sheet with a sheet of parchment paper.

On a floured board, divide the mixture into two parts. Pat each into a roll about 8 inches long and 2 inches wide. Bake in the preheated oven for about ½ hour. The top will split and the rolls should have a nice golden color. Remove from the oven and allow to rest for a few minutes. Then, while still warm, cut the loaves with a very sharp knife into half-inch slices. Separate these somewhat and return to the oven for another 5 or 10 minutes so that the surfaces are just mildly crisp. Transfer to a rack to cool.

This makes about 40 pieces. The size of the loaves can be adjusted according to whether you prefer large or small slices. The slices can be frozen but will also keep very well in a tin at ordinary room temperature. When I have a stock of these in the kitchen, it's like money in the bank.

Now, these recipes are hardly typical of Jewish cooking, which seems to absorb an endless amount of labor and where time is never a consideration. Before one can even begin to cook poultry or a piece of meat, for example, there is an hour-and-a-half-long process of home koshering. Both poultry and meat are required to soak for half an hour in cold water, and are then heavily salted and placed to drain for another hour on a slanting, grooved board. This is to ensure the extraction of every drop of blood.

Everything seems to require a combination of patience and energy. But in its demand for sheer labor in a compressed space of time, nothing can compete with Passover. Although food could be brought in and stored in bags and boxes on the fire escape or in the hallway a day or two before, the real work still lay ahead. The very first sign of the imminence of Passover, in fact, was the arrival in the front hall of a crate containing a gross—twelve dozen—of eggs. This was not extravagance. This was prudence.

The kitchen could not really be attacked until the very day of the first Passover Seder. Ten o'clock in the morning was the magic hour. From that time on, we lived in a kind of limbo between *hometz*—the everyday world—and *Pesach*. It was forbidden to eat any of the ordinary food, nor was one yet permitted to eat mazzah or any Passover food; that was only allowed after sunset. In those intervening hours, the entire kitchen had to be cleared of the everyday kitchenware, and, of course, all the groceries had to be removed from the house. Then the real labor could begin in which the entire kitchen would be scrubbed down, the shelves newly lined with paper, and the boxes of Passover pots and pans and dishes brought out from the basement and the backs of closets. Only now could the actual cooking start for the Passover Seder for twenty or more people.

These preparations required consummate generalship and the marshaling of every hand available. Sometime in the early afternoon, we would be permitted to stop for a snack since preparations were now advanced enough for us to use the Passover saucepans and utensils. What was generally available were innumerable hard-boiled eggs, and broiled chicken livers prepared by being held in a wire grill over an open gas flame. Meanwhile, the men of the household were assigned the arduous task of grating horseradish. This, as they rightly said, made strong men weep and was generally considered too demanding for the women. In some households, the men also prepared the *haroseth*, the mixture of apples, nuts, wine, and spices meant to represent the mortar used by our ancestors in Egypt.

The main thing about *Pesach* was that the food was so strange. Perfectly ordinary things that we ate all year round were suddenly forbidden: rice, garlic, beans. My mother had a kind of illicit thrill every time she drank coffee. The package in the grocery store bore the solemn seal and signature of a rabbi certifying it as kosher for Passover. But "at home," in Galicia, coffee had been forbidden, as had chocolate, both falling into the prohibited category of beans. I think it was not until after World War II that chocolate suddenly appeared in American groceries with large and indubitable seals as acceptable for Passover. My mother did not look too closely—if at all—into the Talmudic argument that forbade coffee in Probuzhna and permitted it in the Bronx. When it appeared on the special shelves of her grocery store among the Passover supplies, she bought it without a qualm. Another of the miracles of America.

We always asked ourselves why we never prepared and enjoyed the special Passover dishes during the rest of the year. With the exception of mazzah balls, all the other treats remained safely within the eight days of the holiday. Our everyday noodles were banished, but my mother made a special kind of Passover noodles that began with the gossamer foam of eggs and ended in a pancake that was cut into broad, delicate bands with a feathery texture. This same pancake could also be filled with a chopped liver and onion mixture and served as a first course.

Passover breakfasts always seemed more interesting than what we had the rest of the year. In any case there was something special about that first morning. The first Seder was behind us; the kitchen had now been organized into its new strange state with the year-round dishes and utensils locked behind doors and sealed with seven seals, and every surface covered with heavy brown wrapping paper. I am sometimes reminded of this today in chic French bistros with their "tablecloths" of white wrapping paper. Although the dining-room table had its festive cloth, in the kitchen we settled down to the brown paper.

In the morning of the first day of Passover, we didn't go to school and there was a festive sense of ease. We didn't need to rush through breakfast and could savor the most delectable taste of Passover, the real signature taste, which was that first bite into mazzah spread with sweet butter and sprinkled with coarse salt. For those who wanted a cooked cereal, there was *mazzah farfel,* but best of all were *mazzah brei* and the *bubbele.* This was why a small family needed a gross of eggs. And it was these eggs that gave me my sense of Passover dishes as particularly airy. A *bubbele,* for example, is an omelette made with the eggs separated and with mazzah meal added to the yolks. This is like nothing in your French cookbook, and it has a lightness and fluffiness that no classic omelette achieves. There was always the struggle at the end over whether to eat it seasoned with salt or with a spoonful of "Kosher for Passover" strawberry jam dribbled over the top; to this day I cannot make up my mind.

The Passover cakes—no leavening, no baking powder—also gained their texture from firmly beaten egg whites, generally a dozen at a time. The varieties were not great but the flavors were unmistakable: a nut cake made with nuts ground to a powder that was flavoring and thickening ingredient all at once, and the classic sponge cake with its few variations—mostly based on whether one used grated lemon or orange rind as the flavoring.

This was the time of year when certain food purveyors in the Bronx went on vacation: the bagel bakers, the dealers in smoked fish and meats, and, of course, the bakeries. The little groceries limped along selling out their stock of Passover goods in the course of the long week and supplementing their income with the sale of milk and dairy products—all marked "Kosher for Passover," of course. In time some of the novelty of rediscovery wore off, and we began to feel like the Jews in the desert who had tired of the everlasting manna. As the week came to its end, we too began to long for the taste of real bread, nor did we mind standing amid the crowd in the bakeries on the night when they reopened. The fragrance of the bread as its aroma drifted out to the street made us remember the old pleasure that awaited us.

These pages have necessarily indulged in some nostalgia for tastes and dishes that are no longer part of our lives. Perhaps their disappearance was inevitable. They were meant for another climate, another style of living. Nor could the heavy soups, the time-consuming casseroles and dumplings, the odd palate of tastes long compete with the soft, rich foods in the American scheme of things. Or was there a fault in the transmission? Sometimes recipes were held as secrets. Tante Shayndel's mazzah balls were legendary in their feathery lightness, but when she made them she disappeared into the kitchen alone.

I have long thought that the making of mazzah balls is in some ways a parable on the state of the human spirit. The individually formed little balls, dense as lead, are slid gently into the pot of boiling water. The pot is covered tightly and there then ensue fifteen minutes of anxious waiting while the mazzah balls cook. If at the end of their allotted time they have risen to the surface, they represent the purified, cleansed soul, floating free in the upper regions,

half out of the water. Those that did not rise were lost. My own mazzah balls were certainly dependable. They rose to the surface. They
were light. But they could not compare with Tante Shayndel's. Yet
no amount of persuasion could begin to extract the recipe from her.
We would speculate, ask questions, suggest this or that magical ingredient. She would only smile enigmatically. Not everyone, of
course, was as secretive as Tante Shayndel.

I think these recipes are so ephemeral because they were part of
an oral tradition. Your old-fashioned Jewish housewife had no
cookbook but had learned what she knew by observation, by apprenticeship in her mother's kitchen, by gossiping with her neighbors about how to make the dishes that were the backbone of her
repertoire. Some, like my Tante Elke, were generous. She would
willingly allow me to stand next to her as she mixed her moist and
rich honey cake for the New Year's holiday. But this would be the
only way to get it down accurately—closely recording everything
she did, making her put the flour in measuring cups before she
poured it into the mixture instead of just pouring it in with a scoop
as she would have done if she were alone. These demands along with
my record of her running commentary on what she was doing has
given me an incomparable recipe. (In her honor, I append it at the
end of this chapter.) But it took very close observation and what
seemed like maddeningly obvious questions to Tante Elke, who
could not understand such a lack of ordinary common sense about
one of her cuisine's most commonplace cakes.

I once tried the purely verbal approach for some simple crisp
cookies that she made. One after another she listed all the ingredients, with some general advice as to the order in which they were
to be mixed. As I looked at my handwritten notes, I realized that
something was missing. "But the flour," I stammered. "What about
the flour?" "*Avade* . . . Well, of course!" she could only reply in some
exasperation. What were these educated girls good for if they didn't
understand that you couldn't make cookies without flour?

As in every cuisine, the ultimate flavor of its style depends not on any individual dish but on the orchestration of the entire meal. The immigrant generation brought this sense of what constituted a meal with them, and it remained intact despite decades in America. In their universe, they simply had no idea where mayonnaise, for example, fit in. There were dairy meals; there were meat meals; there were fish meals. Each had its constellation of dishes, flavors, and balances. And mayonnaise was nowhere.

With their children's generation the mold broke apart, and not just because so many of that generation gave up kashruth. As Sholem Aleichem predicted, in America the regular order of things, the tastes of seasons, holidays, and the working days, would become confused. And however expertly prepared, a single dish does not add up to a cuisine. Many of the old recipes are now presented in glossy cookbooks available to anyone, even to those who have never tasted Tante Shayndel's cooking. But will a newcomer ever know what constitutes true lightness? Even I, who have known those ineffable mazzah balls, also live with a dismembered cuisine. Sometimes, when I serve a mazzah ball soup in a meal that might end with a Tiramisu, I wonder secretly, "Where is the *yidishn tam* . . . the Jewish taste?"

*Tante Elke's Honey Cake*

| | |
|---|---|
| *1 lb. honey*[1] | *4 eggs* |
| *1 1/2 cups brown sugar* | |

*Sift together:*

| | |
|---|---|
| *4 1/4 cups sifted all-purpose flour* | *1 tsp. ginger* |
| *2 tsp. baking powder* | *1 tsp. cinnamon* |
| *2 tsp. baking soda* | *1/2 tsp. nutmeg* |

Beat the eggs thoroughly until thick. Add the sugar and honey. Add the seasoned flour alternately to the egg mixture with:

---

[1]Tante Elke says to warm the honey because how else will you get it out of the jar.

*Juice and rind of 1 orange[2]*        *1 cup corn oil[3]*

*Then add:*
*1 1/2 cups chopped walnuts*     *1/2 cup cold strong coffee*
*1/2 cup raisins[4]*               *1/2 cup seltzer*

Oil two 9″ × 5″ baking pans. Line with brown paper and oil again. (This is the old way. A much simpler method is to use parchment paper.)[5]

Before putting the cakes into the oven, the tops can be sprinkled with slivered blanched almonds.

Bake the cakes at 325° F. in a preheated oven for 1 1/2 hours. Allow them to sit for 5 minutes after you take them out of the oven. Then invert them onto cake racks and peel off the paper while they are still warm.

Good luck!

---

[2]Tante Elke would simply grate the entire orange through a hand-held grater. I have never been able to reproduce this feat and therefore suggest a more conventional route to getting the orange flavor.

[3]Do not use any of the designer oils—safflower, canola, sunflower, or even olive oil. Only corn oil will give the bland background taste that you need.

[4]How to keep the nuts and raisins from ending up at the bottom of the cake is an eternal problem. This method of coating them with flour has science on its side and it generally works.

[5]Tante Elke baked her cake in a roasting pan—lined with brown paper from a grocery-store bag, the pan greased with oil and the paper likewise. With a cake this big, is was cut into cubes rather than slices.

# 9

# Corsets

In the Bronx, the world was always being divided into two parts: law and custom, meat and milk, ordinary days when one was permitted to work, to ride, to cut, to kindle flame, to cook, and then the holidays when all these activities, and more, were forbidden. The minutiae of religious observance that governed traditional Jewish life takes volumes just to enumerate, not to mention the additional volumes of commentary and case law. The sort of problems that would absorb Talmudic scholars—"If a whole mouse is found dead in a vat of wine, is the wine kosher or not? And if it is only a part of a mouse . . .?"—were not the considerations that stirred our interest. We were instead closely informed on all the details that went into running a kosher house, the regulations for the observance of the Sabbath and the holidays, the prayers to be offered at recurrent ceremonials, and how to *behave*. There were ready and expected formulas for coming and going, for sickness and health, for rejoicing and grief. There were also postures of deference and respect toward the elderly and learned. In this universe, there was, as well, a powerful sense of the private and public, and the public began at the threshold of one's apartment.

America, after all, was not like those intimate communities that the immigrants had left behind where everyone was known and called by his or her first name (or names) and perhaps also by a descriptive: an occupation, a father's or mother's name, or a well-known characteristic. Beryl the tailor, Motl Pesi the son of the cantor, Tevye the dairyman, Bontshe the silent are all familiar from the classics of Yiddish literature. In families, these epithets sometimes became even more explicit: Dvorah the crazy; Faybush the crooked one. But in the Bronx, one no longer knew the entire history of one's neighbors, the history of their families, their failings and merits or those of their ancestors. In the Bronx, torn out of all context, the young housewives addressed one another formally as "Mrs. Pfeffer," "Mrs. Pizetzner," and if they had been speaking Yiddish, they would have used the distant form of *ir*. The men, a little brisker, a little brusquer, used simply the family name without the honorific. "Levine," they would say, "how about a game of pinochle?" One had to be family or at least *landslayt* to use the intimate form of address easily. Thus, outside one's door one made an appearance and took on the role of the public person. And this was no casual matter.

In those early years in the Bronx, the well-organized housewife had her work in hand by the middle of the day. In the morning, she cleaned and washed and began dinner. She fed her children who came home from school for lunch. And then in the afternoon she went out to shop and, especially in the summer, to enjoy an afternoon chatting with her neighbors. This meant putting on a corset.

The ladies I knew in the Bronx ran to type: they were little and plump, and at home wore wrap-around cotton house dresses, known in the Depression years as Hoover aprons. These palely floral dresses that tied with a wrap-around sash at the back were originally intended, I always imagined, for the angular bodies of farm housewives. Yet they were very forgiving to all sorts of figures and accommodated themselves to the wearer, including the soft little bodies of the immigrants in the Bronx. But ordinary clothes which had waistlines and necklines required severe adjustments on the part of the Bronx ladies, who were nourished on a diet in which sour cream was a staple, and chicken-fat cracklings—*gribenes*—a treat. They knew very well that sociability and, more than that, respectability had its price. Dressing meant accepting the discipline of the corset, which would contain the softnesses and roundnesses that had not been foreseen in the ateliers of clothes designers. These "garments," as they were called, were serious all-in-ones which bound up the entire body, were intricately fastened with laces, hooks, and eyes, and stiffened with cunningly arranged bones that created the perfect form. Every neighborhood had its corsetière, who, after surveying the supplicant knowingly, would bring out the Iron Maiden best designed for the figure in front of her. This was then further adjusted—a tuck here, an easing there—until it was pronounced perfect. In difficult cases, it might even be made to order.

I always thought of these corsetières as Hungarian, who in the typology of the Bronx had a reputation for worldly chic to which most of the other ladies would not lay claim. They were invariably of a certain age, were themselves visibly and elegantly corseted, and wore their hair in sophisticated up-sweeps, with a hint of henna. While at the most my mother and her neighbors might dab on a bit of face powder and a little lipstick for a special occasion, the corsetière understood the art of makeup, and one knew that her perfectly tinted skin, with its heightened color, had not been supplied by nature—all of which of course only made these sorceresses even more compelling.

The tape measure was applied and whisked away from various parts of the torso with a lightness and dexterity that made it impossible for the subject to see what her actual girth was. But the figures were noted swiftly and quietly by the corsetière, who all the while carried on an absorbing diversionary conversation. Then came the moment of choice. Although these garments were no less cunningly designed than the Brooklyn Bridge, they were also covered with the most delicate and dainty of fabrics—lacy-looking white for summer, and almost universally a "flesh-colored" peach for the rest of the year.

Putting on the corset, then, was a commitment and statement as one prepared to go out. One made an entrance as one stepped out into the street and started on the round of shopping, or went to a park, or even simply took down a chair to sit in front of the house with neighbors. Respectability meant containment, a calculation of the form that one presented. In the privacy of the dressing room, it had been decided with the corsetière whether the bosom was to be flattened or emphasized and how far the waist and hips were to be suppressed. And then over this newly achieved form, finally, came the dress. One neighborhood dress shop owner, in fact, was known to send customers home who arrived uncorseted. How was she expected to fit them properly if they weren't even dressed!

While the corset took care of the inner form, what went over it received equally scrupulous attention. There was a word in frequent use that was at once a descriptive, a term of praise, and an ideal—*balebatish*, "respectable." This meant not only fine quality, but wearing the right clothes at the right time. Anything less was a reflection on the good judgment, on the standing, of the wearer, when it was not an offense against the community. Hence the indispensability of the corset and stockings, even on the long subway ride to Coney Island—or perhaps especially then, since this meant hours in an exposed public place.

Similarly, like the French who use the verb *assister* when they mean that someone attended an event, the guests at an "affair" or a social happening of any kind were expected to appear appropriately dressed for the occasion. They were assisting in its festivity by costuming themselves in a style that heightened spirits and showed deference to the mood and expectations of their hosts. The rules, while unspoken, were strict, and judgment even swifter in this community on what constituted an offense against propriety. When my cousin Sadie chose to wear a printed chiffon dress instead of a white bridal gown at her wedding in her parents' cold-water flat on the Lower East Side, the family relished the scandal for years, using the incident to illustrate a variety of ethical points: the loose morals of the young, the lack of respect for the family, the bad omen such lightheartedness presaged for the marriage.

Everything always came down to *derekh erets*—the proper way to behave—and in this new, unstable world, the manners of home were carefully protected. For the time being, at least, the old forms provided the sure framework—the corset, as it were—for appropriate behavior. To dress elaborately, to wear whatever jewelry was available to a wedding or other grand occasion, was seen less as an exercise in self-adornment than as a sign of respect—*opgebn koved*—just as its opposite was an affront.

The acquisition of jewelry, therefore, was a slow but tenaciously pursued goal of the careful housewives in the Bronx. A diamond, however, was not only a female adornment; it was also the family treasure. My mother's diamond engagement ring was understood to be a resource by which we could raise instant cash in hard times. Over and over again, it was given in to pawn, and in this way got us through bouts of unemployment and medical emergencies, the two specters that haunted working-class families who lived from week to week. My mother had an intermediate stage before the pawnbroker, and that was the teapot. Here she put by the odd change that she could spare, more rarely a few dollars for an emergency. "There's always money for the devil—*Farn tayvil iz du,*" she would say when she had to raid her hoard. When the emergency was over, as soon as there was a little cash, her ring was redeemed—emblem as well as resource.

My parents never had to resort to one of the local, much hated moneylenders who insured their loans by the device of a co-signer who would be responsible if the principal borrower defaulted. On many occasions, I remember a friend or a relative appearing in our kitchen with a much folded piece of paper. My father always had only one answer: "I wouldn't do it even for my own brother!" When one of these moneylenders—albeit in Warsaw—was beaten up by a fellow thug, the song celebrating the event and the universal pleasure it gave traveled across the ocean. "Harshl, where are you with your big hands? You won't be taking your percentage any more."

At weddings, my mother's diamond sparkled on her finger in honor of the bride. For such occasions, my father brought out his one good blue suit and would regard it with satisfaction as *balebatish* when he put it on. There was a kind of magical exchange here in which the suit conferred its qualities on the wearer. By appearing in fine worsted wool, my father felt exalted in his own eyes, subtly adjusting his demeanor, his language, from the everyday to something more festive, thus adding something to the occasion he attended. But lapses, as I have indicated, were remembered. Once, my cousin Milton, who had escaped from the Bronx and returned triumphant from a new job in Los Angeles in time for Passover, made us all realize the fragility of custom, how easily an institution could be broken apart. When he appeared at the Seder wearing only a T-shirt, no jacket, no fine broadcloth shirt, no tie, there was a palpable sense of shock in the room at the lack of *derekh erets*—the disrespect this showed both for the holiday and for his father. It displayed an abdication, a self-segregation from the mood of the evening. We watched Milton narrowly, warily, after that.

Shopping, too, was no simple exchange of goods for money. It was an occasion for sport, for display, for social contact. Neighborhoods in the Bronx were clearly defined by an array of stores so complete that one never needed to step out of a narrow circle of the few blocks around one's apartment building. The sum total of one's needs, edible and inedible, was finely divided among various specialties, each of which represented a craft as well as a source of supply, and each of which was presided over by a personage who made up a part of the housewife's social world. Places like the butcher shop, where she came regularly, where everyone else also shopped, became little clubs where the butcher reigned supreme, dispenser of favors to the harem of the day.

Of course one dressed to go shopping because it was a social occasion in which one established one's character in the neighborhood. There were the complainers, the penny-pinchers, the ones who asked for credit and paid promptly, and others who were dilatory. There were those who lived "with a broad hand—*mit a breytn hand,*" who were imprudent and wasteful. All this was known and inscribed in some invisible account book which added up to reputation. How much or how well people fed their families was open to the scrutiny of the neighbors, as both economy and extravagance were noted and judged. It was not for nothing that my mother let it be known that she never bought bakery cake but always made her own. Ungrateful wretch that I was, I longed for bakery cakes, which were so much softer, sweeter, and more entrancingly decorated than anything my mother could produce.

Bronx neighborhoods by day were female worlds; the only men were the elderly, or the storekeepers who became somehow a target for the remaining coquetry in the lives of these otherwise sedate women. There was a difference between my mother dressed and my mother at home in housedress and slippers. My mother dressed was a woman with a firm step, decisive, on stage, as it were, conscious of her persona, playing her part in the neighborhood. And, of course, each of the neighbors had *her* part, her assigned role in the loosely formed constellation of acquaintances and friends who met together as they shopped, or sat together in little clusters in front of the house. They gossiped about absent neighbors, about what they were cooking for dinner; they complained about their husbands and about "women's troubles." But they hardly ever talked about the Old Country, except to wave it away. That past was over, almost. A sentimental song about the Old Country in a cabaret or on a record could stir a sigh for lost youth or perhaps for lost dreams. Sometimes the village from which they came figured as blurred background for a family anecdote or a childhood recollection; otherwise it simply disappeared. What absorbed them were their daily struggles to make ends meet.

With husbands who owned small, marginal businesses or were wage earners, these women's lives were less than secure, and they thought carefully about every expenditure. Thrift became a habit, a virtue, just as its opposites, wastefulness or self-indulgence, became a sin. A sentence uttered over and over again in these households was "It's a sin to throw it away," whether it was food, clothing, or a worn-out piece of furniture. This was not just morally wrong but entered into that long catalogue of forbidden acts that had been breathed into us from the beginning. We were accountable for these transgressions to God, and on Yom Kippur, the Day of Atonement, the sin of waste was undoubtedly subsumed under that long list, arranged alphabetically, that we recited five times during the sacred day, beating our chests as we asked forgiveness. When something was a sin, therefore, it gave one pause. From time to time, I wonder about all the eating disorders that have been brought on by that homely sentence: "It's a sin to throw it away . . . " How it fills the waiting rooms of psychiatrists across the country and torments the souls of those who haven't freed themselves of its power.

It was, then, a world governed by rules—rules of religious law, custom, social usage, rules dictated by language and nostalgia. And as long as these rules held, my parents and their neighbors knew where they were. To a certain degree, the order of the Old World continued in the fastnesses of the Bronx. Memories of home faded or were suppressed and customs fell away. At Purim, neighbors no longer sent one another plates of *shelakhmones*—cakes and fruits— as they had in the Old Country to celebrate the day. But the rhythm of Jewish life, its essential structure and the sense of *derekh erets*, remained.

I sometimes think that the corset was the main cause of the great Jewish migration to Florida after World War II. Earlier, Florida had been the resort of the wealthy or of those in such delicate health that they could not withstand a northern winter. When I was in fourth grade, a very thin and pale boy was taken out of school to go with his mother to Florida for a few months. As we learned, this happened every winter. His mother had already caught all our attention because she was "American" and slim, and wore suits, and was head of the Parent Teacher Association. She explained in amazing, unaccented English that his health was so poor that he could not survive the cold weather in the northern fastnesses of the Bronx. We were all impressed, not only by his fragile condition but by the thought that she and her husband would then be separated for many months. A divided family was beyond our imaginations. Who would cook supper?

In the late 1940s, however, Florida took on a less privileged aspect. By this time, some of the early immigrants had reached the age of retirement. The blessed Social Security system had been in place for a decade, giving old people a regular if tiny income, and Florida was not only warmer but notoriously cheaper than the Bronx. Its popularity grew, and children who were supporting their parents would also advocate Florida as the place for them to live. As their numbers expanded, the new immigrants built again the neighborhoods that had sustained their way of life in the Bronx: the live chicken markets, the bakeries, the modest kosher restaurants, the cafeterias, where the elderly and lonesome might get to know one another.

It was the warmth and the eternal summer that led to the first confusion, the feeling that Florida was the prelude, the antechamber to the Eternal Life that lay before them. Elderly housewives who had never ventured outside their doors in northern cities without corset and stockings could be seen strolling on the main streets of Miami in the gilded housedresses that the new dyeing techniques made possible, and wearing the soft slippers that meant that they were at home. In certain haunts, over glasses of tea, new acquaintances were made, and to the scandal of their children new alliances entered into. A quirk in the Social Security law was, in fact, responsible for a wave of geriatric immorality. If two people, each receiving Social Security, married, their combined income would be reduced by the federal government, on the quaint theory that two can live more cheaply than one. But in the marginal circumstances of many Florida residents, this sacrifice for the sake of appearances was more than most could afford. And so, many elderly couples, to their own astonishment, ended their days living according to the flaming rules of "free love." A favorite story of the period tells of a son who hears of his father's improprieties and comes down to investigate. He finds his father's hotel, knocks on the door of his room, and enters to find his father in bed with a strange woman. "Sonny," says the father, "calm down. It's not what you think. I'm still keeping kosher."

This rather dreaming remittance world, where the old rules seemed suspended, was yet another way station among the endless wonders unfolded in America. It was all part of a general strategy of survival, acceptance, and adaptability in the face of the absurdities of life. The immigrants' ultimate, unforgiving tenacity had brought these pensioners to America in the first place, and it was this that finally made a mockery of "Sonny's" concerns.

Such readjustments, adaptations, in the lives of the old Jews of the immigrant generation—cataclysmic from the perspective of the shtetl—were all happening just as the first gaudy hotels along the Miami beaches were going up. The first of these palaces, the Fontainebleau and the Eden Roc, quickly received nicknames: the former stubbornly known as the "Fountain Blue" (accent on the

"Blue") and the second sardonically and punningly referred to in Yiddish as *idn raykh,* "rich Jews." But below Collins Avenue, the Bronx lived on in an atmosphere where display was shunned and modesty was a virtue.

In the 1950s, when the Fountain Blue was still new, I went to visit my parents, who were spending the winter in a little hotel below Collins Avenue. One evening, curious about the new pleasure domes and wearing a cotton dress, I took the bus up to 219th Street to the gates of the old Firestone estate, now the site of the hotel, and walked up the circular ramp to the main entrance. Despite the flurry of activity, chauffeured cars coming and going, the uniformed door-keeper spotted me and asked whether I was a guest at the hotel. When I responded truthfully that I was not, he told me that I would not be permitted to enter. And clearly I didn't belong.

I lingered long enough to peer through the magnificent glass panels flanking the revolving door to see in the marble-floored lobby ladies and gentlemen in evening dress, some women even wearing little summer fur jackets, then called shrugs. Of course, I was an interloper in my plain daytime cotton. Day and evening were not alike, and having grown up in the Bronx, I understood that. We had been schooled in differences. Here the distinction was not only between rich and poor but also between the times of day. And for the rich, the evening was different—with different costumes, different pleasures—a time of pure enjoyment. People came to the Fountain Blue to indulge their fantasy of a grand world in luxurious, gilded surroundings. I now understood why my cousin from Elyria, Ohio, and her rich husband came to the Fountain Blue every winter. Here they could live for a few weeks amidst a grandeur that their money made possible, but for which their little town in Ohio was too small.

Every evening after a day of swimming or other play, they could dress in formal clothes and enter the world of a Ginger Rogers–Fred Astaire movie: sumptuous rooms, elegant restaurants, dance bands, and other people just as formally and splendidly dressed as they were. The architect, Morris Lapidus, who saw himself more as showman than as master builder, produced exactly the sort of over-scale environment that fostered make-believe. In the lobby, against an exploded Piranesi etching, Lapidus had curved a glamorous staircase that rose in the forest of black and white marble and glittered with curved and shining brass. French antique-style furniture, French gardens, a main ballroom large enough for five thousand people, and other extravagances encouraged the illusion of another world. It was knowingly and heavily laid on, and it was exactly what my cousins from Elyria wanted.

In quite another key, and responding to other fantasies, was the old Roney Plaza Hotel, a relic of the 1920s, which also prided itself on its formal gardens, as well as an aviary. Built in the Mission style, it was intended for gentlemen in white flannel trousers and ladies in tailored middy dresses. What was delicious about it was its cavernous cool rooms and the quiet, discreet service. As in the best restaurants, plates were changed, glasses were filled, dishes appeared without a word being exchanged. The hushed silence and silver appointments were particularly exquisite at breakfast, but the Roney Plaza could not compete in a new era in which what was wanted was glitter and excitement. The center of gravity moved uptown, and at some point the Roney Plaza was torn down.

My parents, needless to say, went neither to the Roney Plaza nor to the Fountain Blue. Not even to look. They said that the places were not for them and the prices too expensive for plain people like themselves. I think they were wise. They knew how to protect themselves from feeling like outsiders and poor relations. In their neighborhood they were respected, and the restaurants offered the kind of food that they recognized and at prices they could enjoy.

During their declining years in Florida, they positively reveled in the virtue of their modest lives. "We're not fancy," they would say with great satisfaction and with scorn for the new high-priced, high-rise condominiums. In actuality, they and many of their neighbors were too timid or too inexperienced in the ways of the world to enjoy the "fancy," luxurious restaurants to which their grown children would take them when they came for a visit.

Except for Tante Elke—a woman who was getting even with God and who reveled in her outings to Trader Vic and other exotic eateries. When my Tante Elke and uncle Moyshe had come to this country, they settled first in New York with their two sons. But by the 1920s Uncle Moyshe, who worked in a factory making pocketbook frames, had developed asthma. As it grew more acute, his doctor advised him to seek the dry climate of Los Angeles, which would be far better for him than the damp and cold of New York. With great reluctance and renewed fears about starting yet again, the couple decided to accept the doctor's verdict. It was a blow for the rest of us, too, since Elke as the eldest in a motherless family had cared for her brothers and sisters for as long as anyone could remember. On the day they left, the whole family escorted them to Pennsylvania Station with provisions for their long journey across the country. Once again, as on their ship's voyage to this country, they had to take kosher food with them, since they would not be able to eat what was sold on the train. The parting was wrenching for all. Who knew when we would see one another again?

They arrived in Los Angeles in midwinter, and Uncle Moyshe set himself up as a peddler, traveling by horse and wagon among Mexican farm workers selling clothing and basic household articles. He made only a bare living, but when Passover came in the spring, Tante Elke was determined to prepare a real Seder for the family. Far from freshwater fish, and not knowing whether what she had was kosher, she pounded abalone and other strange denizens of the sea into gefilte fish. Finally the moment came, and the family sat down, my aunt glancing with satisfaction at her festive table, knowing what it had cost her to prepare it. Then, shortly after Uncle Moyshe started chanting the Haggadah, the worst happened. He began wheezing, and in a little while he was threatened with a full-blown asthma attack. Quickly, he harnessed his horse and escaped in his wagon to the mountains and the cool light air.

My aunt surveyed the wreckage of the scene and went outside into the quiet night. Furious at how all her work had been reduced to nothing, at her husband's continued illness in this presumed sanctuary, at their separation across a continent from the family, she raised her fist to the heavens. "All right," she declared. "If this is what You can do, I won't keep kosher!" It seemed like a retribution that balanced the calamity that had befallen her. And without telling her husband, she enjoyed her revenge for the rest of her life. When we went to Trader Vic's for a celebration, she would point to the shrimp on the menu as the waiter came round, and without ever actually saying the word, would silently order what she wanted. When her husband asked what was on her plate, she would shrug and say, "Try it. You'll like it."

My aunt and her generation kept score when they retired to Florida, as a way of imposing boundaries on a newly boundaryless world. Gone were the seasons, and without work, day and night too flowed together. Yet the decorum that had been instilled in them in the Old Country remained. And now that they were elders, they knew what was due to them. The missing phone calls or failed visits from children were not only a personal offense, they were also an offense against *derekh erets*—the proper order of society.

Easily intimidated by a strange world, my parents did not share Tante Elke's boldness and sense of adventure. When they finally stopped being "snowbirds" and decided to settle in Florida, they bought into a homey development of modest apartments largely inhabited by elderly Jews from the Old Country like themselves. While it had the requisite swimming pool, by no stretch of the imagination could its barnlike "rec hall" have been called a clubhouse. Nor did it have tennis courts or a golf course, and of course this was before the days of weight rooms and exercise machines. A few of the more athletic types like my father took walks in the early morning around the perimeter of the development and did laps in the pool. But the rest of the inhabitants, like my mother, thought that they had "worked plenty" in their lives and were now intent on resting up for the remainder of their allotted time.

It would be hard to count the number of acrylic afghans that were knitted around the pool while the ladies talked about their children and grandchildren with the peculiar ambivalence of parents who are far away. On the one hand, they wanted to display the achievements of their offspring, since it magnified their own importance and sense of accomplishment. On the other hand, these neighbors gradually constituted a new family for one another, and as they said rather candidly, when their children came on a visit, they felt "twice blessed— once when they arrived, and a second time when they left." They basked in the reflected glory of the doctors, lawyers, and teachers they had produced. They racked up points for signs of devotion: baskets of flowers on Mother's Day and birthdays, attentive phone calls and visits. But they depended on, and cared for, one another.

Then, as newer, gaudier, and more expensive developments grew up around them, they drew even closer together, exuding satisfaction in their own unpretentious and neighborly surroundings at only a fraction of the cost of those needlessly opulent apartments. "Who needs a view of the ocean?" they asked. If you wanted to look at water, they had a man-made pond right in front of their windows. Their rooms were large and air-conditioned. As far as they were concerned, they lived in luxury. And with a pool just at the end of their walkway, it was ridiculous, they agreed, to pay those prices. In this easy, intimate atmosphere even my mother, who had very strict ideas of propriety, would stroll about the grounds wearing a "playsuit," or bathing suit, outside and inside having all merged into one. Corsets had long since gone the way of down comforters, plush living-room sets, kid gloves, and other trappings of northern civilization. They were succeeded by "Florida rooms" with rattan furniture, by wall-to-wall carpeting, by light cotton upholstery, and the complete abandonment of formality. But all of that came decades after those early years in the Bronx.

# 10

# Girls

My father lived to be ninety-eight, and until the end of his life he never failed to introduce my sister and me with a grand gesture as his "two disappointments." We were, very simply put, an offense to his manhood—an offense made the more bitter by the fact that his brother, his ineffectual brother whom he despised, had three sons. To the end of his days my father scanned medical stories in the newspapers for a solution to this riddle, and in his ninety-sixth year he eventually found a study that seemed to rescue his honor. It showed that men who had daughters were more virile than men who had sons. This satisfied him briefly. In one of his rare uses of the telephone, he called my sister and me to tell us about it. But I think it did not make the pain go away. He should have had sons.

I thought so, too. All through my childhood I longed for a brother, and on the many ritual occasions in the midst of our street games when we were supposed to make wishes, chanting with locked pinkies:

> *May your wish and my wish come true.*
> *And do not speak until you're spoken to . . .*

I would always wish for a brother. A brother would be the only possible counterweight to my father, who ruled my mother and his two daughters by fiat. He pronounced and we obeyed. No discussion was permitted, and any slight demurral was immediately perceived as insubordination, punishable by shouts or blows or both. A brother, however, would be treated differently. In my imagination, I could see my father overcome with pride and tenderness toward this male being who would be indulged, listened to, permitted to contradict. This was his *son!* And this son, I naturally assumed, would become a spokesman for his sisters, and would join our life-long conspiracy to rescue ourselves and our dignity from a world in which we were too often helpless and mute.

That girls were lesser beings was made clear from the beginning. On the first Saturday after his daughter's birth, the unfortunate father would be given the honor in the synagogue of being called to read from the Torah and to proclaim her name. Neither mother nor infant were present, of course, and this rather dry ceremony was the end of the welcome. No parties, no gathering of the family. Just a quiet acknowledgment of a fact. It was a powerful tradition, and durable. As a Yiddish proverb puts it: "When one has daughters, laughter vanishes." *("Az men hot tekhter, gayt avek di gelekhter.")*

The kosher butcher in our neighborhood could not face even that moment in the synagogue. Every Sunday he and his brother, each the father of three girls, visited their old mother, who teased them openly about their lack of sons. When word reached him in his butcher shop one morning that his *fourth* daughter had just been born at home, he disappeared for three days into the local Turkish bath, leaving his newly delivered wife to cope with the domestic crisis.

As late as 1950, when my own first daughter was born, this way of looking at the world was still in full flower. I lived then in Manhattan on the Upper West Side where a laundryman, a man of the Old School although not of the Old Country, came every week to pick up and deliver the household linens. On the day after I returned from the hospital, I answered his ring with my baby in my arms. He greeted me in his usual forthright way, taking in the scene: "Ah, *mazel tov*. And what did you have?" "A girl," I answered. "Well," he said, struggling to find something to say, "as long as it's healthy!"

This attitude toward girls did not stop, of course, after the week of their birth, so that girls very early had to sort out a peculiar paradox. During an interview fifty years after her arrival in this country from Minsk, Ida Richter summed up how it felt in two words: "A girl," she said, "wasn't much." Nonetheless, despite her perceived lack of worth, a Jewish girl in the Old Country very early became an effective force in the world. She worked at household tasks, cared for her younger siblings, helped her mother in her business, and often, while still a young child, was sent away as an apprentice while her brother remained at home and studied. As a time-honored system, this division of labor between male and female—the men studying, the women working—shaped the structure of Jewish life. For some six hundred years, it had served the Jews as a way to live in the Diaspora.

In all of Europe, manliness was measured by the use of force and the use of weapons, whether ornamentally as an item of dress, symbolically as in duels, or actually as in war, in civic defense, or even in acts of crime. Since the thirteenth century, when the Jews were forbidden to bear arms by the *Sachsenspiegel*, a widely used code of laws in the German lands, they had been deprived of the European symbol of manhood. But they had responded with a new pattern, ideally suited to their life in the Diaspora. In the closed Jewish communities of Europe, they turned the seemingly harmless occupation of sitting day after day over folios of sacred text into the most significant of enterprises. They created a new hierarchy of values in which command of these texts, and luminous powers of elucidation, stood at the height of all human accomplishments. It gave Jewish men an occupation; it defined their manhood, and gave them status and rewards. Preoccupied within its confines, convinced of its transcendent worth, young men grew into old men, still studying the sacred books that remained a lifetime task.

In a sense it was a democratic system because a talented student at a yeshiva, however humble his origins, could hope for a rich bride and the guarantee of many years of support by his in-laws, who longed for nothing more than to have such a scholar at their table. While these provisions endowed the men with years of leisure, they simultaneously gave the bride permanent responsibility for the day-to-day existence of the family. Many used their dowries to set up yet another tiny shop in the tight circumstances of the Jewish villages. One song is about "the hundredth shop in the street," where the shopkeeper's day reaches its climax when a customer comes in for a kopeck's worth of herring.

The wife as main breadwinner was a custom so long in use, so ingrained in practice that it was not until the end of the nineteenth century that it began to be viewed openly with some skepticism. Sholem Asch's short story *Menachem Breindls* is ironical as he relates the unquestioning devotion of Breindl to her husband. She tends her market stall, cares for house and children, runs to the synagogue to bring Menachem his midday meal, and all the while feels only a glowing pride in his status as a learned man. When she dies suddenly, in the midst of her tasks, we see Menachem still sitting in the synagogue hardly aware of what has happened or of the life that has gone on outside its walls. Some decades earlier the novelist Mendele Mokher Seforim had also railed against this mode of life, calling it "not living, but dreaming."

Similarly, the movie *A Brivele der Mamen*—*A Little Letter to Mother*, which was produced as late as 1937, speaks to an earlier time. The title comes from a song written in 1904, and the movie is set in pre–World War I Poland. Here the public disapproval of the wife for supporting her husband shows how acceptance of the institution was beginning to fray. In a critical scene, the husband, who is renowned in the town for his composition of synagogue music, overhears two customers talking outside his wife's shop. They praise her hard work, but, to his shame, speak slightingly of him as a good-for-nothing. Certainly such behavior could not long survive in the United States, where young single women began to earn their own money and develop a taste for independence.

Although, as we have seen, the old institutions—the arranged marriages, the dowries, the prenuptial contracts—gradually disappeared in the New World, the old attitudes remained. My father would sometimes tell, quite blandly, of the test frequently used in his town for finding a patient, good-tempered wife. The prospective bride was given a basket of knotted yarns and asked to untangle them. As she worked, she was closely observed and her response to this difficult and maddening task became one of the measures of her acceptability. Although I remained prudently silent as I listened, I simmered with outrage as much at the story itself as at my father's smiling acceptance of it with its implication that women were created humbly and cheerfully to serve men. My feelings were relieved only by my thankfulness that I had been born in the Bronx and not in Bialystok.

In the factories where men and women worked together, women were generally paid less for the same work and frequently had to put up with a gamut of offensive behavior from smutty remarks to groping to actual demands for sexual favors from foremen or bosses. Rose Gallup Cohen, whom we have met earlier (see "Hats," p. 110), tells of her moment of revolt. It occurred, significantly enough, not on her own behalf but because of a younger sister whom she had brought to work with her. Since it heightened the sport of the men in telling their off-color stories to embarrass the girls, the presence of a new girl gave them a fresh incentive. Rose Cohen had long attempted to defend herself and the other girls from these verbal assaults by asking that the women be allowed to sit together at a separate table. But as one of the tailors then asked her, "Do you expect to make the world over?"

On the day that she brought her sister, one of the worst culprits began with a story about a wedding. "We girls as usual sat with our heads hanging," reports Rose Cohen,

and I was aware that sister's face almost touched the work in her lap. . . . Suddenly a feeling of rage shook me. "Why did we pretend? Did pretending cleanse our minds from the filth thrown into them?" . . . The blood beat so in my head that I was half blinded with the thought of showing myself so openly. Then I rose, and scarcely knowing what I did, I flung the cape [that she was sewing] from me; its purple silk lining caught on a nail, in the wall opposite, and hung there—and I cried to them half sobbing, "You have made life bitter for me. I pray God that rather than that I should have to go into a tailor shop again I may meet my death on my way home." All this seemed to have taken a long, long time and I gradually realised that it was very still in our corner of the shop and that now it was the men who sat with their heads hung and my sister was standing close to me. I took my coat, gave her her little shawl, and we went out.

In the home, new ground was also being staked out. Immigrant fathers no longer had the final word on the choice of their daughters' spouses, but a residual deference prevailed. And while parents could no longer compel a girl to marry a man she did not want, they often exercised veto power. In many stories in the immigrant community, true love seems to have gone unfulfilled as women told one another with a sigh of early passions that they had renounced. In the Smolinsky family in Anzia Yezierska's *Bread Givers,* three of the four daughters, in turn, are made to give up their true loves and to accept the handpicked suitors found by their father. In two cases, these turn out to be swindlers; and in the third, the father finds a loathsome old man whose very touch makes his bride shudder. Of course, Yezierska in 1925 was writing a tract rather than a novel, but her passion and her illustrations represent truly the dilemmas of many young girls caught between two worlds. This was no longer the Old World where the bride might be carried by force to her wedding, as the journalist Rose Pastor Stokes related of her own mother. In America, the last word lay ultimately with the prospective bride. But there were subtle forces at work: parental pressure, fear of spinsterhood, prudent calculation that may well have led more girls into arranged marriages than they would have wanted.

It was not until they had reached the New World that women felt free enough or became literate enough to write about themselves. In the Old World, men wrote personal memoirs and political manifestoes; they wrote learned works in the old Hebrew and modern poetry in the new. But women were not included even among the new poets. As the literary critic Dan Miron has noted, "Bialik, in his role as editor of the literary journal *Hashiloah*, would have welcomed a woman poet with open arms, if she had sent him a poem that could measure up to his poetic standards." The last "if," of course, creates a tantalizing area of ambiguity. Clearly, none measured up, and from 1890 to 1920, at the height of the "Hebrew Renaissance," not a single woman poet was published in his periodical. We do not know how much was lost to desk drawers, but we do know that women wrote in other languages.

Pauline Wengeroff wrote her memoirs in German although she was born into an Orthodox Yiddish-speaking family in Bobruisk, White Russia, in 1833. Celia Dropkin, who was born a half century later, also in Bobruisk, first wrote in Russian. When she was in her twenties she sent a passionate love poem in Yiddish to her adored Uri Nissan Gnessin, a prominent writer in modern Hebrew. Gnessin promptly appropriated the poem in a lightly disguised story of their romance, published in 1913. Translating it into Hebrew, he "improved" its literary style—which meant overlaying her spare, modern language with biblical allusions and rhythms. The first line of Dropkin's poem reads: "If he comes back to my town . . . " unvarnished and direct. In Gnessin's hands, it becomes: "And if it comes to pass and he will return from his wandering to my country . . . "—a line full of allusions to and rhythms from the Bible. And here, of course, was the nub of the matter. Since women were not educated in traditional Hebrew learning, had no command of the literature, its nuances, its range and breadth, they were simply not qualified as players in the new wave of writing in Hebrew that was creating a modern mode, but delighted in the display and the allusion to the old.

In America, a new country and a new language freed women to write directly. Celia Dropkin continued to write in Yiddish after she came to the United States in 1912. But Mary Antin, Anzia Yezierska, Rose Gallup Cohen, Theresa Malkiel, Rose Pastor Stokes, and Emma Goldman, all of whom arrived as young uneducated immigrants, wrote in English. In their new language, they broke with a past in which they had had no place. They wrote about their experiences as immigrants and workers, and the cauldron of emotions generated in the family by America. Unfettered by old rules, they were admired for the clarity and power of their expression in their chosen language.

At least two of these women reaped fairy-tale rewards. In 1903, at the age of twenty-four, Rose Pastor Stokes moved to New York to become a feature writer and columnist for the English section of the *Yidishes Tageblat*—the *Yiddish Daily News*. In the course of her work, she was assigned to interview Anson Phelps Stokes, the heir of an important New York banking family, a meeting that rapidly developed into a romance culminating in their marriage in July 1905. The newspaper, of course, featured the event on its front page under the headline: "Cinderella Wedding." Two decades later, in 1920, Anzia Yezierska, another young, self-taught Russian immigrant, won a Hollywood contract for her volume of short stories *Hungry Hearts*. Rebelling against her family, she had left home and supported herself with menial jobs while she wrote her passionate stories about the hardships and longings of immigrant life. These created such a stir that a movie studio brought her out to the West

Coast with great fanfare, lavishing on her the breathtaking opulence usually reserved for the stars. That neither of these transmutations succeeded in any permanent way is, of course, the stuff of real life and not of fairy tales.

For many of the young women who worked in the shops, however, reality was fairy-tale enough. Despite brutal and cheating bosses, despite low wages and long struggles, there was ultimately a sense of achievement. They did not remain forever on the bottom rung of the ladder. Of the 1 million Jews who entered this country between 1899 and 1910, nearly half were listed as having "no occupation," the famous *Luftmentshen*—the people who lived on air—who characterized the population of the Jewish villages. At the same time two thirds of the Jews who did have jobs were highly skilled craftsmen: shoemakers, carpenters, painters, glaziers, and above all in various branches of the clothing industry.

But many Jewish immigrants moved very rapidly out of the category of factory workers into entrepreneurship. Sometimes they began with no more than a basket of goods which they peddled door to door, or they rented a pushcart, or even opened a little store. Whatever its form, the move was always in the direction of independence. By 1905, the census showed that those who had been in the country between seven and fourteen years had a very different way of making a living from the newly arrived immigrants. While 55 percent were still at the bottom of the economic ladder in the semi-skilled and skilled trades, 32 percent had started new businesses, mostly as storekeepers, and 10 percent had actually achieved high incomes in garment manufacture, real estate, and construction. A few had also entered white-collar occupations as salesmen, bookkeepers, and office workers. Moses Rischin, that masterful chronicler of East European Jewish immigrants, has calculated that even the number of Jewish professionals was growing visibly. "Between 1897 and 1907," he writes in his *Promised City*, "the number of Jewish physicians had risen from 450 to 1000 in the borough of Manhattan . . . the number of pharmacists from 85 to 235 . . . and the number of dentists from 59 to 350." They made up only a tiny percentage among the immigrants, but a highly visible one, as Jews frequented the doctors and lawyers and pharmacists who spoke their language.

These Jewish professionals inspired the immigrants with hope, if not for themselves, at least for their children. And everyone knew of someone who had started a business. The "happy ending" to Abraham Cahan's *Yekl*, written in 1896, has both couples planning to start businesses: one pair a dancing school, and the other a grocery store. It was against this background of visible accomplishment that new immigrants were emboldened to launch out. Many of the little stores in Jewish residential neighborhoods, as we have seen, were the result of craftsmen going into business, seeking their autonomy. There were the glaziers who also sold picture frames, and measured and installed window shades in front of the glass that was their province. There was the tailor who branched out and sold fabric, but also made slipcovers and draperies to order. Is it any wonder that with a skill and a little capital, or even without skill and just a little capital, they decided to try their luck? Armed with their hopes for these enterprises, young couples dared to marry and committed themselves to building up their businesses. My mother and father were just such a couple, pooling their resources in 1922 to start a stationery store. Here women had a new role as partners in a joint enterprise. What in the old days would have been my mother's dowry was, in the New World, her personal nest egg, saved from her factory labor and contributed to the starting capital.

Following through on their newfound independence, many women immigrants engaged in the kind of public action in America that would have been unthinkable in their old home. In 1902, the housewives in New York conducted a successful strike against the kosher butchers who had raised their prices from 12 to 18 cents a pound. Another was organized by women in Cleveland in 1906, and again in Detroit in 1910. Women workers stood up and spoke at union meetings; they became "chairladies" in the shops, representing the rights of their fellow workers as union spokeswomen. They marched and picketed along with the men and sat on union committees. In their spare time, they attended classes and courses assiduously, and, of course, they went to the theater, the "night school" of the Jewish community, as Irving Howe put it.

What happened later? Many women gave up their jobs when their children were born, taking on instantly the subdued role of household drudge. It is a mystery what happened to those bright-eyed young girls who look out at us from their wedding pictures and who so quickly became unappetizing slatterns. This transformation also became one of the best kept secrets of the next generation. Glimpses of the way it really was are revealed in the novels that were also chronicles of immigrant life. In Henry Roth's *Call It Sleep*, which begins in 1907, he describes what happens to the protagonist's Aunt Bertha after her marriage:

> Aunt Bertha had changed since David had seen her last. Uncorseted, she looked fatter now, frowsier. The last remnant of tidiness in her appearance had vanished. Her heavy breasts, sagging visibly against her blouse, stained by fruit juice and chocolate, flopped slovenly from side to side. Fibres of her raffia-coarse red hair twined her moist throat. . . . She submerged him in a fat embrace that reeked of perspiration flavored with coffee.

The indelible memory of those housewives persisted even in 1956, when Kate Simon wrote of her childhood in *Bronx Primitive* and wanted to emphasize her mother's exceptional qualities. She "was already tagged 'The Princess,' " Simon reports, "because she never went into the street unless fully, carefully dressed: no grease-stained housedress, no bent, melted felt slippers." In this passing sentence, sober and precise, Kate Simon evokes the image that prevailed more often than not in those immaculate apartments. In the anxious fulfillment of all her duties, in her pursuit of perfect cleanliness, the pursuer often forgot herself. Or else she treated herself as only the last vessel to be cleaned in the great Friday marathons that Isaac Rosenfeld described in his novel *Passage from Home* (1946) about Jewish life in Chicago. "It was late on a Friday afternoon," he began,

> and my stepmother, having finished with the house, had just come out of the tub. . . . But her observation of personal cleanliness was more than a measure of health. It was, to begin with, an extension of her housework—done cleaning the floors and the furniture, the rugs, the dishes and the woodwork, she would begin on herself, and in this extended ritual the same motive would continue to operate. For it was no mere going-over she gave to the house; it was a religious ceremony. . . . And as she made the house ready, so she prepared herself for the coming of Queen Saturday, the *Shabbes*.

While his stepmother, with cold cream daubed over her face—the final step in her ritual—dissolves into her inanimate household, the adolescent protagonist's single aunt with her untidy apartment and dusty bookshelves emerges from *her* bathroom in a cloud of perfume and begins to teach him about the world and love. Is it any wonder that in their interminable rounds the housewives sometimes had their doubts? As my mother-in-law said knowingly, "A house is a thief," and a woman needed to guard against being robbed.

At the very same time that Roth published his much praised masterpiece, Daniel Fuchs was writing his *Williamsburg Trilogy* where, with excruciating realism, he lays out the steady hostility that seemed to be the basis of all relationships, and the consequent isolation of his characters. What he catches above all is the tone of voice, the nagging ill-temper, the irritability and sarcasm that characterized daily life among his families in Brooklyn. This was fiction, but it mirrored perfectly the temper not only of Williamsburg but also of the Bronx that I knew. I don't yet understand why it became such a widespread habit and style. But there was undoubtedly always an edge, a brittleness that promised a quick flare-up of temper at any moment.

Perhaps the astonishing contrast between that hostile, everyday reality and the world of novels about other lives and other times was what made reading such an unsettling experience. It may explain why I wept uncontrollably over every page of *Little Women,* and not just at the death of little Beth. The conversations and sentiments of the March family may have been saccharine to my more hardened American friends, but they were a revelation to me. The unfailing kindness and gentleness with which people spoke to one another in Louisa May Alcott's novel was a style in very short supply in the Bronx. Alcott's people cared about one another's feelings. They apologized if someone seemed hurt or offended. In casual encounters, they were charmingly polite. I did not stop to ask whether these pictures were true, but read them as reportage and added another point on my scorecard for America. The despairing self-neglect of our mothers, the rough and sardonic mode of much of what passed for conversation, left us bewildered about the world. Which was more real, we asked ourselves: our books, the movies, the homilies on behavior we learned in school, or our very nervous and impatient families?

These mothers had not grown up as tender hothouse plants. They had journeyed across half the world, had mastered skills, and had earned their living from the time they were tender children. But when they married and became housewives, something went out of them. All too many simply gave up on themselves. In their new country, in their new world, the heavy hand of the past incapacitated them. They had chosen their mates; they hoped to live happily ever after; but they did not know how. In the Old Country, in the traditional world out of which they came, women were, almost half the time, "unclean." In a traditional household, during the week that she was menstruating and until another week had passed before she went to the ritual bath to cleanse herself, a woman could not be touched by her husband. And, of course, couples slept apart, since during that two-week period contact between husband and wife was forbidden. My mother told me that in her home in Galicia, her older sister would not so much as hand over a bunch of keys directly to her father on the days that she was "unclean." She would put them on the table for him to pick up, and this in some way vitiated the contamination. Hence, since a man can never tell when a woman is "unclean," no Orthodox man will even shake hands with a strange woman.

A lot changed in America, but ingrained attitudes did not fade easily. Romantic gestures of embracing, kissing, and hand-holding were not often seen among the immigrant generation. Mendele Mokher Seforim in his autobiography, written around the turn of the century, describes the prevailing attitude. "Love is not the kind of thing the Jewish mind can grasp," he asserts categorically. "Love and lovers are not to be found among Jews, especially not in those days . . . and in a respectable family." Some decades later Kate Simon observes of her parents, people out of Mendele's time and place: "I never saw my mother and father kiss or stroke each other as people did in the movies. In company she addressed him, as did most of the Jewish women, by our family name, a mark of respectful distance. They inhabited two separate worlds. . . . "

Even on the Yiddish stage, passion was expressed more through speech than gesture. Couples may have esteemed and even loved one another, but they had not yet mastered the Western vocabulary of love. The old physical barriers between the sexes exerted their inimical force. Engaged couples did not hold hands or gaze into one another's eyes in public. All of this had to be learned—through novels, the movies, and the photographs of wealthy Americans at play that so fascinated the immigrant press. The departure on ocean liners of magnates, socialites, and other celebrities was standard fare in the rotogravure sections of the popular Yiddish newspapers, where couples stood arm-in-arm, smiling, *happy*. Such frivolity, the newspaper readers must have thought, was not for Jews.

When I pressed one woman friend to describe her childhood in the Bronx, she could only answer starkly, "There was no fun." In a situation where parents worried steadily and visibly about endangered relatives in Europe, about holding on to their jobs, about how to make ends meet, there was neither the will nor the talent for the sporting good times on a shoestring that seemed to be featured in our books about the happy poor. There were no cheerful excursions to a nearby creek with makeshift fishing poles, no happy neighborly picnics. Each household, it must be said, was miserable in its own way.

It seems strange in an epoch so intently devoted to the pursuit of happiness how novel this idea was even among the young newcomers. For the immigrant generation, it was difficult, even dangerous, to acknowledge happiness openly, since lurking evil spirits were ready to pounce on every shred of good fortune. What began perhaps as a feigned posture of defense, hardened into a stony denial of reality.

Even the generation born in this country had to learn what happiness was and how to express it. Daniel Fuchs in his *Summer in Williamsburg* makes much of how both the young men and the young women draw on the latest movies as they compose their speeches to one another, and strike the attitudes that seemed so effective to them as they sat watching in the darkened theater. Inevitably, in the real world, the effects fail and the relationship falls apart as the two speakers stand separated by a mountain of misunderstanding and longing, with nothing left but to revert to their native hostile Brooklynese. Kate Simon as a thirteen-year-old, growing conscious of her developing body, is happier, imagining herself "as desirable as Gloria Swanson, as steely as Nita Naldi, as winsome as Marion Davies . . . like them invincible and immortal." These fantasies may arm her, but they do not bring her closer to her contemporaries.

Married couples had to look beyond their parents, therefore, for models of an American married life, and often failed in the process. In Fuch's *Summer in Williamsburg*, a husband has just driven his wife and two children to Fallsburgh, New York, "to the country," for a three-week vacation. The young couple are about to take leave of one another:

> They stood clumsily and didn't know how to kiss. The last time had been so long ago they felt as though kissing was nonsense and ridiculous, but now they knew they should be kissing each other good-bye and it was difficult to do it.
>
> "Good-bye, Sam," she finally said. "Take care of yourself and remember what I said, you're all I got."
>
> "Don't worry. I'll be all right." He patted her on the shoulder and went out of the room.

Perhaps if there had been more kissing there would have been less fighting. But kissing and endearments were mostly reserved for very young children—and then all the delicious diminutives of which Yiddish is capable would come out. Babies created a free zone where tenderness could be legitimately expressed in language and touch. "Little bird, little crown, my own treasure, little sweetness, little mother, little father," and on and on. Every name with the addition of a few suffixes could be turned into a poem. But they had not yet learned the language of love in English. Sam and his wife are almost ashamed to be loving and kind to one another. They simply don't know how to do it.

What was left? The women of the old generation cleaned their houses and polished their kitchen floors. Every day they cooked substantial meals and baked regularly because it was a source of shame not to have a piece of cake in the house if someone came by. And in the process they grew irritable, shapeless, and neglected. One woman told me that she could not remember what her aunt's face looked like because every time she saw her, she was standing at the sink with her back to the visitors in her kitchen. Later, after World War II, as the Jewish-mother jokes gained form and currency, this sad, humiliating fact is what their children kept secret.

In the jokes, she became the featureless symbol of devotion whose sole function was to provide total, uncomprehending love. The Jewish-mother jokes were only the first outward sign marking the distance that had opened between the generations. With a nod of recognition, the children told one another marriage jokes as they began to cast their parents into manageable and fixed stereotypes. There is, for example, the daughter who is rewarded after she graduates from college with a trip abroad to find a husband. On her return, she telephones from the dock to say that she is arriving with her betrothed. When the doorbell rings, the mother opens the door to see before her a magnificent African adorned with feathers and bells on his wrists and ankles and a bone through his nose. "Oy, Ruthie," she wails as she takes in the scene. "I said a *rich* doctor!" All those Ruthies and Roses and Myrnas who were telling these jokes were, in actuality, gradually moving out of emotional reach. They were afraid of being drawn back into the old vortex. But perhaps without even wishing it, there was simply the distance that came as they quietly moved into another language, another culture, and most important, gained another perspective.

Their mothers, however, provided a powerful—and often negative—model to the American-born generation. One successful woman writer who lived in a sumptuous Central Park West apartment always sent out for food when she invited people to dinner. She frankly explained her aversion to cooking as a reaction to her mother's kitchen. She remembered her mother's grease-stained dress, her heavy body, her laborious lifting of pots, and the hours that she spent in the kitchen. It no longer mattered whether the food was delicious. For the young writer, the kitchen spelled danger. If she lifted a pot, she would turn into an ugly old woman.

Another friend whom I met at college also felt herself placed in an excruciating dilemma. She was a very good student and had an active social life. For her it was marriage itself, rather than cooking, that was the danger. Marriage was the death of the body—and of the spirit. Women were indentured servants to their husbands, perpetual slaves to the needs of their children. In short, they lived for the needs of others, as Philip Roth wrote in a perfect sentence on his mother's life. He describes how his father, in his boredom upon retiring, attempted to take over the household: "only my mother," as Roth points out, "happened not to need a boss, having been her own since her single-handed establishment of a first-class domestic-management and mothering company back in 1927, when my brother was born." These mothers became frightening examples to their daughters of what might happen without vigilance, without self-respect.

Strangely enough, when they drew a moral from their lives, these mothers gave their daughters contradictory messages. On the one hand, they shared the accepted view that a girl who was not married or at least engaged by eighteen was already regarded as an old maid. On the other hand, they counseled escape. But the course a girl took was often less a measure of talent than of courage. One girl who wanted to go to college and become a teacher was warned off such an imprudent course of action by both her parents. They worried that as a teacher, a formidable bluestocking, she would frighten away potential suitors. Faced with this possibility—or threat, as they presented it—she chose a safe "commercial" course in high school. Afterward she found a job as a secretary, which she got, she always claimed, because with her blue eyes and fair coloring she could pass as a Gentile. With this modest job, and a little money in the bank, she was married at twenty. This was the story with the "happy ending."

But Kate Simon's mother—like mine, and I wonder how many others—warned her daughter off marriage as mere subservience, and urged her to take up a career where she would be independent. For my mother, nothing was more glamorous than the women she saw in the morning going off to what she called "business." It meant that they dressed beautifully, that they sat in wonderfully appointed offices where people spoke genteelly to one another, where one might flirt but never grow serious.

I sometimes wonder whether my mother had read the Sholem Aleichem stories about Motl Pesi, the orphaned cantor's son who travels with his extended family to New York. On their way they stop in London, where they seek out a refugee assistance organization. There, the officials sit quietly at their desks, smoking cigars and saying, "All right. All right." Sholem Aleichem puts these two words in English to contrast their reassuring calm with the frantic anxiety of the destitute immigrants. My mother's dream, then, was of a woman in charge of her own life, who worked in such an office without husband or children to disturb her. But the closer I got to eighteen, the more she postponed this fantasy, and worried ever more openly about my "prospects."

The responses to these contradictory signals with their ultimate ground tone of disparagement for being a mere girl were understandably varied. At the extremes were the girls who simply rebelled: who moved away, who married Gentiles, who took up careers and lives that ultimately estranged them from their families. Most chose a middle way that would maintain their self-respect, permit them to use their innate gifts, and yet afford them some independence. It often left a bitter aftertaste. This was not the unfulfilled love of the earlier generation, but unfulfilled dreams ultimately hurt as much.

We recognize one another now with our "corrected" New York

speech, our commitment to the betterment of the world, and a certain hardheaded insistence on rationality that cannot be seduced by astrology or aroma therapy. We are a little earnest, dogmatic even, in the American scheme of things, but none of this can hide our wistful longing to be cared for and esteemed. One afternoon, I found myself sitting at a luncheon table with a group of women who had come out of such families as mine and had attended one or another of the New York City colleges. We had assembled to honor a mutual friend and most of us did not know one another. But we immediately hit on what seemed to be a universal theme. One after another, each explained how she had not meant to go to a city college at all. Several had won scholarships to universities outside the city; others had parents who could have afforded the tuition elsewhere; but in every case their fearful mothers had objected to their leaving the family roof. Reluctantly and resentfully, therefore, they had stayed, but feeling cheated for the rest of their lives by their mothers' timidity.

Many of the women who went to college did carve out some kind of career. Few aimed for or expected anything illustrious, but they did useful work. In some families, however, where money was short, it was expected that the girls would give way while the boys went on for higher education. One woman who ironed her brothers' shirts while they attended college was persuaded to take a secretarial course that would quickly prepare her for a job. It did not even occur to her to question this family strategy until much later. Those girls who did go on to a higher education were often closely questioned to make sure that what they were studying would be useful, would get them a job when they graduated. Even so—how long would a girl work? Some left their jobs when they married. At the very latest they left when they became pregnant with their first baby.

What was insidious about this atmosphere was that it often left young women with a powerful sense of self-doubt. One of my college friends who had a brilliant academic record found her confidence so undermined that although she was offered a scholarship for a doctorate in economics at New York University, she could not bring herself to accept it. Her faith in her ability was not as great as that of the scholarship committee. In the end it was simply not sufficient to support her through the arduous and lonesome process of writing her dissertation. Now, as she contemplates this period in her life many decades later, she reminds me that in any case the outside world was not particularly welcoming to young women scholars, and if they were Jewish the barriers were all but impossible to scale. No, she couldn't cope with it all.

In her family they had been very closely ruled by a despotic father who demanded absolute obedience and absolute silence in his presence. Once a year the family drove to the Catskills from the Bronx for a vacation. At the beginning of the trip the father displayed a cat-o'-nine-tails, which the oldest of the three girls was made to kiss. The whip then sat on the seat by his side as an open reminder to his children of his readiness to enforce compliance. How did girls respond to the violence, the threats, the quarrels, the ill-temper, and the cutting remarks that were so characteristic of their childhood? Differently from the boys, who were born, as it were, into the ruling clan. This was why I so desperately longed for a brother.

It was not only language and customs and social styles that separated the generations. It was also their aspirations. For the immigrants, it was enough to learn to manage the New World. Their children wanted to enter it. For the older generation, every new skill, every new stage was a miracle. When the illiterate owner of the poultry market in Kate Simon's *Bronx Primitive* buys a car and learns to drive, it is not a simple rite of passage. It is a marvel to himself and to the entire neighborhood. I can imagine that twenty years later when his son bought a car, he wanted to drive to places and enter precincts whose very existence were unknown to his father. These misunderstandings about what was enough, about what one "needed," marked the differences between the generations.

In the Passover Haggadah, there is a long poem of thanksgiving in which the ancient Israelites recite the miracles that God performed for them in their Exodus from Egypt, and after each pair, the refrain is *"Dayenu—we should have been satisfied."* Thus:

> *Had he satisfied our needs in the desert for forty years,*
> *but not fed us manna,*
> *We should have been satisfied.*
> *Had He fed us manna,*
> *but not given us the Sabbath,*
> *We should have been satisfied.*
> *Had He given us the Sabbath,*
> *but not brought us to Mount Sinai,*
> *We should have been satisfied. . . .*

The immigrants to America, like the ancient Israelites, were satisfied after each miracle in their own exodus and hardly thought to ask for more. They lived in the New World, but with the expectations of the Old. When my cousin in Ohio graduated from high school in the mid-1930s, she was given a trip to New York City as her present. I am sure that coming to stay with us in a tenement apartment in the Bronx and sleeping on the living-room sofa was not exactly what she had in mind when she told her friends she was going to New York. Fortunately, the trip was rescued for her by some young cousins who knew how to show her around the city, could introduce her to some interesting young men and give her the thrill of being part of the New York scene.

But all the while she stayed with us, my mother had quite a different scenario in her head. The good times that my cousin seemed so fixed on were, according to my mother, a mere pretense, a ruse.

Actually, in my mother's scheme of things, she was here to scout out the scene, hoping to find a job for herself, establish a base, and then gradually bring the rest of the family, including my mother's beloved sister, to New York. That is certainly what my mother would have done in my cousin's place. She could not believe that my cousin would travel a thousand miles just to enjoy herself.

But the world had definitely changed. For my cousin's generation, good times were on the agenda. The sense of imminent danger, of the precariousness of life itself, that had so dominated immigrant thought was no longer in the forefront of the next generation's imagination. If my mother or her contemporaries had composed a "Dayenu," certainly the rescue from physical peril represented by America would have been prominent, not to mention *parnose*, "a livelihood," which was also satisfied here. Even good health had a better chance of being realized.

I think that the immigrant generation did not see happiness as a legitimate goal in life. It was what happened when all one's obligations had been fulfilled. In announcing the call letters of WNYC, the municipal radio station in New York, they used to add: "a city where seven million people live in peace and enjoy the benefits of democracy." Similarly for the immigrants, if at the end of their lives they could fold their hands and enjoy the benefits of peace and prosperity, the affection of their children, did they have the *right* to ask for more?

Many of the women did ask for more, albeit guiltily. They longed for education, for position, for respect, for baubles and finery, for pleasure. But then, as my mother reminded me, when someone died, broken bits of pottery were placed on the eyelids as a sign of the vanity of the things of this world. I sometimes wondered whether she told me this in order to remind me of my own frivolity in my passion for the variety and wonders of the world around us.

"Dayenu" was a stern creed, and not altogether appropriate to the richness of American life. It was perhaps a creed that worked where poverty was so widespread that a roof over one's head and enough to eat were all that one could hope for. But in the New World, immigrant women saw stretching before them infinite possibilities, and their restlessness with their constricted past and their wish to capture something of the richness of the present led to those mixed signals that their daughters received.

While many of those daughters hesitated, living by the cautions and fears of their mothers, like my partners at the luncheon table, others accepted the invitation of America. It was perhaps not such a generous invitation in the twenties and thirties as it later became. But, as a start, "Dayenu." The large numbers of Jewish women who entered the professions as teachers, social workers, librarians, government workers, who entered the business world as bookkeepers, secretaries, administrators, felt a profound satisfaction in their accomplishment and in their work.

There were even those stalwart exceptions who became doctors and lawyers, entered the academy, or made their mark in the arts. I think that that generation never ceased to marvel at how far they had come. Although they had not known the fear of persecution and pogroms, they had tasted at first hand discrimination fueled by anti-Semitism and the dread of joblessness that the Depression left behind. This did not leave them unmarked. In their later years, they nourished a hidden fear that their fine positions and beautiful houses could, might, all vanish overnight. So they worked out their secret, fallback positions, the place perhaps where they "ought" to have landed if American opportunity had not propelled them so far. Once, as I talked with a very successful child psychiatrist about these widespread fantasies, she immediately confessed her own. "I suppose," she said very seriously, "I could always find a job as a nursery school teacher."

So much of all of this has been kept secret. Just as the immigrant generation kept silent about their primitive lives in the villages from which they came, about customs that they feared would elicit laughter or contempt from their American children, these very American children have kept their own secrets. Among ourselves, around that luncheon table, we said: "Dayenu." We knew how far we had come. We were pleased with our work. We had encompassed a whole new civilization and had devised a way to live in it. But we knew how much more our brothers and husbands had accomplished, how we had lagged behind them, and a little of that shame prevented us from facing our own daughters. It was their fathers and uncles who were the doctors and scientists, the university professors, the world-renowned musicians and Nobel Prize winners.

In the last quarter of the twentieth century, my generation has watched the dividing and subdividing women's movement with something like bemusement. In view of the long journey that we have made, some of the details that have preoccupied the next generations seem no more than wearisome. As for us, we are still contemplating older issues: What is the good life? What is happiness?

## 11

# Winter

The sound of winter was the ring of snow shovels on the sidewalk late at night as the "super" cleared the sidewalk of the falling snow. This, with the clank of tire chains on the passing cars, foretold the changing landscape that would await us in the morning. We knew we were lucky because we lived in a steam-heated building and were warm no matter what the outside weather. But other houses in the neighborhood had "cold-water flats," which actually had both hot and cold water but no central heating. For the families in these flats, the falling snow and the clank of car wheels meant more expense as their kerosene or electric heaters worked overtime. For us, however, winter meant a saving.

With the first frost my mother discontinued her patronage of the iceman, and put out on the fire escape the winter icebox, actually a galvanized-tin chest. All the hardware stores in our neighborhood featured these contrivances as soon as fall came, so that gradually the streets bloomed with their glitter. Neatly built, with two sliding doors and a shelf inside to divide the space, they offered a secure and tidy way to store food during the winter months. With all the world an icebox, it would have been an unthinkable expense to continue to buy ice for the kitchen. On days of severe frost, we covered the box with newspaper or cardboard to provide a little extra insulation. But sometimes even these precautions failed to prevent that frozen cap of cream from rising above the milk bottle or the butter from turning into a brick. If the sill at the kitchen window were wide enough, some families lashed their boxes with wire to whatever framework they could find in order to keep them at a more convenient location. When the fire escape was off the bedroom, it was not particularly handy. Nonetheless, it was very satisfying to save that 75 cents a week, $3.00 in a month. That began to be real money.

With so many engaged in piecework labor or small businesses where profits were measured in pennies, it is no wonder that this habit of close calculation became ingrained in the immigrants' way of thinking. Every few cents represented a measurable amount of time spent at the sewing machine or the pressing iron. It was hard to think of prices in any other way. Many of the young girls living at home hardly saw the money that they earned. Among sixteen- and seventeen-year-olds working as store clerks in New York around 1909, 85 percent gave their entire earnings to the family. Among Italian women, no matter what their occupation, the same proportion also surrendered their entire earnings, while the remainder gave a part. Among girls who worked in factories, 90 percent turned over their wages. A little money in hand, then, became a precious thing.

The coming of winter was also marked by a careful inventory of last year's clothes—the heavy overcoats, galoshes, and hats that were required to get through the season safely. With the terrible fear in immigrant families of catching cold and its possible escalating, ultimately fatal consequences, these were not just clothes, they were components of one's armor in the war with the elements. The anxiety to outfit children adequately was intensified, however, by its financial burden. The moment when we tried on last year's winter coat was always fraught with suspense. Would it be big enough for another season? The sight of the inevitably protruding wristbone was always followed by that tug at the sleeve, suddenly too short, and then a close examination of the amount still in the seam beneath to see whether there was enough to let out. Where necessary, there was the stratagem of the "false hem" that permitted my parents to use every last fragment of cloth to make up the length.

Ohrbach's, the bargain department store for clothing, gauged its audience perfectly in an ad it ran just before the winter of 1938. It showed three children on skates, warmly dressed in fashionable tweed coats, under the headline: "Now you needn't sacrifice in order to dress your children for winter." Without ever mentioning prices, they were hinting not too subtly, a mother could protect her children's health and still have enough left over for something stylish for herself. "Dress your children well," suggested the text, "but don't deprive yourself."

It was not only with the allure of savings that Ohrbach's beckoned to its immigrant customers. Their ad writers understood the powerful pull of imagination. These immigrant mothers saw their children, even without prompting from Ohrbach's, as little lords and ladies. And here they were shown by a photographer who had clearly made his picture on his knees, looking up at these charming, friendly young aristocrats so perfectly turned out in their captivating and debonair outfits. It had nothing to do with what girls and boys in the Bronx actually wore on skates, but it made a mother's heart swell with pride.

Orhbach's ads appealed to the Bronx way of thinking. They avoided all issue of price, simply making the very advanced and daring social point: Don't wait. You can have everything. And you can afford it because of Ohrbach's low prices. Another ad promised successful marriages to women who kept themselves well dressed. "For happy homes . . . dress beautifully but avoid extravagance." Furthermore, the ad promised there would be "no more squabbles over bills!"

It was not only immigrant mothers who modeled their children on English nobility. Best & Co., a Fifth Avenue specialty store at the high end of the price spectrum, in a similar appeal, advertised a little boy's "Royal Middy Navy Chinchilla Reefer. Tailored in England." The ad pressed its claim home with a bit of manufacturing history that instantly made the buyer a part of the English Admiralty: "This coat is made for Best's in England by a commissioned naval tailor, and is 'regulation' in every detail down to nautical brass buttons and a red flannel lining."

The inevitable conflict and charge of "sissy" was handled firmly in the advice columns by dividing clothes between play and "dressy." In the "dressy" category, our young heroes were delivered up to their mothers' whims. At play, however, both interests come together. "A regular he-man your son will feel," wrote one advertiser in what reads like a transcription of Bronx syntax, "(and his mother'll know he's safely warm) in a big young mackinaw. . . . " Firmly bundled into his mackinaw, our young Bronxite was off to the intense life of the streets and his session of ring-a-levio. This utterly absorbing game that could go on for an entire day was played only by the boys. They formed two competing teams, each seeking to capture the other's players and imprison them in a "dungeon" marked off by chalk on the street.

As Ohrbach's so cleverly suggested, Bronx mothers did not confine their dreams to their children's wardrobe and welfare. Somewhere in their hearts was the wish, closely held, deeply cherished, for the fur coat. And here different kinds were kept strictly separate as appropriate for different ages and stages in life. From the very species of the fur one could read an entire marital history, not to mention the state of the husband's balance sheet.

In the movies, for example, when an actress flounced across the screen in a silver fox stole, it was clear that she was not the "good girl." There is an echo of this convention in the famous opening scene of *Born Yesterday* (1950), in which Judy Holliday as the gangster's moll enters a hotel lobby trailing several long-haired fur coats over her arm. In the Bronx, the young married woman, the *yinge vaybl*, whose husband was just beginning to feel a sense of security in his business, might begin to look around for a gray squirrel coat. Often closely tailored to the youthful figures of the women who wore them, perhaps with a small silver fox collar, as a harbinger of things to come, these coats were worn with more pleasure, it seemed to me, than the more expensive Persian lamb coats that marked a later and more affluent station in life. These rather heavy, serious coats for rather heavier ladies were far less cheerful, although they were substantial and conveyed standing in the world. They seemed more a reward for service than an indulgence, dully functional rather than luxurious. Seal coats, the next step on the ladder, by contrast, were soft, silky, and expensive. They draped flatteringly around the body; they seemed always somehow perfumed. Their wearers, I thought, must be happy. This perhaps was what ladies on the Grand Concourse wore.

It seems bizarre, at the end of the twentieth century, to write about this, as fur coats are spray-painted on the streets by ecologically minded citizens and major designers are afraid to use anything but "faux" fur. Yet in the early decades of the century they represented way stations and realizations of the fantasies in the immigrant population. My cousin Anna, who had been brought to this country from Poland as an infant, was the only child of her parents. She was indulged and petted and developed a rather daring style. One day she came to visit with her boyfriend and was wearing for the first time something that she called her "monkey-fur jacket." It was short, with wide sleeves, and hung loosely on her tiny frame. The shape of the jacket somehow emphasized the rather long, black, hairlike fur. It frightened me, and I thought it repulsive. But she seemed to wear it almost as a joke. And even I had to admit that, in its wildness, it rather suited her.

Then, as now, the ad writers and the tinkerers in the trade knew how to satisfy the wish that represented a hope. Here the plentiful and inexpensive muskrat was pressed into service. The close reader of the ads by Russeks, the standard-bearer of fur sellers in New York, could buy "seal-dyed muskrat" or even "mink-dyed muskrat" for the price of the humble squirrel. Sometimes even the ubiquitous squirrel was garnished with the adjective "Russian"— a descriptive generally reserved for sable, that most exquisite and sumptuous of furs, beyond anyone's dreams. In this new evocation, "Russian squirrel" suddenly seemed quite glamorous.

At a time when all these coats were available for about $150, equal to perhaps a month's work, a mink coat soared into the stratosphere at $1,000. No one even thought of mink. Once, during the crowded Christmas season, I stood next to the wearer of such a coat at Macy's. As we waited for the cashier, she pulled a little silver compact out of her purse, glanced into the mirror, and then slipped the compact, with her gray, suede-gloved hand, into the pocket of her coat. It was a powerful moment because the carelessness of the gesture only heightened the confluence of so much luxury. But even in the case of the unobtainable mink, the ingenious ad writer could coax the imagination: with the help of a little French, one could buy a mink-dyed *lapin*.

My mother never owned a fur coat when we lived in the Bronx. But she had a fur scarf, which, judging by its antiquity, I think she must have bought as part of her extravagant habits when she was still a working girl. As she proudly told me, it was stone marten, and she preserved it carefully in tissue paper with cakes of camphor. It had beady glass eyes set in a very lifelike miniature animal head that fastened the scarf by seeming to bite its fluffy tail. She wore it casually, ornamentally, over a dress or suit when we went for ceremonious walks in the park, and of course on family visits. Although I liked to stroke the fur, I found the head even on that diminutive scale too lifelike and somehow bizarre. Nonetheless, it had its uses when I wanted to torment my little sister and made the head approach and seem to snap at her.

Winter was one time of the year, in our city fastness, when we felt that the elements came to us. Summer happened in the country, but in winter we had snow and ice in the streets, and frost on our window panes. When the snow came, and then froze into lakes of ice on the street, sleds materialized from their basement storage places and we took turns pulling one another up and down in the roadway. For older people with business to accomplish, it was a less cheerful time. Everything took longer and was harder to do. The short walk to the bank or the grocery store suddenly was effortful and filled with danger.

It was in the midst of such a winter in the heart of the Depression years that my father was once again jobless and began an earnest and desperate search for work. He had owned, in succession, several small stationery stores, the last of which had failed. He had also worked as a window washer, as a streetcar conductor, and as a button and notions salesman in the garment district. Now, with the family living on the last money from my mother's pawned engagement ring, he was ready to take anything that meant a regular wage. Saving of carfare, he walked long distances in the cold from one interview to another, and after some fruitless weeks answered an ad for a milkman at Sheffield's. The impediment, it turned out in the interview, was that he was Jewish. The company had never hired a Jew and saw no reason to begin now since they doubted that Jews had the stamina for such arduous work as running up and down flights of stairs bearing loaded metal carriers full of milk bottles. My father, as he told the story, made a speech citing his army service, his perfect health, his dire need for a job, and his promise of total loyalty and dedication to his work if he were only given the opportunity to prove himself. Whether moved by this speech or on a hunch of his own, the interviewer decided to violate company precedent and hire the Jew standing before him.

My father's gratitude was in proportion to his fear, and he rededicated himself every day to the welfare of his company and his job.

He gave it the unswerving fealty of the vassal to his lord, and no trade union could ever have come between him and the company. It was his safe berth during the worst years of the Depression, and he stayed on the job for nine years, until he collapsed with an attack of angina. But he looked back on this as a golden time, when he had somehow single-handedly vanquished the system and taught those "others" that a Jew was as good as any other man.

It was not as if the pay was particularly lavish. In fact, there were a few dark times when there had even been pay cuts. But by the midthirties when the economy stabilized, he made a steady $40 a week. My parents considered it prudent to allot one fourth of their income for rent, and they stayed strictly within that boundary when they looked for an apartment. Half of my father's pay went for food for a family of four and the remainder—$10—had to cover everything else. According to the New York Budget Council, we lived extravagantly well. In September 1938, it published a budget for families "in the low marginal income group," and allotted $8.25 for food for a family of five. That family, according to the Council, "would live on the cheaper cuts of meat . . . and eat plenty of fish. . . . Other food would include evaporated milk as well as fresh milk, potatoes, macaroni, cheap cereals and oleomargarine as well as butter."

What the Budget Council did not reckon on in its calculations was the cost of kosher food, where the meat could be double what it cost at the A&P food stores. Nor would my mother buy anything but unsalted butter, on the perhaps unfounded but widely held belief that salted butter was not kosher. And, of course, she wouldn't even approach margarine, made of mysterious ingredients and even looking like lard! She also bought only white eggs, which cost a few cents more than the brown. But this was as insurance against the possibility of finding a blood spot in the egg that would render it unkosher. The white eggs were "candled," literally held up to a candle in a darkened room; because the white shell was so translucent, an expert could see instantly whether there was a telltale fleck.

The freshwater fish that she bought to make gefilte fish were also rather more expensive than the cod and haddock recommended by the Budget Council. Nor could my parents see the point of eating Wonder Bread at 8 cents a loaf when they could get a pound of good rye bread for 15 cents. My mother could only shake her head in dismay. *"Povatine,"* she said dismissively of Wonder Bread. "Cobwebs." It had no substance, no body.

On all these points my parents were united in what seemed to them the self-evident choices. But even with prudence it cost $20 a week, as they said, "for the table." I received 50 cents a week for my carfare to high school, but brought my own lunch from home every day. From time to time as I needed school supplies, I received supplements. Textbooks were, of course, distributed free for the semester by the school, but were required to be returned in perfect condition at the end of the school year. In June came the moment of reckoning when they were inspected for pencil marks, rips and turned-down corners, with a fixed scale of prices for each defacement. Needless to say, a lost book was a catastrophe for the family. In my four years of traveling back and forth on the subway, I only lost one.

We devoted a certain amount of time to the care of our books. Some years, we used large brown paper bags, saved from the grocery store, to make book covers. And sometimes my mother actually bought oilcloth that we would cut to fit and then sew onto the book to preserve its pristine condition. Knowing how money was counted out led me to keep my handwriting small and I was always shocked to see friends in class doodling on a fresh sheet of notebook paper. This sense of thrift was not peculiar to my family, but was part of a world just recovering from the Depression that retained a lingering respect for every penny.

The General Electric Company played on these feelings in an advertising campaign in October 1938. Drawing on the talents of Helen Hokinson, who was usually a fixture at *The New Yorker*, the ad in the *New York Post* showed a group of her affluent suburban matrons in the electrical appliance section of a department store. One of them has just dropped a coin, and as a man scrambles to retrieve it, the caption reads: "Don't bother! It's only a penny." Here the writer rolls up his sleeves. "But see how much these appliances will do for a penny's worth of electricity . . . 1 cent will bring you more than four hours' entertainment with a new compact radio or nearly an hour's correct reading light, or heat an automatic iron for more than 20 minutes . . . etc." When even General Electric cared about a penny, I could do no less.

Like many of his fellow milkmen, my father had a sideline to help augment his income. It grew up so naturally beside his annual wine-making that it took me some time to realize that it was illegal. It all seemed quite straightforward. Some days he arranged to finish his work early and went downtown, returning in the late afternoon with a five-gallon can of pure alcohol wrapped in plain brown paper. With this and some cherries and sugar, he made a kind of brandy. It was very strong, and if he allowed it to stand for any length of time, it developed a certain body. Sometimes when he couldn't make the trip, the alcohol was delivered late in the evening by Mr. Kronpolski, a giant of a man whose cheeks had two telltale spots of bright red. He seemed too large for our small living room and would only rarely consent to sit down for a visit. Generally he stood, shifting uneasily from one foot to another, turning quickly if the door opened unexpectedly.

Mr. Kronpolski was no gangster. If anything, he saw himself as a victim, forced into his accursed business by circumstances, by the times. He knew that he was unwell, that his heart was bad and his blood pressure high. He knew also that the constant fear, the sudden alarms with which he lived were the worst possible conditions for a man with his ailments. But what was he to do? This was a living. And then there was his daughter, Zelda, the source of his pride and joy and redemption, who was a student at Hunter College. A brilliant student, a diamond among students. After she finished, perhaps he would look around for something else. Meanwhile, he took care of his customers, dealt with the gangsters, and paid off the police.

My father sold his bootleg brandy at work. At Sheffield's a strict hierarchy prevailed that placed on some higher level the milkmen who actually delivered the milk and cream to the door, made out the bills, and collected the money. Below them were the stablemen who tended the horses and cared for the delivery wagons. The milkmen were "Americans." The stablemen were largely newly arrived Irish immigrants and were even more poorly paid than the milkmen. But it was mostly among the stablemen that my father found a market for his brandy, which he put up in reused glass milk bottles. The men would stop by at our apartment after work to pick up a quart, standing for a moment in the dark corridor and quickly disappearing.

One of his steady customers was Johnny, the stableman who was in charge of the horse assigned to my father for his deliveries. Dissimilar as they seemed, my father and Johnny shared a rural background and had found some bond in the stables on Webster Avenue. My father had grown up in a tiny village near Bialystok where, as a boy, he had hung around the nearby farms, ridden horses, and helped care for the animals. Something of a delinquent as a child, he had been allowed to run wild because he was regarded as uncontrollable. When her neighbors asked his mother whether she didn't worry about his climbing trees, leaping onto the logging rafts in the river, swimming near the falls, she would respond with a Russian proverb to the effect that the Devil will never take a devil. Released from the confinement of the *heder* (the all-day religious school), my father was simultaneously released from the world of Yiddish. Visiting the Tsar's soldiers in the nearby barracks, he spoke Russian. On the rare occasions that he met the great landowners of the region and their servants, he spoke Polish. But mostly he spent his time with the peasant boys of his age, speaking Russian to them and to the horses, participating in their day-to-day life in the fields and orchards.

Although he and Johnny had grown up more than a thousand miles apart, they now shared a language and spoke to one another as well as to the horses in English. They shared also that unsentimental interest in animals of country people. They didn't "love" them, but they knew how to care for them and how to get the best out of them. They saw one another every day and they talked—mostly about horses and a little about their lives. On the infrequent occasions when my father drove his horse and wagon to our street, he loved to show off a trick by which he could get his horse to say no. He would lean forward and whisper into its ear (whether in Russian or English I never knew), and then the horse would invariably stamp the ground and shake his head.

When Johnny came to pick up his quart, unlike the others he was invited in to sit down. Even I, as a child listening to the talk, could tell that there was something terribly wrong. Without knowing the word, I knew that Johnny and his wife were alcoholics, that they lived in terrible squalor, that their teen-aged daughter, to Johnny's distress, lay about all day on a bed without linen and drank along with her parents. In our house his story was yet another proof of that old, obnoxiously smug Yiddish song, *"Shiker iz er, trinken miz er, vayl er is a goy.* (He is a drunkard and he must drink, because he is a Gentile.)" My father pitied Johnny, but he continued to sell him his quarts of brandy.

Minor, home-bred illegality was well known in the Bronx. There were, for example, the card games that went on in certain apartments at all hours of the day and night. The owner of the apartment essentially ran these games as a business. There was an entrance fee, and she (it was usually a woman) also made a little money selling refreshments—sandwiches and drinks. But for some women (and men) card playing was a kind of mania, and there were neighborhood types simply known as "card players," who spent all their waking hours in one or another of these gambling houses. Of course it was illegal, but that disturbed the neighbors less than the immorality of a woman (or man) neglecting their familial obligations to follow their obsession. There were very rigid ideas in the Bronx as to wifely duties, and paramount among them was the obligation to cook an evening meal. Opening a can, or buying cold cuts from the delicatessen, no matter how delicious, were seen as a breach in the marital contract. In this, of course, the Jewish community in the Bronx only shared the strongly held conventional views of the rest of America at the time. The letters to the advice columns in the newspapers not infrequently featured complaints by husbands who felt neglected because their wives did not see housekeeping as a serious responsibility. At the same time, husbands who gambled away their pay checks were the mirror image of the problem, occasioning just as many letters of distress.

I must confess that on the rare occasions that I was permitted to visit, I rather liked the atmosphere in these gambling parlors. I liked the ladies who looked so different from my mother and her neighbors. The gambling ladies, the *kurtn shpiler* (card players), were loud, brightly gotten up, often with vividly dyed hair. They smoked; they told off-color jokes; they weren't afraid of the men. In fact, they weren't afraid. The man who would have the temerity to reproach one of them for failing to cook his dinner would soon regret it. These women in their independence had a different view of life from the one I was used to. They understood that it included *good times*. The men also exuded the same indulgent sense of enjoying life, as they smoked their cigars, spread themselves at ease in their chairs, rumbled their bids, kibbitzed and told stories. My father was drawn to these houses, and occasionally would go to spend an evening despite my mother's tight-lipped disapproval. A man who never really had friends, he went as much for the conviviality, I think, as for the game itself. He was never trapped into an obsessive need, but without my mother's opposition, he probably would have been more of a regular than he was.

Then there was the sale of goods of uncertain origin out of apartments. The contraband was generally clothing—new but available only as unique items. As a cover story, they were referred to as "samples." In the bedroom of the apartment a clothes rack displayed an array of dresses, coats, and jackets in a variety of sizes. If the buyer were lucky, she found the dress she liked in her size. But it was understood that there was no source from which to order an alternative in another size or color. These were samples! What hung on the rack, however, was much better, by far, than what we were accustomed to in our usual forays to Third Avenue, the main shopping street in the East Bronx. In these bedroom transactions, beautiful dresses and coats were sold for a fraction of their true worth. We didn't ask, they didn't tell, yet everyone knew there was something not quite regular in the way these items had arrived there. We shrugged; we were glad of the chain of acquaintance that secured our entrance and the opportunity to buy something fine. We wished the seller well, and hoped that she and her suppliers would not be caught. For the moment, the arrangement satisfied both her need for money and our hankering for something better than we could afford. We took advantage of it.

Both my parents had a taste for the grand gesture and for what seemed to them lavish expenditure, and the money that my father made from his bootleg business gave them just that little extra margin. It permitted, for example, a shopping expedition of a Saturday night to the open-air market on Bathgate Avenue in the East Bronx. There they dallied along the street, looked into store windows, craned their necks at the goods on the pushcarts each brightly illuminated by a naptha lamp, bought fruit candies from Eastern Europe in their highly colored wrappers, slices of halvah, sometimes some household linens, or a knitted sweater, a shirt for my father, whatever caught their fancy in a free-spending mood. I was left at home to take care of my sister during these excursions, but we were rewarded on their return with some of the treats that they had bought.

That was the good part. But sometimes the openwork lime green sweater that they brought back for me with such delight was nothing more than a torment. With feigned pleasure, I would accept it, hoping never to wear it. As a teenager who had, as they used to say, "developed" early, wearing anything clinging was a misery. My parents seemed oblivious to my embarrassment and only exclaimed at how well the color suited me.

Bathgate Avenue and I soon parted company as I began to ponder the dress of my high school classmates and wonder where they found subdued tweed jackets and dark plaid skirts. The clothes on Bathgate Avenue ran to what my mother was pleased to call *Italyeynishe farbn* (Italian colors), a less than complimentary phrase on her lips. Nonetheless, however exquisite and careful her taste for herself, she always seemed to choose *Italyeynishe farbn* for me. I must admit that I was rather a sullen child, a *mruk*, as I heard all too often. My mother may have been trying to brighten the atmosphere with her choice of garish reds and yellows, or "maize," as she liked to call it. But these selections only sent me deeper into despair as I continued my silent observation of the quiet, well-fitting clothes of my classmates.

The mystery of their origin was finally revealed by one of the girls who, even to me, was visibly a social climber. In explaining how she removed a label from a dress bought at the elegant De Pinna's department store on upper Fifth Avenue and sewed it into something bought off a pushcart, she inadvertently revealed the source of all those beautiful things I coveted. I could never see the point of her label game; but someday, I resolved, when I had worked up the courage, I would go to De Pinna's and look at their clothes.

In winter the great holiday that lay across the end of the year, dominating its last weeks, was, of course, Christmas. Even in P.S. 90—presided over by Mr. Rabin and Miss Goldstein as principal and as-

sistant principal, respectively—where the students were predominantly Jewish, Christmas held sway. Paper Christmas trees and
snowmen were glued to the windows. In some classrooms, little
trees appeared on the teacher's desk, and in music class we learned
to sing Christmas carols.

But this was only the beginning. The whole city was suffused
with the atmosphere of Christmas. The parks had their decorated
trees. Some churches displayed their crèches out of doors, and the
stores were, of course, filled with brilliant, glittering decorations. I
loved looking at the infinitely fragile glass balls, as evanescent as
bubbles, with their shimmering colors and elaborate ornamentation.
The shining tinsel, the tiny colored lights, created an irresistible atmosphere of festivity and gaiety.

We resisted. Actually it was not even resistance since all these activities had nothing to do with us. There was a chasm of difference
separating us from the festivities that was even wider for my parents than for me. I doubt that my parents and their contemporaries
even saw, much less were able to take any pleasure in the spectacle
that lay open on the streets and in the stores. For them, the associations with any Christian celebration were of potential danger. In
the Old Country, holidays were periods of heightened tempers
when an unlucky word, a misunderstood gesture, could have violent consequences. We who were born in America had no such
fears and could enjoy the cheer, the music, the parties to which we
were invited, and the seductive atmosphere.

There were no forked tongues around in the early decades of the
century to explain that this was just a midwinter solstice, an ancient
pagan festival taken over equally, albeit with different content, by
both Christians and Jews. The immigrant generation could never
have been made to believe that there was any equation between
Hanukkah and Christmas because fortuitously they fell together in
the calendar. Nor did we think that Christmas was a secular holiday. To us, this was clearly a Christian celebration of the birth of

their Saviour, just as it had been in Europe in our parents' villages. And we were still onlookers. It was no more possible for us to have asked our parents for a Christmas tree than to have asked for a suckling pig for dinner. There was no context for a Christmas tree in our lives. What would have been the blessing to pronounce over the tree, over the lights? The more one contemplated the anomaly, the more ludicrous it became.

Hanukkah, like Purim, is one of those festivals without arduous religious obligations and without the tragic overtones that mark so many of the holidays that punctuate the Jewish calendar. Also like Purim it has an aura of easy enjoyment—families gathering to spend a winter evening, eating potato pancakes, playing cards or dominoes—and even the children came in for their share of notice in the reenactment of a miracle.

Hanukkah celebrated not only the triumph of the Maccabees over the wicked Antiochus in the second century before the Common Era, but also the miracle of a vial of oil sufficient only to keep a lamp burning for one day that actually burned for eight. Commemorating this event we lit candles, increasing one each day for eight days until the candelabrum was fully alight. The charming, miniature, twisted orange candles added an additional playful note to the proceedings. On the first day of the holiday, after the first candle had been lit at dusk and the appropriate prayers had been said, the children were given gifts of coins *(Hanukkah gelt)*. These coins were vital to our happiness since my cousins and I played a kind of matching game, throwing them against a wall. And in order to stay in the game for the longest time it was best to have a fistful of small coins. There was no point losing a whole half-dollar at one throw! Once, my uncle Jake, possibly in a fit of absent-mindedness, arrived with a gift of a pencil sharpener for me, which we all found most disconcerting. For me it was particularly distressing because now I didn't receive money, as all my cousins did. Uncle Jake had been reading the American newspapers, it seems, and had absorbed the seasonal lesson of gifts but had clearly forgotten the usefulness of a handful of change.

This blissful, unconscious distance could not last. More people than Uncle Jake read the paper and observed what was happening around them. Christmas was not only an overwhelming event in America but each year, it seemed, it grew larger. Family gatherings, engagements, office parties, class reunions—every good thing seemed to center on Christmas, and at the center of it all were wide-eyed children. The immigrant generation was interested, sometimes amused, but unmoved. The generation born here grew uneasy. In which direction should they spring? Was it true that Christmas was a secular holiday? Should they be just like other Americans and have a tree in their living rooms? Or should they see what was to be done about Hanukkah?

The experiments with the celebration of Hanukkah that took place over the middle decades of the twentieth century have been wonderfully chronicled in Jenna W. Joselit's book *The Wonders of America*. As she describes the search for Americanized varieties of the holiday, they range from the ludicrous to the pathetic. Finally the gift-giving essence of the season prevailed, putting its imprimatur also on Hanukkah. By the end of the century, done with experimenting, we are firmly bound up in the "traditional" practice of eight presents for each child, one for each night of Hanukkah.

Puffed up in the home, the holiday has not escaped being pressed into service as the visible public rival to Christmas, the opponent with its seven-branched candelabrum extending its arms starkly over parks and city greens where it was never meant to be. The fantasy that has gone into the manufacture of the Hanukkah menorah, not only in Eastern Europe but wherever Jews have lived, has been formidable, and its products have been imaginative and beautiful. Except for those originally designed for use in the synagogue, they have always been on an intimate domestic scale, often rich in biblical allusion and sometimes drawing on local symbols.

I feel sad now in December when I see the huge, overscale, brutal menorahs that give no one pleasure, except those who are using them to establish some kind of false parity. The charm of the Hanukkah celebration is that it is quintessentially domestic, and it would never have occurred to the immigrant generation to parade its observance. Nor would it have given my parents and their *landslayt* any satisfaction to have seen these public displays. If anything, it would have evoked that old, familiar anxiety, which had considerably diminished in America, evolving here into something more like caution, and drawing a wall of privacy around celebrations and practices that had no place in a Christian world.

The immigrants did not need to exhibit their way of life. On the contrary, they preferred to cultivate it within their own precincts, an extension of the secrecy or perhaps the silence that surrounded so much of their transplantation. Of course, as some of the immigrants and their children grew more affluent, they built substantial synagogues, and other institutions: orphanages, hospitals, old-age homes. But at the beginning, at least, these were built within Jewish neighborhoods to serve Jewish needs—in fulfillment of that long-standing obligation to give charity. Substantial as they now seem, the synagogues built by the immigrants in the early decades of this century were constructed with hardly a glance at the impression they would make on the surrounding world. They represented the pride and confidence of the immigrants as they established themselves in their American incarnation.

Nonetheless, in America they saw themselves often as mere epigones, palely repeating the rituals of their youth which had occurred in some real world. Their synagogue services, their home celebrations seemed shadowy, faded, lacking in authority, a diminished version of what they had known. It was with all the more reverence, therefore, that they regarded the old men who stood at the front of the synagogue wrapped in prayer shawls that hung to the ground, their collars embellished with dense silver embroidery.

In their very persons these men carried the tradition, the connection with the Old World. And on Yom Kippur when they invoked the mercy of God as they delivered the priestly blessing, falling heavily to their knees and then rising, a gesture that occurred only once a year, every congregant could not help but feel fear and awe.

Gershom Scholem recounts a Hasidic tale about the loss of tradition that beautifully captures the feeling of the immigrants as they saw their own familiar practices suddenly become elusive. "When the Baal Shem had a difficult task before him," writes Scholem,

> he would go to a certain place in the woods, light a fire and meditate in prayer—and what he had set out to perform was done. When a generation later the "Maggid" of Meseritz was faced with the same task he would go to the same place in the woods and say: We can no longer light the fire, but we can still speak the prayer—and what he wanted done became reality. Again a generation later Rabbi Moshe Leib of Sassov had to perform this task. And he too went into the woods and said: We can no longer light a fire, nor do we know the secret meditations belonging to the prayer, but we do know the place in the woods to which it all belongs—and this must suffice, and sufficient it was. But when another generation had passed and Rabbi Israel of Rishin was called up to perform the task, he sat down on his golden chair in his castle and said: We cannot light the fire, we cannot speak the prayers, we do not know the place, but we can tell the story of how it was done. And, the story-teller adds, the story which he told had the same effect as the actions of the other three.

Much like the rabbis in the story, the immigrants felt that they had once seen the fire burning but now could only tell the story. They relived the holidays, therefore, as much in memory as in practice. Despite skeptical, bored children and scattered family, they lit their candles, invited relatives and *landslayt*, and talked, remembering family stories, catching up on the latest news, at ease in one another's company. Drinking tea.

In the Bronx there was a dedication to the healing power of talk and tea. There was much to discuss since they all read the newspapers with the greatest intensity as they looked for signs and portents. In some fundamental way, the immigrants had never outgrown their early belief that the world was essentially an unreliable and dangerous place. It required watching. My parents and their *landslayt* studied the news, then, from two perspectives: Was it good or bad for the Jews? Was it good or bad for working people? My mother saw it very simply, and whenever there was a new report of a conflict starting in some part of the world, she had a ready comment. "No matter who wins," she said, "it's the working people who get killed." The search for the right way did not stop at the public level, but entered also into long narratives of perceived slights and injustices. Over and over again I heard these minutely circumstantial accounts conclude with the ringing question: "Is that a way to behave?"

Here the narrator took the high road where his or her injury became simply the opening illustration for a discussion of a broader question in ethics. Another round of tea would now be poured to strengthen the participants for the ensuing debate. The point was that people came together to *talk*. It was as if life were an eternal exploration and examination with friends and relatives of the passing scene. What had happened was only the opening sequence of the narrative. What followed was the eternal question: Was it right or wrong?

The favorite tea in the Bronx came in gold-striped red tins, miniatures, with their domed lids and printed straps, of trunks that would have been at home in any eighteenth- or nineteenth-century coach. They bore the name of the great Russian tea-importing family, "Wissotsky," and carried the transliterated Russian slogan: *Sweetouch-nee* (Flowery Tea) arched over the central medallion of a

Chinese gentleman with cap and queue examining a box of tea. This popular blend, which was basically a Chinese black tea with an admixture of Darjeeling and Oolong for flavor and aroma, produced a deep orange color, highly visible in the glasses out of which it was drunk. In an old memory from home, my mother sometimes added a spoonful of strawberry jam to her glass instead of sugar. When, on special occasions, I too was allowed to have jam, I would let it sit in the bottom of the glass, watching the bright color seep away before savoring the sweetness of last summer's strawberries.

My parents learned to drink coffee in America, but it never moved past breakfast. Coffee implied cream, and since cream was not permitted in a kosher household after a meat dinner, the natural conclusion to the evening meal was tea. The cakes that accompanied it, of course, came under the same prohibitions as the meal itself, so that Jewish bakers specialized in cakes without dairy products. They were sometimes dry—sponge cakes, egg cookies *(kichlech)*, almond bread *(mandelbrot)*, poppy-seed cakes—and sometimes moist like the honey cakes and nut cakes rich in oil and eggs. But layer cakes with whipped cream or frostings, the hallmark of the American bakery, were outside their repertoire. In any case, the immigrant generation took a long time to develop an appetite for these unfamiliar textures, and for fundamental satisfaction always went back to what they knew.

During the long winter evenings when family came to visit and sat around the table drinking tea, the white tablecloth would be covered with bowls of fruit and nuts, an assortment of plain cakes cut into cubes, and the delectable dry cookies that went so well with tea. Here my aunts and uncles reverted to the old European way of eating fruit, peeling an apple or an orange slowly in a long spiral and then slicing it into small, decorous bites. At the same time, the nuts offered a challenge to some of the men who, rather than use the nutcracker, preferred to crush them between their palms with a loud noise and then spend a long time picking out the morsels from the shell. The evenings generally started in a rather boisterous mood, as people caught up, exclaimed over the children, shifting back and forth between Yiddish and English, exchanging the latest news. But as the evening wore on and the children were put to bed, the voices became quieter, the mood softened, the language settled into Yiddish, and as I fell asleep, I would hear only the murmur of voices and the clink of teaspoons against glass.

# 12

# Beds

During the 1930s the Simmons Mattress Company ran a series of advertisements in popular newspapers and magazines for its Beautyrest mattress. "You spend one-third of your life in bed," the text proclaimed, and then showed the bedrooms of the rich and famous. The dizzying implication was that the lucky owner of a Simmons mattress could spend one third of each day in circumstances identical to those of, for example, the Roosevelts or the Tafts whose bedrooms were shown. In an earlier series, the company had cast its net even wider and won the endorsements of such notables as George Bernard Shaw, Guglielmo Marconi, "the inventor of the wireless"; Gordon Selfridge, "founder of London's largest store"; and our own rubber tycoon, Harvey Firestone.

These parallels touched a deep chord among readers, as the advertising department at Simmons must have known. When the scarcity of jobs and a dim economic situation made life so precarious, those of us preparing to enter the working world developed a very special view of "life." We knew that one had to take whatever opportunity offered in order to earn enough to live; but with that basic foundation laid, one's real life, one's fantasy life was given full rein. Among my friends, we planned our future along two independent courses. First, how we would earn our bread; and secondly, what we wanted to do. One of the purest examples was of a couple, each of whom had majored in the classics in college. Vocationally, there was no place to go with such an education. But how were they to live? They decided to open a little grocery store in Harlem, and then in between customers, they thought, they would continue to read the Romans and the Greeks. As the story was told, they could be found on any day with their books spread before them as they weighed out cheese and butter and bagged groceries.

In another case, my brother-in-law who loved blues and Western music had also calculated his prospects pretty realistically. He decided that he would study optometry, open a store in some appropriate neighborhood in the Bronx, and strum his guitar in his idle moments. A rather more pessimistic friend of mine who was afraid that she would never find a job—no matter how lowly—had worked out a plan if she were forced to "go on relief." In that case, she would take a room in the neighborhood of the New York Public Library, and thus saving the carfare would continue her dedicated study of French medieval poetry. Without a doubt, there were good and beautiful things in this world; there were elegant ways to live. We had not yet figured out how or whether it was possible for us to achieve such ends.

It was in such an atmosphere, therefore, that every accomplishment counted double—first in the pleasure in the event itself, and second in the wonder that it had come to pass. It was in this spirit that my mother-in-law used to recount the story of her life in America as a parable based on the achievement of *"a giten gelayger*—a good place to lie down." In an echo of the Simmons Beautyrest ad, she along with the majority of the immigrant Jewish community set great worth on their beds and bedding. Whether they stayed at home and cared for house and children, or went out to work in the shops, or tended the little neighborhood stores that they owned, their days were long and toilsome. They stood on their feet most of the time or bent over close work in a shop for unrelieved hours, then stood in the subway all the way home. It was the climax of the day when they could finally lie down and relieve their aching bones.

Is it any wonder that Jewish immigrants who carried very little else with them from the Old Country almost always brought a down comforter? My mother-in-law, of course, brought two—one for herself and one for her husband since, as traditional Jews, they naturally slept in separate beds. My mother-in-law, who had a feeling for the absurd, and acknowledged that there was something slightly ridiculous about her relentless search for perfect comfort, did not, however, allow these doubts to interfere with her close pursuit of this goal. In her account, my in-laws' first beds on the Lower East Side were high, white-painted iron beds with flat springs and thin cotton-batting mattresses. The cotton batting soon shifted; the springs sagged here and there. One slept with a shoulder down and a hip up, or vice versa, so that one arose in the morning feeling that one's torso had been dislocated in the course of the night. When there was just a little extra money, my mother-in-law's first move was to sell the cotton mattresses and replace them, of course, with Simmons Beautyrest. This was, after all, not just a mattress; it even had cunningly coiled springs inside. What did it matter if the flat spring had its breaks and its bends when one actually slept on such a marvel? Yet, as it turned out, it did matter, and there was now no help for it. They had to gather enough money to buy the box springs. But when this was accomplished it turned out that a box spring and a coil mattress, nearly a foot and a half of upholstery, had not been intended for the spidery framework of an iron bed.

What was needed for stability was a low wooden bed with broad sidepieces and sturdy horizontal slats that could contain the box spring with no danger of its sliding. The Beautyrest mattress then floated lightly on top, at a comfortable height for changing sheets and for that voluptuous moment of getting into bed. All of this meant expense and trouble and took time. It was not until my in-laws had been some decades in this country, therefore, that my mother-in-law finally managed to put together all the pieces that made for *a giten gelayger*. It was also a story that she told with both amusement at her naivete and a growing wonder at her own "need" for something that would have been the ultimate in luxury in the Old Country.

The sense that luxury was something to be attained and experienced privately, almost in a clandestine way, was the point perhaps where my mother-in-law's ethos and that of the advertisement converged. Very much like Oblomov in Goncharov's novel, who decided that no one could find him out or fault him for his invisible expenditures for food—for the whitest of veal, the subtlest of mushrooms—so our immigrants learned to treasure the invisible luxury of *a giten gelayger*: the down quilt and pillows, piled with a comforting fullness behind the head and shoulders, the perfectly ironed sheets and pillowcases.

As we have seen earlier, Jews were used to living with the idea of a divided world—the rules of behavior, what one ate and drank, time itself were all separated into aspects of the holy and the profane. This bifurcation of life was no more than the permanent division within the self that had been for so long an attribute of Jewish life in Europe. Publicly, Jews were the outsiders, the despised butt of jokes and scorn, if not worse. But at home, within their own community, they lived within a totally different system. In 1828 in the midst of a narrative of his travels in Italy, Heinrich Heine interrupts his observations with an account of the peddler Moses Lump, also known as Lümpchen, of Hamburg. Heine brilliantly captures this dichotomy as he first describes how Moses trudges about all week in every weather with a pack on his back. "But when he comes home on Friday evening," writes Heine in quite another key,

he finds the lamp with seven candles lit, his table covered in white linen, and he puts away his pack and his worries and sits down at his table with his crooked wife and his even more crooked daughter, and with them eats fish that has been cooked in a tasty white garlic sauce, sings the magnificent songs of King David, and rejoices with his whole heart about the exodus of the children of Israel from Egypt, rejoices also that the evildoers who did them evil have died, and that King Pharaoh, Nebuchadnezzer, Haman, Antiochus, Titus and such people are dead, but that Moses Lump is still alive and is eating fish with his wife and child. And I tell you, Herr Doctor, the fish are exquisite and the man is happy, he does not need to torment himself with education; he sits, happy in his religion and in his dressing gown, like Diogenes in his barrel, and he gazes with pleasure at his candles which he does not even have to trim. . . . And if Rothschild the Great were now to arrive with all his brokers, accountants, agents, and managers with whom he conquers the world and were to speak: "Moses Lump, ask me for a favor. Whatever you wish will be granted to you," Herr Doctor, I am convinced that Moses Lump would answer quietly, "Trim the candles!" And Rothschild the Great, with much astonishment, would say: "If I were not Rothschild, then I would like to be such a Lümpchen."

This delicious fable, however, was not so far off the mark of reality even a century later. The habit of the division of the world into the necessary, the workaday, the instrumental on the one hand, and the freely chosen, spiritual, or fantastical on the other, was a way of living that survived the constraints of the Old World, survived even the constraints of religion, and blossomed anew in secular America. As a Lümpchen, one worked all week tending a grocery store, or as a shoe clerk at Macy's or trudging door to door selling insurance. Even a well-known Yiddish poet like Morris Rosenfeld worked as a presser in the sweatshops along with his fellow immigrants, writing his verse when he could. But at the end of the day, at the end of the week, the real world, the real self waited. Sometimes it could even be managed so that one did not need to wait. When the mens' wear garment factories were concentrated in the area below 14th Street, one machine operator, a passionate bibliophile, used to spend his lunch hours browsing amongst the second-hand book shops on Fourth Avenue. Over the years, in an unending hunt, he gradually assembled his sets, volume by volume, of Dickens, Scott, Hugo, and the *Encyclopaedia Britannica*.

In our part of the Bronx, Mr. Kamen's commission bakery offered another example. Here he sold breads baked by various large Jewish firms and delivered fresh every morning to small stores such as his, to groceries and luncheonettes. Early risers could sometimes see a large brown paper bag of rolls left leaning against the door of a store awaiting the owner's arrival. "Moishe's," "Darling," "Pechter's"—each bakery had its distinctive paper label attached to the bread and baked onto it. Moishe's used as its illustration the head of Michelangelo's *Moses;* Darling showed a little boy in a sailor suit looking earnestly into the camera, clearly the darling of the owner; and Pechter's, proud of its fleet of trucks, used a drawing of one of its earliest models, high and square, with its name prominently displayed on the side. Mr. Kamen's breads were stacked on slanting shelves on the wall behind the counter, except for one or two which he reserved for his books.

As the years went on, and as Mr. Kamen grew more and more into the custodian of neighborhood morals and mores, the number of shelves devoted to books increased, and one had to arrive early in the morning to be sure to get a bread from the dwindling supply. During his leisure moments he stood in his doorway or gazed out of the window watching the local scene, so that for him there were no surprises. When one of his customers tearfully told him that her husband had suddenly left her, only she was bewildered by what had happened. Mr. Kamen had long observed the erring husband and his mistress strolling arm-in-arm while the unsuspecting wife went off to work.

Selling bread was clearly his avocation, what he did to keep body and soul together. Of course, everyone knew that Mr. Kamen was a writer since during the summer when his favored customers left the neighborhood, Mr. Kamen wrote them long and flowery letters. But whether he ever bundled all their confidences and his own observations into some epic work remained the subject of speculation. Was he writing a novel, poetry, philosophical essays about the human condition that came under his scrutiny? At any hour of the day, there was sure to be someone standing at the counter earnestly confiding some long, convoluted tale. He or she would reluctantly break off while a customer sheepishly asked for a rye bread *with* seeds, only to resume as the transaction was completed. On other, less fraught, occasions, one came, fell into conversation, lingered, got to know the neighbors, and left with an excellent bread and feeling a little better about the world.

Most of us, of the first generation born in this country, did not have to test my friend's dire theory of what to do should all stratagems fail and one had to go on relief. The burgeoning defense industry at the end of the thirties opened new jobs, and when the United States entered the war in 1941, many of the men were drafted into the army. The veterans who came out at the end of the war took advantage of the free college education that was offered to them, and young Jews surprisingly found themselves in a new world. In the universities the old quota system broke apart, and academic careers were actually possible; industry, which had been forced to open its doors during the war years, offered yet another outlet for talent; suddenly, instead of choosing between undesirable expedients, Jewish college graduates were able to consider what they truly wanted to do in the world.

It was a heady experience to be soaring in that very empyrean we had known only from afar. In the years after the war, young Jews were finding employment as editors in publishing houses, as writers for magazines from *Fortune* to *Partisan Review*. They could hope for careers in the university, where the tide of the times overtook the old guard, secretly horrified at the presence of "Hebrew gentlemen," as they were sometimes referred to by the Old Blues at Yale. The Hebrew gentlemen could now even hope for careers in the mainstream of law and medicine and the sciences.

In the arts, the explosion was both visible and verbal. Poets and writers like Delmore Schwartz, Saul Bellow, Bernard Malamud; art critics like Clement Greenberg and Harold Rosenberg; painters on the order of Adolph Gottlieb, Helen Frankenthaler, Mark Rothko, Ben Shahn, and the Soyer brothers were producing daring work with a new vision of the world. From the periphery, Jewish critics in literature and the arts moved to center. Alfred Kazin and Leslie Fiedler looked at American literature from a fresh viewpoint; while Lionel Trilling, whose early years in academia had been made painful by the usual social anti-Semitism, became an eloquent arbiter of literary taste as well as a significant commentator on current politics.

Suddenly in New York it was chic to be Jewish. The editors of *Partisan Review*, which canvassed literature, philosophy, and politics, were unaffectedly so. Philip Rahv, one of those editors and an arbiter of literary standards for a whole generation of writers, took as his adopted name the Yiddish word for rabbi. In November 1945 the American Jewish Committee launched a new magazine, *Commentary*, under the editorship of a brilliant, sophisticated editor from Mobile, Alabama—Elliot Cohen. Cohen, who had been a child prodigy, going off to Yale at the age of fourteen, was committed to the idea of fostering Jewish learning in the context of the modern world. He had no use for the closeted study of Jewish sacred texts behind the impenetrable walls of the yeshivah.

His mission was the reclamation of the young Jewish intellectuals who, newly intoxicated by the riches of Western civilization, were about to abandon their own heritage. His weapon in this struggle was *Commentary*, and he drew into its orbit as editors and writers exactly those young Jews who needed to be brought back to the fold. Meanwhile, he gave it an aura of unparalleled sophistication.

He asked Warren Chappell, the chief of the art department at Alfred Knopf, to design the magazine, and chose as headings for the regular columns unmistakable indicators of his intentions. In the "Cedars of Lebanon," he printed classical Jewish texts with excellent headnotes to guide the uninformed; "The Study of Man" was devoted to the social sciences, which seemed to be about to unravel the mysteries of man and society. Then in "The American Scene" he borrowed from Henry James to give a collective title to the vignettes he encouraged on American Jewish life.

It was in this department that Cohen published my first public work, an article on the Jewish delicatessen. It was a heady experience for a young writer, and made all the more exciting by the fascinating mail that the magazine received. Everyone seemed to have views, and, even then, nostalgic feelings about the Jewish delicatessen. Most unexpected and flattering was a postcard from Orson Welles, whom I had admired since the time I had seen him nearly a decade earlier in his production of *Julius Caesar* at the Mercury Theatre. There, playing against the bare brick wall of the stage, he had transformed Shakespeare's play into a parable for our times with Caesar as Mussolini in the Roman Forum. We were swept away by the daring and the passion of the production. And now, here was a postcard about pastrami sandwiches from Orson Welles himself.

Apart from its sentiment, this article, which was humorous and affectionate, opened a new vein for mining the American Jewish experience. It imposed a little distance and a certain indulgent style, and other writers also adopted the tone to write about what we already saw as a vanishing past. There were essays on Jewish types, such as the *paintner* (the standard Bronx pronunciation of "painter"), the idea of *yichus* (lineage), a report on Grossingers, the ultimate Catskill hotel, reminiscences on growing up in Brooklyn. I was, myself, too constrained to plunge boldly into a writing career. But hesitantly, once a year or so, I would offer the magazine a new piece, and, for a while, such pieces were invariably accepted. One rather lighthearted article on Jewish weddings, however, was rejected by Clement Greenberg in his famous gruff style. "Jewish weddings," he told me, "are no laughing matter."

What we were doing in "The American Scene" was trying to come to terms with what felt like an awkward past, trying to salvage it, retell it in a new voice. We had moved on from the rather savage snobbery that was sometimes visible in an earlier generation, as in Meyer Levin's unforgettable Passover scene in *The Old Bunch*, published in 1937. There, the chic young pair who are the hosts, made doubly self-conscious by the presence of a Gentile couple, choose as their theme for the evening Marie Antoinette's famous quip. The atmosphere at this parody of a Seder is set by the centerpiece, a layer cake topped with a figure representing Moses. "I get it," says one of the guests. "If you can't eat bread, eat cake!" Worse is yet to come as the goblet for Elijah is filled with gin instead of wine, and the main dish is, of course, ham.

Ten years later, we could only read such a scene with the painful embarrassment that Levin intended us to feel and more. By then, we knew what had happened to the Jews of Eastern Europe. The revelation of the death camps as they were discovered by Allied troops at the end of the war now dominated our consciousness. As the stories and pictures came out day after day in the *New York Times*, they had a deeply sobering effect. They left us somehow with a sense that we had become the custodians of a tradition we had thought was being securely tended abroad. Suddenly old Socialists were getting up at five in the morning to put in an hour studying Hebrew. New reading circles were formed as we sought teachers and help from the once-scorned seminaries. "I cannot allow a tradition of five thousand years to die with me," said one of my friends, a longtime and by then former Trotskyite.

We drew closer together and began to realize that we were friends. Among the many things that our lives at home had not prepared us for was friendship. It is striking in Irving Howe's memoir of his early years how distant his relationships are with colleagues, where encounters become part competitions, part sparring matches. It takes a long time for him to learn how to make friends. He wants it, but he doesn't know how to get there. During the war, he is consigned for two of his four years in the army to a remote station in Alaska where his dissimilarity from his fellow soldiers is so immediately apparent that he is called "the prof." "While there was respect behind that label," Howe notes, "it also carried a charge of hostility, not violent but nervous, expressing a fear of difference."

Among the men on the base is one Ira, "a clever New Yorker," with whom Howe talks on the telephone for hours at a time during the tedious days when they are on duty at different parts of the base. They talk about what Ira's wife is reading, about pastrami sandwiches, "anything at all," writes Howe, "as long as it was not *immediately* personal, which is to say, too sensitive and painful." On Sundays the two men walked together to Anchorage, a dismal walk to a dismal town, it would seem, a distance of two or three miles. And again, "we talked about family and books in a careful, low-keyed way. . . . But we rarely fell into private feeling, still more rarely into self-pity." Similarly, Howe's recollections of his first years back in New York are full of rueful accounts of missed opportunities with people whom he admired and liked but did not know how to approach.

And how could he? In the immigrant world in which he grew up, there seemed to be ceaseless social activity—family visits, people dropping by, weddings, bar mitzvahs, landsmanshaft banquets. But when we observe it closely, we see that by and large the cast of characters is made up of blood kin, and as for the *landslayt*, they might as well have been relatives. In fact, many of them probably were in some distant branch of cousinage. But friends, strangers, were accorded only a wary welcome. Women sometimes confided in one another, yet often only in extremis, and then standing on a landing still clutching a bag of groceries as the story of imminent economic collapse, of sickness, a faithless husband unfolded. But this was not yet friendship. This was the cry for help or solace of a despairing, wounded creature.

We still had to learn about friendship as a durable way of sharing and even creating life's pleasures, as well as bearing its sorrows. Irving Howe's description of intellectual life in the postwar years catches perfectly the edginess of cocktail parties where conversation was seen as a war of words, and postmortem accounts reveled in reciting slashing ripostes. We were too shy and unsure to be kind, and it took a while for us to learn that generosity or openness did not necessarily make one vulnerable.

One glamorous young couple, Jews from the Midwest, who were the Dick Diver and Nicole of our group, taught us about enjoyment. They arrived in New York newly married, just returned from their Caribbean honeymoon. There they had bought Danish china, Jensen silver, Steuben glass, and various other carefully chosen and, to me, dazzling articles for their new apartment. I stopped by one afternoon as they were unpacking one of their crates of china and marveled at the depth of the colors and the delicacy of the porcelain as it emerged from the excelsior. Thinking of how my own world was ordered, I contemplated all these exquisite pieces and asked: "But what will you use for every day?" Dick looked at me in surprise, but understood my meaning. "Why, this of course," he said. "After all, I am my own most honored guest."

This was a revelation. That one could be kind to oneself, that one could enjoy *every day* the treasures that fortune had placed in one's hands, was a way of thinking that was simply not in my stock of received ideas. While we—my liberal, high-thinking friends and I—had thought deeply about politics, national and international, about society and social justice, we had not a clue as to how to live. It was self-evident that the framework of our parents' lives was totally inappropriate, and without a word or moment of reflection, we had simply rejected it as a model. Unfortunately, socialism with all its compassion for the working class offered only a bleak philosophy for the cadres. I heard more often than I wanted Lenin's famous remark comparing sex to a drink of water. Ever politically unreliable, however, I seem not to have extirpated successfully the bourgeois longing for love. Nor was I alone. What to do, then, about weddings?

In a retrograde move, these were relegated to the province of the parents, who for the last time took charge of their children's lives, and to the best of their financial capacities put on weddings as they understood them. But perhaps out of embarrassment we did not invite one another to attend. These were strictly for family and *landslayt*. How different the story of our Dick and Nicole, who had had a party for some dozens of their friends in a downtown hotel the night before their wedding and whose intimates reappeared the next day as ushers and bridesmaids to cheer them on, to share their joy.

Even the friendly *New York Post* offered little guidance, since the weddings it covered were of high society. We could read, for example, in great detail about the dinner dance to be given by Mr. and Mrs. George F. Baker for Priscilla St. George and her fiancé Angier Biddle Duke in honor of their forthcoming wedding. Originally, the *Post* informed us, this event had been scheduled as a debutante ball for Miss St. George, then it was to be an engagement party, and finally, overcome by the rush of events, it was to celebrate the imminent nuptials. Very nice. We could sympathize with the happy confusion of Mr. and Mrs. Baker in the piling up of happinesses, but there didn't seem to be much of a match here for our own circumstances. The etiquette column, which was called rather brusquely "Behave Yourself," was not much help either, taking a very strict line on which names were to appear on wedding invitations. One stepfather who wrote in discovered that although he would be paying for the wedding and giving the bride away, "etiquette" did not permit him to be named on the invitation.

And here, of course, was where Jewish families simply abandoned all the rules and created their own forms. In Jewish weddings, after all, the two principals are not the only ones to march down the aisle. Both sets of parents accompany their children to the wedding canopy and stand with them during the entire ceremony. Jewish invitations reflected this indisputably significant fact, so that both sets of parents requested the honor of your presence at the marriage of their children. It seemed a better fit with reality than the rather punitive rulebook used by the *Post*.

In the case of weddings, I think a blissful ignorance of the rules that guided the St. Georges and the Dukes led to a freedom of invention that more vividly than anywhere else brought American forms together with Jewish needs. The immigrant generation had already embraced Western dress, as we noted earlier, brought in mixed seating at wedding dinners as well as ballroom dancing. But certain things remained immutable: the wedding canopy, the escorting of bride and groom, the Hebrew marriage contract *(ketubah)*, and the crushing of the glass underfoot by the groom. Since among the immigrants parents were often missing—still in Europe or perhaps dead—another married couple, a sister and brother-in-law perhaps, filled in this role as *interfirers* (escorts) at the wedding. Meanwhile the band played the familiar celebratory wedding music from Eastern Europe that they knew and expected.

All through the Depression and during the war years, however, austerity prevailed. Gone were the old East Side weddings with a hundred guests and festivities that lasted into the early hours of the morning. The lean years marked the age of the wedding parlor, the brief afternoon wedding with the refreshments confined to a "sweet table." The event took place in what was called the rabbi's study— a small enough room so that twenty or thirty people would feel pleasantly crowded. After the ceremony there was wine, some tea or coffee, a wedding cake, a few sandwiches, and after three hours it was over. Many of these young couples did not even have the means to set up their own apartment, but moved in with parents.

And during the war, with young men about to leave, the bride often went back to her old bed after a brief honeymoon, and awaited news.

It was not until after the war that a new tide of prosperity put the caterers back into business, but now with a new clientele, who began to demand a more American wedding with different kinds of food and music and decorations. The exuberance of the Jewish wedding was not to be contained by "Behave Yourself" or "The Correct Thing," but spun off into a sphere of its own making. It took a while, however, for the full-blown Marjorie Morningstar wedding to develop, as so vividly described in Herman Wouk's 1955 novel. And in that twilight between the old and the new, the parents prevailed with their idea of what constituted a celebration.

In a turn that would have been worthy of O. Henry, my first marriage bed was made of iron, with a flat spring. It stood on four short pipe legs, low to the floor, and on it was a cotton-batting mattress. But what had seemed like hardship to my in-laws seemed original and chic to us. Neither we nor our friends would dream of having a bourgeois headboard. Its absence together with our rejection of the bedroom set, as well as of all other sets, left my in-laws baffled as we continued to reinvent domesticity, home, marriage, and life. They had long since grown used to the existence of the double bed invariably chosen by their children. After all, my mother-in-law had herself given up the mikveh (the monthly purification ritual) shortly after arriving in New York. And just as we had boundaries beyond which we could not go, she had hers. Separate beds seemed to her right and decent. But she was in no position to insist.

That none of her children kept a kosher kitchen was another source of sorrow and also an impediment to entertainment. She and her husband were too modest and too kind to make a fuss by word or deed to shame us. There evolved then an unspoken rule. They would eat a light meal at their children's houses, which did not include meat. Mostly they came, inspected the grandchildren, asked about our lives, and had tea and cake. This was the easiest solution and caused the least social strain. But large events, Seders, celebrations on any scale, naturally had to be at their house where these constraints did not exist.

It was not until after World War II, with the arrival of the adamant and fierce Hasidic sects such as the Lubavitch, that things took an ugly turn. Then, in a reversal of roles, newly Orthodox children refused to visit their parents because they could no longer eat in their houses. Forgetting the overriding commandment that it is forbidden to shame someone publicly, and wrapped in their newfound virtue, they brought grief and despair to bewildered parents who saw not newfound virtue but the disappearance of their children. The immigrant generation, at least on the score of kashruth, had reached a more humane solution.

The need of the immigrants for their children superseded every rule—almost. Intermarriage, however—that rare but exigent visitor in Jewish households in the first decades of the twentieth century—left no one undamaged. It did not matter that the numbers were tiny. Between 1908 and 1912, for example, a minuscule 1.17 percent of American Jews "married out." However rarely it occurred, such an act nonetheless tested the deepest feelings of observant immigrant Jews. At the end of the twentieth century it is hard to imagine the profound sense of otherness that immigrant Jews felt for everyone outside their own world. As we have seen earlier, in their experience those who were other inevitably turned out to be *sonim* (enemies), ready to murder, pillage, and drive out of their homes whatever Jews came into their power. And those without power were inevitably just as anti-Semitic. Living in dense Jewish communities, few Jews of the immigrant generation had ever experienced an intimate relationship with a Gentile. Intermarriage then aroused such fear and loathing that it was the rare Christian girl (and generally it was a girl) who met her prospective in-laws under any but the most strained circumstances. Some families, like Tevye's in Sholem Aleichem's story, totally gave up on their child, mourned her as if she had died, and never spoke her name again.

One such intermarried couple of my acquaintance had three children, but despite repeated efforts by the son (who was the Jew in this case), the father remained adamant and never spoke to him again after his marriage. A more unusual but possibly more diplomatic solution was to keep the entire relationship a secret. In this case, the son seemed to be the eternal bachelor, who visited his parents regularly and was invited to all the family *simkhes*. But this involved a lifelong conspiracy on the part of his siblings and whatever other relatives were reliable enough to be let in on the secret. It had the advantage, of course, of keeping the family bond intact.

In a fragile world, however, few immigrant parents were ready to sacrifice their happiness on the altar of principle. And while there might be storms and arguments before the marriage, once the deed was done, parents accepted the inevitable with whatever grace they could muster. Family opposition must surely have been as keen on the other side. Despite estimates of intermarriage as high as 50 percent by the end of the century, in the early decades these cases were rare enough to make headlines when they occurred, most frequently among "emancipated women" such as Rose Pastor Stokes, the "Flower of the Ghetto," or celebrities like Irving Berlin. The wildly improbable *Abie's Irish Rose,* which was published first as a novel in 1926 and then became a Broadway hit as well as a movie, was perhaps a harbinger of times to come as the love of the Jewish boy and his Irish bride eventually overcomes the opposition of both their stubborn fathers. In Jewish homes, however, these stories, whether real or fictional, served mostly as cautionary tales for the unwed as examples not to be imitated.

Estrangement did not occur only because of marrying out. As we have seen earlier, education, language, and a change in social status brought about the odd, somewhat baffled equilibrium characteristic of relations between the immigrant generation and their children. As the children went to college and then left home, both generations began to feel the undeniable gap that opened between them. In the presence of family, we of the college generation learned to modify our speech, to arrange our accounts of what we did and whom we met to accord with the older generation's expectations or experience. With the best will, we had become self-conscious and awkward. This subtle but fundamental shift in our family life also left us feeling deprived.

We needed that web of unqualified closeness to which we felt entitled and we made up for its loss at home by transforming our friends into family. On the night of the first Passover Seder, we scattered and joined our families, but the second night was reserved for friends. We did not have kosher households. The table was not adorned with special Passover china; but we were earnest about holding to the traditions. Some of us, quietly, abstained from bread during the Passover week, just as some of us, quietly, fasted on Yom Kippur whether we went to the synagogue or went to work.

We invented as well a special kind of conversational style, in which we camouflaged our wariness of being personal by wrapping it in distancing generalities. We would move rapidly from an intimate anecdote to some telling theory for which, by implication, the anecdote was only the merest illustration. We had strict standards for ourselves and one another, cherishing what we thought of as good conversation. After we had children, we refrained from telling adorable stories about our offspring and anyone who persisted was immediately marked as an outsider. While our conversation could sometimes sound like a seminar, with the inevitable tedium induced by a monologist, in our private meetings we trusted one another to help unravel the puzzles of daily life. We knew one another as well as if we had been siblings. Jewish families in Brownsville or East New York were no different from my family in the Bronx. None of our assumptions or anxieties needed to be explained since we all shared them and knew exactly what they were.

Were we too self-denying when we didn't talk about our children, too austere in our standards? I think not. This style satisfied another hunger, for another kind of conversation that seemed far more necessary and gratifying to us. This was not just desultory gossip, nor small talk meant to ward off intimacy. These were explorations of ideas and meanings. A way of testing the world, and the turmoil in our heads. In any case, by then we were used to division, and it seemed self-evident that the domestic scene was not fit for the dining table where we talked and talked, as if all the talk would save the world and ourselves.

Malleable as we may have been in the hands of our parents on matters of ceremony, such as weddings and circumcisions, we were immovable on matters of taste. My mother-in-law used to talk about her idea of a beautiful room. The main elements in its decoration were *tishelach un lompelach* (little tables and little lamps). Soft lights and bibelots on the table represented for her the height of gracious living. Her children, however, were emphatically not of the *tishelach un lompelach* persuasion. In 1938, when the Ludwig Baumann furniture stores were advertising in the *New York Post* "3 piece Living Room suites. Carved frames, fine tapestry—$79," the Museum of Modern Art, then still on West 49th Street, launched a show of Bauhaus artifacts. The *Post* covered it on the women's page under the rather wary headline: "Bauhaus Exhibit at Modern Museum Interests Thoughtful Decorators." Further, the *Post* suggested: "This Modern show should interest any woman decorating her own home."

But for us, Bauhaus was not decoration. We saw it as it was meant to be, a new movement in the arts, and its ideology as well as its forms had a powerful influence on us. We had all read the Alfred Loos essay where he denounced decoration as crime, seeing it as the product of exploited workmen. And we knew with Mies van der Rohe that "less is more." We swept our tables clear of objects, unless it was an "interesting" piece of driftwood. We prized natural fabrics and materials, just as the Scandinavian designs of Saarinen, Aalto, Wirkaala seemed to us to represent a clarity of spirit as well as of form. Our favorite colors were earth tones of beige, gray, or at the outer edge terra cotta. No more rosebuds. We bought pure white china and stainless-steel cutlery. It was also a time for "honest" unfinished furniture, which we painted or stained ourselves. A brother-in-law, who was showing me some of the finer finishing techniques, had worked in a shop making "antiques." He described how they had banged on new tables with chains to "distress" the wood and then blew dirt into the crevices. But we scorned antiques of any kind old or new, and sought the same purity in material goods that we had earlier looked for in politics.

In those days of discovery we were enchanted with the pale birch woods from Sweden, the pale broadloom carpeting, the antithesis of the garish designs of the Wiltons or Axminsters. At the most we tolerated texture or a geometric pattern cut into the surface of the carpeting. The final effect of austerity and simplicity was very gratifying to young Socialists or former Socialists trying to find their footing in the all too tempting world.

Unreliable again in matters of taste, in my heart I lusted after color and pattern. Fortunate in my place of work, on my lunch hours I strolled through the furniture showrooms of B. Altman, Lord & Taylor, and W&J Sloane, studying their displays. The fantasy sample rooms with their carefully matched colors and their completeness all suggested as yet unsavored ways of life. W&J Sloane, for example, showed a book-lined library with the walls painted a deep green and featuring a long low sofa. Not cordoned off, the furniture was available to be examined and experienced by passers-by. I tested the sofa and felt the sort of deep comfort that I had never known was possible. These were not Ludwig Baumann's tapestry-covered springs, but soft, yielding down cushions. And underfoot in this luxurious room was not beige broadloom but a sumptuous Oriental carpet. I began to have secret, subversive thoughts and started exploring the floors where high piles of carpets were on display.

Has anyone ever hymned the department store as an educational institution? Richard Hofstadter certainly thought of them as such. One summer in Wellfleet, I heard him defend American supermarkets against a rather snobbish European visitor who complained about their vulgarity. Hofstadter instead praised them for teaching by example principles of cleanliness and order. In the same way I saw the department store as the school of taste. Antique departments with carefully labeled and dated pieces taught me about American pine and Biedermeier fruitwood. I talked to bored carpet salesmen who explained the techniques of Oriental rug knotting, showed me the difference between tribal rugs and those made on power looms. They told me about the Nichols Carpet Company, which established factories in Tientsin and Peking in the 1920s, and produced thousands of carpets for the Western market. Using traditional Chinese motifs, as well as scenes from classical Chinese drawings, Nichols created an entire repertoire that for decades defined Chinese rugs in the Western world. These were not the chaste, geometric patterns in pale gold on the floors of Frank Lloyd Wright's "Taliesin," but in their fin-de-siècle mauves and greens, in their intense blues, they aroused a terrible covetousness in me.

It did not matter that the furniture in my apartment consisted of a metal bed on pipe legs and some shellacked bookcases. They were merely necessary. But a Chinese rug, I thought, would glow forever underfoot like a jewel, changing color with the light and according to where one stood. My conversations with the rug salesmen grew more pointed and I began to consult my bank book, which had been somewhat fattened by $140 in wedding presents. But even that was not enough. The rug I longed for cost $500, the equivalent of a quarter-year's salary. The finest broadloom would cost only a fourth of that. But the mania had caught me and now there was no turning back. I can no longer reconstruct how long it took me to bridge the gap between my bank account and the purchase price of the rug. But one day, I did have the check in my hand and could at last order the long-desired green rug with its Chinese water scene framed in purple. Again I had to wait, this time the better part of a week, as I scheduled the delivery for a day when I would be home. It arrived, finally, the next Saturday, and as it was unrolled before me, I thought that with such richness in my possession everything was possible.

# Part IV

# Here

What happened *here* to the immigrant generation has been blurred in the telling as their children and grandchildren achieved a solid, even spectacularly successful place in American society. For the immigrants, success came at many levels, but always accompanied by the sense that they were strangers. *"Zayt ir a higer*—Were you born here? Are you from these parts?"*, a first question upon meeting in the Old Country, became superfluous in the new. The number of those born in America, *hi-geboyrene,* was a tiny minority among the Jews in New York City in the first decades of the twentieth century. By 1890, nearly half of New York City's population of 1.5 million people were foreign-born, and if we add in those who had a foreign parent, we arrive at an overwhelming 80 percent. This meant that even many of the *hi-geboyrene* had begun life speaking a foreign language, had grown up in a household ruled by ideas from another culture, and were themselves confused as to whether their "American" status was as genuine as that of their classmates in public school who so effortlessly understood the teachers and found their ideas and expectations neither outlandish nor unreasonable.

In the fever to leave their homes that gripped young Jews in

Eastern Europe between 1881 and the outbreak of World War I, the rational considerations that drove them out of their villages were quickly overtaken by their fantasies of how life would be in America. In their new country they were no longer condemned to the perpetual posture of the humble Jew, but could feel a sense of control in life, even of the grand gesture. Over and over, the young men, eager to assert their dignity in a foreign land, devised elaborate stratagems that almost inevitably collapsed in the reality of the New World, but which expressed their longing to command.

One earnest young rabbinical student taught himself English so that on his arrival he could, in his mind's eye, saunter up to a news stand and request the city's best-known newspaper. Unfortunately, never having heard a word of English, he pronounced it "Nev Yorrrk Timm-ess," to the bewilderment of the news vendor. Another, who planned to visit a relative in Trenton after settling in New York, had laboriously studied timetables in Warsaw and had even discovered the cost of a trip between the two cities. He, too, envisioned himself as the debonair traveler. He would utter the word "Trenton," hold up two fingers for tickets for himself and his friend, and push the money across the counter. But, alas, at the counter his fantasy evaporated. The ticket seller only pushed the money back and uttered a string of incomprehensible sounds. As it turned out, the prices had changed since his careful preparation in Warsaw. These seemingly harmless, humorous incidents, related only many decades later when the teller could also laugh, are nonetheless symptomatic of the disappointments and compromises that the young immigrants met with in America.

Young women, too, had their dreams. They hoped to be liberated from a system of betrothal and marriage in which they had no voice. Anzia Yezierska in her novel *Bread Givers*, which takes place in New York, describes the outrage of her heroine at being presented with a match made by her father. "I no longer saw my father before me," she says, "but a tyrant from the Old World where only men were people. To him I was nothing but his last unmarried daughter to be bought and sold. . . .. I saw there was no use talking. He could never understand. He was the Old World. I was the New." In that New World these daughters hoped for some regard in a society different from their own, where even the word for a grown woman, *yidene,* was entirely pejorative. In America, it seemed, life would be different. Whatever ailed the young immigrants, whatever pinched in the Old Country, they thought, would be remedied in the new. The reality proved more complicated.

Above everything, they sought work, as simple survival in the Old Country became ever more difficult for Jews. But even work in America would be different. In 1897 in Borszczow in the district of Lemberg, the Jewish tailors found the custom trade dwindling because of the growth of the clothing factories in the large cities nearby. Without work, without bread, most of them left for the United States. But in America too, the moment for fine hand-tailored suits was passing and they were forced to seek jobs in the hated clothing factories. And yet, there was a difference. Working in a factory in New York was not the same as working in a factory in Lemberg. There they would have exchanged a skilled trade for a place in a factory, and yet everything else would have remained the same: their irredeemably low status in the world as a Jew, their poverty, the hopeless outlook for their children. In America, at the turn of the century, the context of a job in a clothing factory still held out hope to the immigrant. Many of his countrymen had also started as "operators" and moved on to become entrepreneurs. Or conditions in the industry might improve, as they did with unionization in the first decade of the century, and a skilled operator might make a decent living and enjoy comforts that he had hardly dreamed of at home: running water, indoor toilets, heated apartments, paved and lighted streets.

Skilled artisans were only one class of Jewish worker displaced by the industrialization that was slowly encroaching on Eastern Europe. The wagon drivers who transported people, livestock, and goods over the local rutted roads were deprived of their livelihood by the railroads; tavern keepers were threatened by higher rents and legislation depriving them of leases. Even the moneylenders began to feel competition from the newly accessible banks. Nor could storekeepers in the villages keep their customers, who also found it more advantageous to shop in the towns.

While the search for work and safety, especially after the Kishinev Massacre of 1903, were the main forces to propel Jews out of their villages, in time the life of the New World itself beckoned the young and adventurous. New York with its immense concentration of Jewish newcomers quickly became a thriving center of immigrant cultural, social, and political activity. It is no wonder that new arrivals from little towns with a single muddy street were dazzled by the Jewish theater district on Second Avenue with its bright lights, its restaurants and cafés, its elegantly dressed theatergoers. It may not have been America, but it opened vistas to the imagination. One immigrant whose business led him to settle in the South around the turn of the century spoke ruefully about the consequences of his isolation in a small town. "If I were still in New York," he said, "I would go to the Yiddish theater in the evenings, hear a lecture, visit people whose conversation I enjoy, join a club or take part in some movement. In short, after working hours, be a man! Here I have nowhere to go, no one to talk with and nothing to do." Another Jew, who moved to Atlanta in 1905 after having experienced the squalid tenement life of New York, reflected in a similar vein on his choice: "In New York," he wrote somewhat wistfully, "I would have found my soul but without my body, and in Atlanta, a body without a soul."

New York, as any big-city dweller knows, has always been an agglomeration of villages. While most of these villages are the consequence of the accident of settlement, the villages of turn-of-the-century New York were no accident. They were the deliberate constructs of people who spoke the same language, who came from the same country, and who regrouped in the new land for support and comfort. The Irish, the Germans, the Italians all had their centers of concentration. Among the Jews, more than among other immigrants, the passion for organized life through which to express their concerns, to demonstrate their affiliations, to offer charity led to an early proliferation of organizations. Coming from a traditional world in which the synagogue had been a social as well as religious center, at least for the men, the little *shtiblach* (little rooms) for prayer were the first to spring up on the Lower East Side. As in the Old Country, many were organized by trade. The milliners in New York, for example, for decades maintained their own synagogue in the district where their workshops were concentrated. Sometimes they were organized by place of origin, but mostly they were organized by neighborhood to be within easy walking distance of its members. Yet even these *shtiblach* had a precarious existence, as irreligion swept over the young immigrants.

Freed from the narrow confines of the enclosed communities of Europe, these Jews made choices that were dictated more by need than by policy. With Sunday as the only day of rest in factories, some reluctantly worked on the Jewish Sabbath rather than risk their jobs and livelihood. Others temporized, absurdly attending early morning services in the synagogue and then going to work. Others again sought out Jewish employers who closed their shops on Saturdays. But, in any case, the drift toward piecemeal observance of religious injunctions had become almost universal. By 1906, it was estimated that some 90 percent of the immigrants no longer adhered strictly to the code that had ruled their lives at home. In fact, by 1913 60 percent of the Jewish businesses and pushcarts on the Lower East Side of New York operated as usual on the Sabbath.

And yet there was nothing dearer to the heart of these "law-breakers" than *"a shtikl khazonish*—a little bit of cantorial singing." The best-known cantors of the time—Yossele Rosenblatt, Moishe

Oysher, Moshe Koussevitzky—were no less than popular stars, giving concerts across the country and recording well-loved portions of the synagogue services on the newly invented gramophone records. The melodies and chants of the synagogue were inextricably part of the texture of everyday language, and the inconsistency of immigrant life was probably nowhere better shown than in the way these passages were admired and cherished while the institutions out of which they grew were being undermined.

An indigenous American invention for creating a bit of home in a foreign world were the Benevolent Associations, which offered their members a very fragile safety net against the catastrophes of life. In 1938, when these organizations were at their height, some 2,500 were functioning in New York City alone, with a membership of more than a quarter million. Even more than their tiny benefits, the landsmanshaftn offered the easy sociability that the Jewish immigrant craved: meetings, outings, lectures, all in the company of friends, culminating in a gala annual banquet with speeches in Yiddish, of course, toasts, music, and dancing.

Irving Howe has written about the "sense of collective fate . . . implanted in almost every Jew's personal experience." This collectivity was quite unconsciously realized in the web of life and custom in which Jews lived in their sequestered villages or dense city neighborhoods in the Old Country. In America, however, this collectivity no longer meant the resigned acceptance of a malign fate where the sighs and watchfulness of being in *"goles*—exile" were the groundtones of Jewish life. The two contradictory political movements that sprang up in Eastern Europe at the very end of the nineteenth century, Zionism and socialism, grew out of centuries-old despair, but were also the first political attempts actively to confront the Jewish situation since the Enlightenment.

It was no longer enough to await the coming of the Messiah. In New York these same movements had less immediate practical consequences than they had had in Europe, but they continued to represent broad philosophical and social ideals. Zionists from the Russian Empire who had chosen to emigrate to America in the first place were not likely to emigrate yet again to the Holy Land. But with the wonderful inconsistency which marked so much of their lives, these new arrivals in America never found it necessary to give up a shred of their convictions about the correctness of the Zionist program. In America, the Zionist as well as Socialist movements imported, along with their fundamental principles, the refined doctrinal splintering that had marked their European history. The Zionists ranged from the radical Hashomer Hazair on the left to the religious Zionists—the Mizrachi—on the right, and in the Socialist movement the manifold divisions, from Social Democrats to Trotskyites, were elaborated by such exotic America factions as the Lovestonites. With so many shades of opinion, everyone could find a home.

It is no wonder that Yiddish-language newspapers and periodicals proliferated, scrutinizing world news always from a wary Jewish perspective. Representing every possible political and religious direction, the daily Yiddish newspapers and the 150 periodicals published between 1885 and 1914 made no pretense of impartiality. They were in business to provide their readers with a vigorously partisan perspective on the issues of the day. Reflections on the collective fate and future of the Jews in the New World were integral to the thinking of political and religious organizations, of the Jewish trade unions, of cultural groups of every kind, and were aired vociferously in the cafés of the Lower East Side. David Blaustein, who became head of the Educational Alliance in 1898, made this observation of the establishments in his neighborhood: "The East Side café is a café par excellence. One drinks tea there . . . but tea drinking is secondary. The main office the café performs is to serve as a meeting place for discussion-hungry souls. . . . Above all the café is the place where communal questions are informally discussed and the plans of action are formulated."

But all these passions, entertainments, and diversions came later, after they had found a way to earn a living. The U.S. government began tracking immigrants in 1819, listing them according to country of origin, which made the tabulation of the number of Jews among all the many entering nationalities a matter of guesswork. Only in 1899, when the immigration services introduced the category "Hebrew," did it become possible to compile accurate statistics.

Although the overarching rubric "Hebrew" obliterated country of origin, it was still possible to make out the special character of Jewish immigration. Where it differed most notably from the others was that the Jewish immigrants came to stay. Although before the Kishinev massacres and the Russian Revolution of 1905, many returned home, perhaps as many as 15 or 20 percent in a year, we do not know for how long, nor how many re-emigrated. By 1908 only a minuscule number went back, a mere 5 percent, which is striking compared to a return rate of 90 percent for the Bulgarians and Serbs, 60 percent for the South Italians, and 66 percent for the Romanians and Hungarians. On the whole, those returning were young men who had come to America to earn a little bundle of cash, enough to buy them their dreams in the Old Country—a business, a farm, some livestock. With their American money in hand, they could return to a new and better place in their homeland.

The Jewish immigration was not only different in intent but also different in its population. As we saw earlier, it was made up predominantly of children. A quarter of the Jewish immigrants were under the age of fourteen, and if we include those up to sixteen years of age, children make up a full third. They came with little schooling and a smattering of languages. They were the recipients, but not yet old enough to be the carriers of their culture, bringing with them only the "Little Tradition"—the traditions of home, of daily life, the general mores and morals of their community. The "Great Tradition"—the tradition of higher learning, of religious exegesis—remained behind.

The Russian census of 1897 counted 6,000 rabbis in its domains, and in the next twelve years only some 350 left for the United States. Those who remained warned against the peril to Judaism in America and they were not wrong. Well-to-do communities in America could afford to send for distinguished scholars, but on the whole the little *shtiblach* made do without rabbinical help, or elevated one of their own to lead them in prayer. A Jewish prayer community, after all, needs no more than ten men, and a rabbi is not indispensable to the conduct of religious life.

One young Hungarian rabbi, Moses Weinberger, who arrived in 1887, was shocked not only by deviations from religious practice but even by changes in daily life. He took it as a sign of beginning apostasy that housewives now demanded fresh food when they went shopping. Those women, he writes, "who a year or two ago ate salty fish and stinking lentils in Jaszmigrad or Radomyshl and certainly did not sense any bad odor in day old meat . . . were then not so spoiled that everything had to be new, brought into being that very day." He is no less incensed when men and women abandon the old forms of address and accept the American "Mr." or "Mrs." as honorifics. Quite correctly, he perceives the abyss ahead that awaits the abandonment of old forms. "The Enlightenment of Berlin and Europe put together," he warns, "did not accomplish so much in half a century."

Contributing to the general corruption of tradition, Weinberger found, were the unqualified religious functionaries who imposed on the Jewish public. As he investigated, he saw negligence everywhere—in the supervision of the ritual baths, in the credentials of the circumcisers, in the behavior of ordinary Jews who paid little attention to the central prohibitions of the Sabbath relating to "carrying, handling forbidden items, and doing indirect business."

Rabbi Weinberger's observations were made just before the great East European immigration crested. But he understood very clearly that the tempo and demands of the metropolis were not conducive to replicating the atmosphere of the enclosed communities that he knew. Since Jewish law was surrounded and maintained by custom, any breach in the practices of the community inevitably endangered the law. As a folk saying puts it: "A custom breaks a law . . . *a minhag brekht a din.*" And troubling as the negligence and even crimes of the various functionaries of the community were to him, Rabbi Weinberger rightly worried about the consequences of even seemingly trivial changes in popular behavior.

What was happening to Jewish life and belief was that it was proceeding, as it always had, on two almost unrelated levels. On the one hand, in the "Great Tradition," the scholars continued their studies, wrote their treatises, and established yeshivas and seminaries, although gradually the old ways began to be disturbed by the rumblings of modern scholarship. On the other hand, in the "Little Tradition" among the immigrants, the practice of Judaism, which was ruled by custom, was slowly evolving largely unaffected by learned debate.

A decade before the arrival of the East European immigrants, in 1873, the adherents of Reform Judaism organized a Union of American Hebrew Congregations. Drawing upon the changes that had started earlier in the century in Germany, they developed their own *Minhag America,* or American way of worship, published a new prayer book, and in 1875 founded a seminary, the Hebrew Union College in Cincinnati. The Conservative Jewish Theological Seminary followed in 1887, and the Orthodox Yeshiva University ten years later, both in New York. Despite their varying views on the practice of Judaism and even on some of its fundamental tenets, all these seminaries were united in their acceptance of the standards of modern secular scholarship, approaches that were practically heretical in the old yeshivas.

The yeshivas on the Lower East Side that continued where they had left off in the Old Country pursued their studies as they always had, referring to the accepted and revered authorities inside Jewish tradition, using a mode of study perfected over millennia. The new seminaries, whether Orthodox, Conservative, or Reform, were part of the modern world; they placed Jewish learning in the context of modern theology, considered the Higher Criticism, examined the law and history of related peoples in the Near East, and studied the language, literature, and political context of the ancient writings. In the new seminaries, scholars were not isolated from the outside world of learning but shared the standards of international scholarship.

Even the colorful folk tales, legends, and parables came under the scrutiny of Louis Ginzburg at the Jewish Theological Seminary. In publishing a multivolume compilation of Jewish lore and legends, he organized the scattered anecdotes thematically, just as other scholars put the commentaries of thinkers such as Philo and Maimonides into the continuum of Western and Islamic philosophy. But this level of scholarship was beyond the reach of all but the most highly educated immigrants, even as much of the traditional learning had been beyond them.

Whether in the cities or villages of the Old Country, poor and poorly educated Jews, if they were so minded, absorbed their tradition through the continuing study of the sacred texts—the Bible and its commentaries. This study was not for the advancement of scholarship, but for its own sake, and in pursuit of moral teachings. A visiting student or rabbi might bring a new reading to the table, and the itinerant preachers *(magidim)* who raised sermons to an art form also suggested new interpretations to the eternal texts. But for the ordinary Jew, study was as much recreation as learning, a time when he sat together with his companions in the hour before the evening prayers and ruminated on a page of text.

For ordinary Jews, then, Judaism meant the practices and customs of their family and village, what Charles Liebman has called the "folk religion." It included as well the fellowship and familiar melodies of *their* synagogue, and meant being embedded in a community where these rituals were indissoluble from life itself. Of course, they needed their scribes, their ritual slaughterers, their bath attendants; they needed their teachers and cantors and rabbis. But for Jews attendance at the synagogue played only a small part in their steady observance of the Law, which touched every part of their day "from their lying down at night to their rising up in the morning," just as the Lord had commanded. For women, who in any case were not required to attend, the synagogue was less significant than the way they ran their households, which lay at the heart of observance and teaching. Inextricably entwined, undifferentiated in practice, law, custom, local lore, and habits made up the potent mixture that was traditional Judaism.

Yet in America, as the wise men had predicted, the old ways would bend and yield. In part the changes reflected the youth of the immigrants, who were less embedded in the tradition than the older generation. The young arrivals, overwhelmed by the need to earn their bread, quickly came to very pragmatic solutions on the demands of Jewish tradition. As we have seen, the shaved head and the wig required of every married woman was one of the first customs to fall, just as the earlocks that marked Jewish men in Eastern Europe were also quickly abandoned. Other steps followed as Jews, young and old, aspired at least to *look* like an American. Or, more important, not to look like a *griner*—a greenhorn.

Once in America, they had all the more reason to work when their hopes of achieving more than the marginal life of the shtetl glimmered before their eyes. Yet in the America of the nineteenth century, child labor was rampant. In 1890, the U.S. Bureau of the Census revealed that nearly one child in five between the ages of ten and fifteen was at work. These figures did not include the children under ten who were not counted, but many of whom were employed at often dangerous jobs that required their small size for tight places. By 1900, 2 million children were estimated to be in the work force. They worked in coal mines; in textile factories; in the furnace rooms of glass factories; in the food industry shucking oysters, cleaning shrimp, or packing fruits and vegetables in the canneries. Only eight states prohibited children under fourteen from working after ten at night. On the whole, Americans seemed to think that child labor was not cruel but beneficial, keeping children out of the way of crime and removing girls from the temptation of prostitution. Despite a long, weary struggle by reformers, it was not until 1941 that the Supreme Court, in upholding the Fair Labor Standards Act of 1937, finally outlawed the regular employment of children under the age of sixteen.

The immigrant children who arrived in the United States before World War I not only wanted to work; they were required to work. Even children who arrived with their families were not spared from this necessity. There is hardly an immigrant narrative that does not begin with the search for work, and only the younger children in such families finally had the luxury of attending school. Sometimes this attendance was at the cost of the older children, who contributed to putting the younger ones through school. In 1911, an Italian artificial flower maker, who worked often until the early hours of the morning to make her quota, described how she wept with pride and joy when her brother, whom she and the rest of the family had supported, finally graduated from medical school as a doctor.

Although many industriously went to night school to learn English or study American history in anticipation of getting their citizenship papers, on the whole these young workers never really overcame the fact that their basic education had stopped when they were eleven or twelve. It was not that they were not diligent. In 1906, for example, Jews made up the majority of the 100,000 students enrolled in New York City night schools. But when they learned English, they did not move much beyond a basic vocabulary, and fluent though they may have become, their English remained to the end a primitive tool. In 1938, the interviewer in the Works Progress Administration (WPA) study of the landsmanshaftn notes of one of the typical members that "His English is imperfect and ungrammatical and his accent foreign. His Yiddish is a jargon of English and Yiddish words. He was amazed to hear the writer who was interviewing him speak flawless Yiddish. 'Look! What a fine Yiddish he speaks,' he said to his wife, 'just as it is spoken in the old country.' " When the interviewers inquired about the education of the members in the Old Country, they learned that "At the ages of eight, nine, ten and twelve, they were apprenticed to builders and coachmen, or sent to work in near-by textile factories. There was no time or energy left for the acquirement of an education." The pressures to make money and to save were even greater in America, where passage for those at home had to be squeezed out of the meager wages of the new arrivals. The poverty of their parents, which had deprived them of education as children, was translated into their own poverty as beginners in America. Working for long hours every day left them with neither the will nor the time for schooling.

The seemingly endearing malapropisms of Hyman Kaplan, the creation of Leo Rosten, who followed his hero through a saga of English-mangling sessions in night school in the 1930s, are less than funny when we consider how awkwardly Hyman Kaplan had to negotiate between two worlds, his Yiddish fading and his English ludicrous. This was a generation that provided an inexhaustible fount of humor for comedians, who with unerring clarity limned the helplessness of their subjects in the New World. Sam Levenson, one of the gentler of the humorists, loved to tell stories about what he called "the little ladies." In one anecdote, he asks one of his "little ladies" what she thinks of the problem of Red China. "Well," she replies, "on a yellow tablecloth it wouldn't look so bad." There is a lot of condescension in this joke, but it is also a symbol of the hopelessly large gap that would open later between the immigrants and their children.

Those who stayed in the Yiddish-speaking world, with its rich range of reference, its traditions—verbal and literary—retained a real vigor in their language. The crudely carpentered-together English that became the medium of expression of so many of the young immigrants as they gradually lost their native Yiddish of course conveyed their meaning. But they had lost the flash, the control, the subtlety that the lifelong Yiddish speakers always enjoyed. Yet, as we all know, fractured English did not stand in the way of communication in families where stories were told, ideas and moral principles were conveyed, and parents and children loved one another—or not—with or without language. Inevitably, as in other immigrant groups, the native-born children spoke a native English, accepting and adjusting to their parents' speech as something they had always known. But there is no doubt that the highly educated children had two vocabularies, two ways of presenting themselves, as they adjusted and simplified what they wanted to say at home to a level that was comprehensible and reserved a different mode of speech for their peers. Older immigrants who spoke Yiddish to their children learned to accept the fact that they would be answered in English. Others gradually abandoned Yiddish, using English even at home.

Even so illustrious a Yiddish writer as Sholem Asch could not escape the Americanization that overtook his family. In 1910, when his sons were still little, he traveled to New York and wrote his wife in Warsaw with wild enthusiasm for the New World. He urged her to pack up everything and join him to start a new life, although even then he had a presentiment as to how it would go. *"We* perhaps will have a dark time out of it," he wrote, "but our children will become happy and fortunate people . . . an able child can achieve any level of education he wishes, and everything free . . . I am writing you, Madzhe, to sell everything and come even on foot. Bring our children here and the quicker the better, because here is their future as free and healthy people who will be able to work for themselves. In a few weeks they will speak English and will even be able to teach their parents how to speak."

His wife and children did indeed move to America, but in 1917 when Asch's son, Nathan, was in college in Syracuse, it appeared that things had turned out oddly. "My dear son Nathan, I have long wanted to write to you," Asch begins in his letter in Yiddish, "but I did not know in which language to write. That is my tragedy— that I cannot write to my son in the language in which I speak to the people. I don't know English and you don't know Yiddish. . . . " In the Asch family, Yiddish was at least preserved as the language spoken at home. In other households it was even more evanescent.

Inevitably, as linguistic roots weakened, something of the past slipped away as well. Of course, what the young immigrants brought with them (as we have seen earlier) was often only a tenuous remembrance of Jewish life—its mores, its history, its heroes. And sometimes these were recalled only in garbled form. In 1938, the WPA embarked on an ambitious project to study the folklore of the ethnic groups in the United States. The Federal Writers' Project undertook to interview people, state by state, to collect life histories, beliefs, superstitions, and so far as possible to record the speech of their informants in writing. Thousands of such interviews were conducted in New York City alone.

In these narratives, the speakers appear to have been frozen in time at the moment at which their formal schooling ended. One woman told a story about her response as a child to the episode in the Passover Seder when the door is opened for the prophet Elijah. Here is how her story is recorded:

> At de time of pesach dey say an Elenoovie (spirit) comes in to drink de wine. You sit and sit and imagine how it got lower in de glass de wine. I remember when I was a girl, so my heart used to beat, I was afraid I would see when dey opened de door. Evvyting was still; so we watched and tought de glass got a liddle bid less.

What is striking here is that the woman who is telling this story— in very typical immigrant English—does not really know that what she calls "an Elenoovie" and which the interviewer interprets as "spirit" is really the Hebrew phrase *Eli hanovi*—Elijah the Prophet." The literal meaning of the words, as well as the tradition of Elijah in Jewish life, have been lost to her, and consequently, as we saw earlier, are lost to the next generation. She conveys vividly in her inexact English what she felt as a child, with all the verbal and conceptual confusions of a child. But having left her world very early, she has never filled in this gap or clarified her understanding of what was really happening at that moment in the Seder. When we multiply such confusion, such limited knowledge of the Jewish past by the thousands of child immigrants, it leads us to question how much of that past actually sifted down to the next generation.

In America, in the little after-school Hebrew classes, often semi-literate teachers taught the boys to read Hebrew by rote and drilled them in a ready-made Bar Mitzvah speech in English chosen from a well-thumbed book of mysterious origin. In the 1880s, they received 10 cents a week per pupil. In the 1930s, in the Bronx, tuition had risen to 50 cents. Living in another world, in another time from their restless pupils, often with rudimentary English, these men had no way of conveying any tradition to their young students. How much could they teach, when they could barely communicate? On this sort of level, which was all that was available in many Bronx neighborhoods, boys learned little and girls learned less.

Despite their inadequate schooling, these immigrant children had lived long enough at home to be caught up in the "Little Tradition." It gave them a consciousness of themselves as part of that collectivity of which we have spoken, of being part of the long Jewish past. And it was expressed in a multitude of attitudes and homely practices that made up the texture of daily life. But this collectivity brought with it also a sense of responsibility for engagement in the world. The indefatigable Mary Van Kleeck, who studied the artificial flower workers in New York in 1911, noticed something special about the Jewish girls "from Russia, Austria or Germany.

Briefly stated," she wrote in her survey, "it may be said that when the Italian girl exhibits an interest in her trade it is an interest in craftsmanship or in her own wages rather than in general trade conditions. The Jewish girl, on the contrary, has a distinct sense of social responsibility and often displays an eager zest for discussion of labor problems."

As we know, Jewish workers were prime movers in organizing the trade unions in the needle trades where they were so heavily concentrated. The International Ladies' Garment Workers Union (ILGWU), the largest of the Jewish unions, was organized in 1900, and in 1909 was able to muster a strike of 20,000 shirtwaist makers that definitively changed the conditions of work in the industry. Celebrating that bloody strike, the women workers wrote this hymn to their cause:

> It was deep in the winter of 1909
> When we fought and we bled on the picket line.
> And then in the winter of 1910,
> We helped to organize the men!
> Hail to the Waist Makers of 1909,
> Shedding blood on the picket line!

Following its own organizing strikes in the men's clothing industry, the Amalgamated Clothing Workers of America (ACWA) did indeed gain recognition in 1914. By 1920, the ILGWU had over 100,000 members and the ACWA 170,000. Other unions in New York—the bakers', painters', milliners', and furriers'—were also brought into being by an overwhelmingly Jewish work force.

The "Little Tradition," then, while it may have been thin in content, was potent in its moral force. It remained alive among Jews as it did in every ethnic group in densely settled areas. Quite unself-consciously each group perpetuated ideas about the community, the family, education, the treatment of children, manners, and morals, and even its own inflections and patterns of English speech.

Among the immigrant Italians, where loyalty to and support of the family took precedence over the individual, children left school early in order to work and contribute to the family's well-being. At the turn of the century a census of New York schools showed that there was a wide variation in the completion rates for different nationalities. While none of the Italian children completed high school, 10 percent of the native whites and 16 percent of the Russian (mostly Jewish) children received degrees. Even after several generations, in dense Italian settlements grown and married children will tend to settle close to their parents, often following in their occupations. Among Jews, the first American generation had already moved from a predominantly skilled worker, small storekeeper base to a white-collar professional level by taking advantage of the free education in New York City. In 1917, Jewish men made up 73 percent of the students at City College, while 44 percent of the women at Hunter College were Jewish. As a consequence, by 1925 the generation born in this country had moved up a rung in the occupational ladder. More than 50 percent were either in professional or white-collar occupations. This included jobs in both private industry and in the Civil Service, ranging from clerical to administrative positions. These were all occupations that required an education. The immigrant generation, by contrast, also moved up, but along a different route, from jobs as skilled artisans or peddlers to owners of businesses. The growing difference between the generations led inevitably to moves by the children to other, better neighborhoods, or even other cities.

The widening disparity was not only one of place. It also had its darker side, and sometimes led to serious estrangement. The America of the 1920s was a rigidly defined society in which there was a single white Christian, generally Protestant norm. Anything other was at the least laughable if not actually scorned. Social anti-

Semitism as well as a general tone of condescension toward all ethnic groups was simply part of the landscape of America, with its dialect jokes, real estate covenants that excluded Jews and blacks from selected neighborhoods, not to mention quotas in higher education, and job limitations. The 1920s, then, became the heyday of Jewish name changes, nose changes, and even the attempt to "pass." In one of the bitter jokes of the period, a Jewish mother comes to visit her son in his Park Avenue apartment building on a Sunday afternoon. When she does not appear at the expected hour, the son goes down to the lobby of the building and finds her sitting in one of the grand chairs. He is amazed and asks, "Why are you sitting here, why didn't you come up?" "Oh, I wanted to," she says, "but I couldn't remember your name."

With the Depression, economic necessity pressed some Jews, who had no intention of actually giving up their Jewish identity, into living double lives. Many a fair-haired, blue-eyed girl passed at her job as a typist in firms that did not employ Jews. Living a guarded life all day, she could only reclaim her real self after work.

In the 1920s the synagogues, the Benevolent Associations, the cultural associations were all still securely in the hands of their founders, the Yiddish-speaking immigrants. The *Forward,* its name emblazoned in lights across the sky on East Broadway, and other Yiddish newspapers were still appearing daily, and the Yiddish theater was thriving. It was only later that the first generation born in America realized that the tradition was slipping away from them. This was a shock that emerged after World War II as the news of the death camps arrived in the United States. It became evident that the world out of which most of the immigrants had come had been destroyed along with its inhabitants. Unlike other peoples, who could depend on a home country to continue their language and culture, the Jews in America suddenly realized that they had inherited an awesome responsibility. The largest remnants of that destroyed people were in the United States. Filled with a new remorse and guilt, the carefree, careless second generation took up the burden of Exile.

It was a burden that was somewhat lightened by the founding of the State of Israel in 1948, but only in part. Israelis, who were proud of achieving statehood, were also ashamed of what they saw as the servile Jewish past. They preferred to begin their history with Abraham and skip lightly over the intervening two thousand years until the founding of the new Israeli state. Yiddish had been defeated in a hard struggle with Hebrew for the right to be called the national language, and so-called ghetto culture was also repudiated in the first heady years after independence.

The responsibility for remembering, for preserving East European Jewish language and culture fell, then, to the American Jews. Many of their near relations had been killed in the camps and they took up with wonderment the survivors who came to the United States after 1948. It was only then that many understood how much of East European Jewish culture had already slipped away and how ill-prepared the American Jewish community was to continue the traditions of the Old World. The reclamation of that past has grown into one of the guiding passions of the American Jewish community.

Although most Jewish activity is centered in the synagogue and in fund-raising, even the secular past is being remembered in the reawakened interest in Yiddish. The publication of the textbook *College Yiddish* by Uriel Weinreich in 1949 marked the beginning of its formal revival on a new level: as a subject in college and university curricula. And with the language, of course, came the study of the literature and history in which it was embedded. Apart from its survival in the self-segregated Hasidic groups, however, the moment has passed for a distinctly Jewish culture in a Jewish language. But there are many ways of being Jewish in America, from "Jewish lite," as one celebrity said in defining herself, to adherence to the tenets of Orthodoxy.

The traditional Judaism that was brought from Eastern Europe at the beginning of the twentieth century has not stopped changing. In America it collided with modernity in a way that was different from what happened in Western Europe. There, native-born Jews spoke the language and understood the culture of their country, and the integration of Jews and Judaism into the modern world was a process that proceeded over generations. Here, the East European immigrants had to make the same enormous linguistic, cultural, and social leap in one generation. And every generation since then has remade it, seeking to bring ancient faith and practice into some alignment with contemporary life. From the viewpoint of the shtetl, it has been an astonishing century: beardless men, mixed seating in the synagogue, girls being called up to read from the Torah in recognition of their becoming subject to the commandments, women rabbis, acceptance of homosexuality. In the 1920s, Aaron Lebedeff recorded his amazement at these first changes in his song: *"Gevald, gevald, vi kon dos zayn*—Help, help! How can this be?" But by the end of the century, the turning wheel of fortune has brought about a revival of Orthodoxy, its new adherents often coming from far less observant households. In the New York metropolitan region alone, some 230,000 people or 13 percent of the Jewish population were counted as Orthodox in 1983.

What has transfixed the generations since the end of the war, of course, has been the Holocaust and its remembrance. Major museums in New York, Washington, D.C., and Los Angeles are dedicated entirely to that portion of Jewish history. Countless groups are collecting histories of survivors, while books, movies, memorials, and exhibitions keep this unforgettable subject in the forefront of public attention. The constellation of Jewish institutions is different now from what it was at the beginning of the century, when the emphasis was on economic aid, care for orphaned or needy children, burial societies, and credit unions. Now the agglomeration of defense organizations, research centers, university programs, museums, and the myriad of Jewish publications from popular to scholarly indicate that Jewish life in America will enter the twenty-first century with new scholarship, new quarrels, and its immutable agenda—survival.

# A Note on Sources

## Part I Introduction, and Part II, There

The indispensable work on Jewish immigration before World War I is by Samuel Joseph, *Jewish Immigration to the United States from 1881 to 1910* (New York, 1914). Additional statistics are in the *American Jewish Yearbooks* for the years 1916–17 and 1917–18. Important works on Jewish immigrant life in New York include Irving Howe, *World of Our Fathers* (New York and London: Harcourt Brace Jovanovich, 1976); Moses Rischin, *The Promised City. New York's Jews 1870–1914* (New York: Harper & Row, 1962); Rischin, ed., *The Jews of North America* (Detroit: Wayne State University Press, 1987); and Gerald Sorin, *A Time for Building: The Third Migration, 1880–1920* (Baltimore: Johns Hopkins University Press, 1992). This work is Vol. III of a five-volume series, *The Jewish People in America.*

On the history of Jewish life in Eastern Europe, the great classic is by Simon Dubnov, *History of the Jews in Russia and Poland from the Earliest Times Until the Present Day* (reprinted New York: Ktav Publishing House, 1975). More recent works used here are: I. Michael Aronson, *Troubled Waters. The Origins of the 1881 Anti-Jewish Pogroms in Russia* (Pittsburgh: University of Pittsburgh Press, 1990); Salo Baron, *The Russian Jews Under Tsars and Soviets* (New York: Schocken Books, 1987; first published 1964); the report of Henry Hammond Dawson Beaumont, quoted in Eliyahu Feldman, *The Russian Jews in 1905 Through the Eyes and Camera of a British Diplomat* (Tel Aviv: 1986); John Doyle Klier, *Russia Gathers Her Jews. The Origins of the "Jewish Question" in Russia, 1772–1825* (Dekalb, IL: Northern Illinois University Press, 1986); Isaac Levitats, *The Jewish Community in Russia, 1844–1917* (Jerusalem: 1981); Jacob S. Raisin, *The Haskalah Movement in Russia* (Philadelphia: Jewish Publications Society of America, 1913); Michael Stanislawski, *For Whom Do I Toil. Judah Leib Gordon and the Crisis of Russian Jewry* (New York and Oxford: Oxford University Press, 1988), and *Tsar Nicholas I and the Jews. The Transformation of Jewish Society in Russia 1823–1833* (Philadelphia: Jewish Publications Society of America, 1983); and Steven J. Zipperstein, *The Jews of Odessa. A Cultural History, 1794–1881* (Stanford, CA: Stanford University Press, 1986).

Memoirs cited include: Isidore Kopeloff, *Amolike yorn. Iberlebungen fon a idishn ingel in der alten haym* (New York: Mtnah Verlag, 1931); Shmarya Levin, *Childhood in Exile*, trans. Maurice Samuel (New York: Harcourt Brace, 1929); Barbara Meyerhoff, *Remember Our Days* (New York: Simon & Schuster, 1978); Arthur Ruppin, *Tagebücher, Briefe, Erinnerungen* (Königstein: Jüdischer Verlag Athenäum, 1985); and Pauline Wengeroff, *Memoiren einer Grossmutter. Bilder aus der Kulturgeschichte der Juden Russlands im 19. Jahrhundert* (Berlin: Verlag von M. Poppelauer, 1913). The translations from Kopeloff, Ruppin, and Wengeroff are by RG.

The quotations from Sholem Aleichem in the opening chapters and elsewhere through the book are translated by RG from the following cassettes, issued in the original Yiddish by the National Yiddish Book Center at Amherst, Massachusetts. *Humorous Stories*, read by Rita Karin and David Rogow (1988); *Motl Peysi dem Khazns (Selected Chapters)*, read by Ruth Rubin (n.d); *Tevye the Dairyman*, read by Shmuel Atzmon (1990). For Sholem Aleichem stories in English, see Irving Howe and Ruth R. Wisse, eds., *The Best of Sholem Aleichem* (New York: Washington Square Press/Pocket Books, 1979). The quotations from Y. L. Peretz are from the cassette *The Best of Y. L. Peretz*, Vol. 2, read by Miriam Kressyn (Amherst, MA: National Yiddish Book Center, n.d.). The quotations from Mendele Mokher Seforim are from his *Selected Works*, Marvin Zuckerman, Gerald Stillman, and Marion Herbst, eds. (New York: Pangloss Press, 1990). The complete poem by Hayim Bialik on the Kishinev Massacre is in Hebrew and English in *The Penguin Book of Hebrew Verse*, T. Carmi, ed. (New York: Penguin Books, 1981). The letter to the *Forward* is given in full in Isaac Metzker, ed., *A Bintel Brief. Sixty Years of Letters from the Lower East Side to the Jewish Daily Forward* (New York: Schocken Books, 1971).

## Part III   The Bronx

### 5 Hats

The novels referred to in this section include: Abraham Cahan, *Yekl. A Tale of the New York Ghetto* (New York: D. Appleton and Co., 1896); Henry Roth, *Call It Sleep*, Introduction by Alfred Kazin (New York: The Noonday Press, Farrar, Straus & Giroux, 1994; first published 1934); and Anzia Yezierska, *Bread Givers. A Struggle Between a Father of the Old World and a Daughter of the New* (New York: Doubleday, 1925).

Other quotations are from Rose [Gallup] Cohen, *Out of the Shadow* (New York: George H. Doran Co., 1918); Alice Kessler-Harris, *Out to Work. A History of Wage Earning Women in the United States* (New York: Oxford University Press, 1982); and Elie Paretzi, *Die Enstehung der jüdischen Arbeiterbewegung in Russland* (Zandfoort: 1971).

### 6 Papers

The autobiographical citations are from Irving Howe, *A Margin of Hope. An Intellectual Autobiography* (New York: Harcourt Brace Jovanovich, 1982), and Milton Klonsky, "The Trojans of Brighton Beach," in *Commentary* (May 1947).

### 7 Work

The quotations on the colony near Peekskill come from David Leviatin, *Followers of the Trail. Jewish Working-Class Radicals in America* (New Haven and London: Yale University Press, 1989).

## 9 Corsets

For an excellent study of Jewish life in Miami and more, see Deborah Dash Moore, *To the Golden Cities. Pursuing the American Jewish Dream in Miami and L.A.* (New York: The Free Press, 1994).

## 10 Girls

Autobiographical accounts are taken from: Susan A. Glenn, *Daughters of the Shtetl. Life and Labor in the Immigrant Generations* (Ithaca, NY: Cornell University Press, 1990); Sydelle Kramer and Jenny Masur, eds., *Jewish Grandmothers* (Boston: 1976); Philip Roth, *Patrimony. A True Story* (New York: Simon & Schuster, 1991); Kate Simon, *Bronx Primitive. Portraits in a Childhood* (New York: Viking Press, 1982); and Rose Pastor Stokes, Unpublished autobiography, in Rose Pastor Stokes Papers, Group no. 573, Microfilm HM45. Yale University Library, New Haven, CT.

The references to Celia Dropkin are based on an article by Naomi Seidman, "Gender Criticism and Hebrew-Yiddish Literature: A Report from the Field," *Prooftexts. A Journal of Jewish Literary History*, 14 (1994). Excerpts from Dropkin's work in English translation are in *Found Treasures. Stories by Yiddish Women Writers*, Frieda Forman, Ethel Raicus, Sarah Silberstein Swartz, and Margie Wolfe, eds. (Toronto, Ontario: Second Story Press, 1994).

Paula E. Hyman has done pioneering work on the lives of Jewish women on both the micro and the macro levels. Two examples used here are "Immigrant Women and Consumer Protest: The New York Kosher Meat Boycott of 1902," *American Jewish History* 70, no. 1 (1980), and *Gender and Assimilation in Modern Jewish History. The Roles and Representation of Women* (Seattle and London: University of Washington Press, 1995). Other historical sources are Thomas Kessner, *The Golden Door. Italian and Jewish Immigrant Mobility in New York City 1880–1915* (New York: Oxford University Press, 1977), and Gerald Sorin, *A Time for Building. The Third Migration 1880–1920*, op. cit.

Novels cited in this section are: Daniel Fuchs, *Summer in Williamsburg* in *The Williamsburg Trilogy* (New York: Avon Books, 1972); Henry Roth, *Call It Sleep*, op. cit.; Isaac Rosenfeld, *Passage from Home* (New

York: The Dial Press, 1946); and Ruth R. Wisse, *A Shtetl and Other Yiddish Novellas* (Detroit: Wayne State University Press, 1986).

## 11 Winter

Historical works used here are: Jenna W. Joselit, *The Wonders of America* (New York: Hill & Wang, 1995), and Alice Kessler-Harris, *Out to Work* . . . (New York: 1982). The parable about the Ba'al Shem Tov is from the conclusion of Gershom G. Scholem, *Major Trends in Jewish Mysticism* (New York: Schocken Books, 1971). Quotations from the *New York Post* are cited for issues between November 19, 1935, and October 3, 1938.

## 12 Beds

The passage on Moses Lump is from Heinrich Heine, "Die Bäder von Lucca," in *Sämtliche Schriften* (Munich: Carl Hanser Verlag, 1969), vol. II (translated by RG). Also cited are Meyer Levin, *The Old Bunch* (Secaucus, NJ: Citadel Press, 1937), and Jenna W. Joselit, *The Wonders of America,* op. cit.

# Part IV Here

Major sources used in this section:

Sholem Asch, *Briv (Letters)* (Tel Aviv: Beth Sholem Asch, 1980). The letters in the text were translated by RG.

Myron Berman, *The Attitude of American Jewry Toward East European Jewish Immigration, 1881–1914.* Ph.D. dissertation, Columbia University, 1980.

Miriam Blaustein, ed., *Memoirs of David Blaustein. Educator and Communal Worker* (IL: McBride, Nast & Co, 1989).

Susan A. Glenn, *Daughters of the Shtetl* . . . (Ithaca, NY: Cornell University Press, 1990).

Irving Howe, *World of Our Fathers,* op. cit.

——, Introduction to David Berger's *The Legacy of Jewish Immigration: 1881 and Its Impact* (New York: Columbia University Press, 1983).

# A Note on Sources

Thomas Kessner, *The Golden Door* . . . (New York: Oxford University Press, 1977).

Hanna Kliger, ed., *Jewish Hometown Associations and Family Circles in New York* (Bloomington, IN: Indiana University Press, 1992).

Charles S. Liebman, "Orthodoxy in American Jewish Life," *American Jewish Yearbook*, LXVI [1965].

———. "The Religion of American Jews," in Marshall Sklare, ed., *The Jew in American Society* (New York: Behrman House, 1974).

Raphael Mahler, "Jewish Emigration from Galicia," in Deborah Dash Moore, ed., *East European Jews in Two Worlds: Studies from the YIVO Annual* (Dekalb, IL: Northwestern University Press, 1989).

Deborah Dash Moore, "The Construction of Community," in Rischin, ed., *The Jews of North America*, op. cit.

Diane Ravitch, *The Great School Wars* (New York: 1974).

Walter I. Trattner, *Crusade for the Children. A History of the National Child Labor Committee and Child Labor Reform in America* (Chicago: Quadrangle Books, 1970).

Mary van Kleeck, *Artificial Flower Makers* (New York, 1913).

WPA Federal Writers' Project, File 24012403, Bronx, NY, December 28, 1938. Library of Congress, Washington, DC.

Moses Weinberger, *People Walk on Their Heads. Jews and Judaism in New York*, trans. and ed. Jonathan D. Sarna (New York: Holmes & Meier, 1981).

# Acknowledgments

In writing this book, I have sought to gather the reminiscences of others to confirm or enlarge on my own. Many friends and relatives were liberal with their time and reflections as they pondered events and experiences now many decades old in order to fill in details of the picture that I was trying to construct.

In particular I would like to thank Jerome Berson, Ruth Burstein, Henry Glazer, Mildred Glazer, Rose Glazer, and Gail Klebanoff for telling me stories and reflecting on their youth in the Bronx. Esther Briskman, Benjamin Harshav, Edward Stankiewicz, and Howard Stern were helpful on linguistic matters, and Claudia Naurot supplied valuable details on the history of the Simmons Mattress Company. I owe a great deal to the support of Peggy and Dick Kuhns for their careful readings and comments on early drafts.

My daughter Sophie Glazer was a corrective voice from another generation, and with her unerring literary eye she came to my aid at a number of places. Sarah Glazer Khedouri, my eldest daughter, read portions of the manuscript to my great benefit with both professional and familial care. Lizzie Glazer, my youngest daughter, together with my son-in-law Bill Montgomery, was the inspiration for at least one of the chapters, while their comments elsewhere were often telling and enlightening. I am indebted to my sister Shirley Gorenstein for many things, but especially for her generosity in connection with this book.

My old friend Jean Staschover and I have mused on the questions discussed in this book in many meetings in the half-century that we have known each other. With her permission, I have used some of the anecdotes she told me. Shirley Lavine has generously allowed me to publish her family's recipe for Greek Salad, rare in being one of the few ever written down.

While collecting music for this book, I had the good fortune to have Jenny Romaine as an expert and patient guide through the record collection at YIVO (the Yiddish Scientific Institute at New York). I also want to thank the knowledgeable librarians and technicians at the Music Division of the Library of Congress in Washington and at the Record Collection of the New York Public Library for the Performing Arts at Lincoln Center. Zalman Mlotek was kind enough to advise me on texts and sources for traditional Jewish songs. Henry Sapoznik at Living Traditions was the person to whom all roads led. He proved an amazing and prodigal source of information on Yiddish music and has become the spiritual godfather of the record connected with this book. Daniel Bell, out of his inexhaustible knowledge of the Jewish labor movement, gave me the texts of several old workers' songs and was kind enough to sing one on cassette so that it could be included on the record. Joe Glazer, who has long experience as both composer and performer in the field, also generously gave me his counsel about immigrant and union music. Donald S. Lamm, chairman of W. W. Norton, has earned my gratitude for taking on the simultaneous roles of publisher, editor, and agent in bringing this work to light.

Lawrence Graver at Williams College and Marion Kaplan at Queens College in New York City kindly invited me to speak at their respective institutions and thereby gave me an opportunity to test my ideas in public. I was also glad to have been invited to present a part of the book for discussion at the Muriel Gardiner Seminar on Psychoanalysis and the Humanities in New Haven at the invitation of Albert Solnit.

My last and most loving thanks go to my husband, Peter Gay, who supported me in every way in this enterprise, as he has throughout our lives together. He was also my unwearying in-house editor, reading every section in turn with his fine eye for logic and style.